Going to Shakespeare

Going to Shakespeare

J. C. Trewin

London
GEORGE ALLEN & UNWIN
Boston   Sydney

First published in 1978

© George Allen & Unwin (Publishers) Ltd, 1978

ISBN 0 04 792010 6

Photoset by Northampton Phototypesetters
in 10 on 11 point Baskerville
Printed in Great Britain by
Unwin Brothers Limited
The Gresham Press,
Old Woking, Surrey

For

ARTHUR COLBY SPRAGUE
First Chronicler

Contents

Introduction   *page* 11
William Shakespeare   15
King Henry VI, Part One (?1589–90)   17
King Henry VI, Part Two (1590–1)   22
King Henry VI, Part Three (1590–1)   26
King Richard III (1592–3)   31
Titus Andronicus (1593–4)   38
The Comedy of Errors (before 1594)   45
The Taming of the Shrew (1593–4)   51
The Two Gentlemen of Verona (1594)   59
Love's Labour's Lost (1594–5; revised 1597)   66
King John (1594–6)   74
King Richard II (1595)   81
Romeo and Juliet (1595–6)   91
A Midsummer Night's Dream (1595–6)   98
The Merchant of Venice (1596–7)   107
King Henry IV, Part One (1596–7)   113
The Merry Wives of Windsor (1597–8)   120
King Henry IV, Part Two (1598)   127
Much Ado About Nothing (1598–9)   132
As You Like It (1599)   140
King Henry V (1599)   147
Julius Caesar (1599)   153
Twelfth Night (1601–2)   160
Hamlet, Prince of Denmark (1601–2)   169
Troilus and Cressida (1601–2)   177
All's Well That Ends Well (1602–3)   183
Measure for Measure (1604)   190
Othello, the Moor of Venice (1604)   197
King Lear (1605)   204
Macbeth (1606)   212

Antony and Cleopatra (1606–7)   *page* 221
Timon of Athens (1607–8)   228
Coriolanus (1607–8)   235
Pericles, Prince of Tyre (1607–8)   244
Cymbeline (1609)   251
The Winter's Tale (1611)   259
The Tempest (1611)   268
King Henry VIII (1612–13)   276
Some Books   283
Index   285

Introduction

PANDARUS: Who play they to?
SERVANT: To the hearers, sir.
PANDARUS: At whose pleasure, friend?
SERVANT: At mine, sir, and theirs that love music.

Troilus and Cressida, III, i, 20–3

I

Shakespeare, actor-dramatist, wrote his plays to be performed, yet how many of the thousands of books and millions of words about them discuss their effect in performance, take them from page to stage? What follows is a spectator's discursive notebook. Intended first for relative newcomers, who are still finding their way about the Folio in the theatre, it suggests some of the things to watch and listen for: the shape of a play, lines, speeches, cuts, recent or traditional business. It is not an academic exploration but something informal that I would have liked, and could not find, when I was discovering Shakespeare in the early 1920s: a look from the house itself at the acting texts as the theatre diversely interprets them, the people, their movements, and their music. It will answer some questions and prompt others.

Not so long ago, few collectors had seen and heard everything in the Folio (plus *Pericles*). It is far easier now: from time to time even the furious contention of the *Henry VI* trilogy and the frenzies of *Titus Andronicus* reappear. It took me more than three decades to complete the list, beginning with a provincial *Tempest* on an icy March night and ending with the Jackson-Seale revival of *1 Henry VI*. In 1,500 or so performances I have not yet heard spoken from the stage every line Shakespeare wrote, but the hour must be approaching.[1]

New Shakespearians soon become collectors. They find themselves

asking how the latest Lady Macbeth will stress 'What, in our house?';
a Malcolm, 'O, by whom?'; a Laertes, 'O, where?'; and a Hamlet,
'in your philosophy'. They want to see whether Benedick and Beatrice
avoid the laugh on 'Kill Claudio'; whether any fresh business has
joined the clotted mass in the interlude of Pyramus and Thisbe; how
long Isabella can hold her pause before pleading for Angelo; how
Macbeth will point 'Hang out our banners on the outward walls';
whether Euphronius is allowed his 'morn-dew on the myrtle leaf';
whether Claudius looks at the dumb-show, or Mistress Ford is asleep
on Falstaff's entry, or Iago keeps those early lines when Roderigo
is summoning Brabantio:

RODERIGO: Here is her father's house. I'll call aloud.
IAGO: Do, with like timorous accent and dire yell
           As when, by night and negligence, the fire
           Is spied in populous cities. (I, i, 76–8)

Who will speak 'You that way: we this way' at the end of *Love's
Labour's Lost?* Does a Richard II use Maurice Evans's gesture at
'Northumberland, thou ladder'? When was a Lavache last heard
subtly varying the repetitions of 'O Lord, sir!'[2] or a Henry V
imitating the 'mock' of tennis-balls in the Elizabethan effect of the
Rebound? Does Orlando recognise Rosalind? Are Petruchio and Kate
in love at first sight? Does Portia know of the 'jot of blood' when she
comes to court? Is Hubert also the Citizen of Angiers? How will the
masque be presented in *The Tempest?* Will the ghosts encircle the
sleeping Posthumus, and Jupiter descend on his eagle? And how does
Isabella respond to the Duke's proposal?

      Dear Isabel,
   I have a motion much imports your good;
   Whereto if you'll a willing ear incline,
   What's mine is yours, and what is yours is mine. (V, i, 532–4)

Then how much sympathy can we afford Shylock? Does Lear seek
to outcry the storm? What does Octavius do at the end of *Julius Caesar?*
And what is the position of Maria in Olivia's household? (Who, for
that matter, is Fabian?) The more one asks, the more the questions
bristle: questions about the ages of Horatio and Juliet's Nurse, about
the grouping at the end of *Lear*, the bear on the Bohemian shore, the
doubling (or not) of Thaisa and Marina, Hermione and Perdita, the
retention of the last scene of *Romeo*, of Valentine's absurd fifth-act
magnanimity, of Coriolanus's salute to Valeria:

The noble sister of Publicola,
The moon of Rome, chaste as the icicle
That's curdied by the frost from purest snow,
And hangs on Dian's temple – dear Valeria! (V, iii, 64–7)

So it goes on. Is Owen Glendower the Welsh Captain of *Richard II*?
Does Titania have the Indian boy that an early Victorian playbill
described as a 'sable pledge of hope'? How is the banquet treated in
Timon? Is Eglamour burlesqued? How far is the fooling taken in *The
Comedy of Errors*? Does Fluellen carry in the dead Boy? Who is the
Third Murderer? And who are Innogen, Violenta, Varrius, Kate
Keepdown?

II

For the moment, leave it there. I am thankful for so much excitement
through the years, beginning at a lost Theatre Royal behind its Ionic
pillars in the far south-west; at Stratford-upon-Avon when Bridges-
Adams, in the interregnum between the two Memorial Theatres, was
directing upon the shallow stage of the Picture House; and at the Old
Vic during the reign of Harcourt Williams. Since then, at home and
abroad, a legion of delights. If directors (some are my friends) appear
to be the book's collective villain, that is only because I wish now
and then that they would let Shakespeare speak unimpeded and avoid
remembrance of Bottom's 'What beard were I best to play it in?'
     No doubt the epigraph should be Arnold's

> Ere the passing hour go by,
> Quick, thy tablets, Memory!

I advise playgoers who pursue the subject to look at the brief biblio-
graphy. The order of the plays is arguable; my dates are from the
Riverside Shakespeare (1974); quotations are keyed to Professor Peter
Alexander's edition (reprinted many times since 1951). A few phrases
have been borrowed from work of mine long out of print. Just one
thing: there can be trouble when a name becomes hyphenated late
in a career, and for the sake of consistency – though it is easy to err
in these matters – I have given the hyphen to Granville-Barker
throughout.
     I am deeply grateful for the aid and encouragement of Professor
Arthur Colby Sprague; that unchallengeable authority is not responsible for any of my *gaffes*. The book owes an immense amount to my
wife Wendy, who has listened to Shakespeare with me so often and in

so many places. Enlightening talks with Martin Holmes, the late Sir Barry Jackson, Robert Speaight, Ivor Brown, Baliol Holloway, Ernest Milton, and A. V. Cookman, are clear in memory.

Thanks, finally, to my friend Herbert van Thal; and to my publishers for their tolerance and editorial perceptiveness.

Hampstead, 1977   J.C.T.

NOTES

1 Every word is spoken in the Argo/British Council recordings directed by George Rylands.
2 *All's Well That Ends Well*, II, ii.

William Shakespeare

I

William Shakespeare, eldest son of John Shakespeare, a glover, and his wife (who had been Mary Arden, of Wilmcote) was born in Henley Street, Stratford-upon-Avon, on a date traditionally believed to be 23 April 1564. He was educated at the local Grammar School. In 1582, when eighteen, he married Anne Hathaway, of Shottery. They had three children: Susanna (1583–1649, who married John Hall, a Stratford physician, in 1607); twins, Judith (1585–1664; married in 1616 to Thomas Quiney), and Hamnet (1585–96).

The facts of his life between 1585 and 1592 are highly conjectural: a reference in 1592 shows him to be firmly established as a London actor and playwright. In 1594 he was a prominent actor and 'sharer' (that is, a part-owner of the company) with the Lord Chamberlain's men; five years later they opened the Globe Theatre on Bankside in Southwark. On James I's accession in 1603 the company became the King's Men; it rented a second and private theatre, the Blackfriars, in 1608. Shakespeare had retired to Stratford before 1612, though he kept his London associations. On 23 April 1616 he died – the cause is unknown – at New Place, the big Stratford house he had bought in 1597. He was buried in the chancel of the Collegiate Church of the Holy Trinity where Gerard Janssen's bust commemorates him.

The First Folio collection of his plays, edited by former colleagues, John Heminges and Henry Condell, was published in 1623 (*Pericles* remained outside until the second edition of the Third Folio, 1664). Ben Jonson wrote a tributary poem, honouring him as 'the applause! delight! the wonder of our Stage!' and including the lines:

> Sweet Swan of Avon! What a sight it were
> To see thee in our waters yet appear,

>And make those flights upon the banks of Thames,
>That so did take Eliza, and our James!

His plays speak for him. The parts he acted in them can only be conjectured: among suggestions are Adam *(As You Like It)*, the Ghost *(Hamlet)*, Duncan *(Macbeth)*.

King Henry VI, Part One
(?1589–90)

I

'Enter with drum and colours.' This stage direction should be the epigraph for the turbulent early trilogy of *Henry VI*. Its dating is as complex as its narrative is uninhibited, a swirling race of incident seldom channelled into any sober-flowing history. All we need to know in the theatre is that several men may have worked on these dramatised dynastic broils that audiences wanted and managers supplied. Scholar after scholar has enjoyed dismembering the trilogy, *Part One* in particular, and assigning the better scenes to Shakespeare: a process that reminds me of the *Twelfth Night* exchange between Olivia and Viola: 'Is't not well done? – 'Excellently done – if God did all.' A young man learning his trade could write as badly as the next, but Shakespeare and his partners, whoever they were, could keep a stage in tumult.

Though the plays are rare in the theatre,[1] and *1 Henry VI* rarer than any, a bold recreation in the 1950s surprised the critics. One of these, after the Birmingham Repertory revivals had been brought to the Old Vic, could say only that they were 'very noisy'. I doubt on earnest consideration whether either the wars in France or the English Wars of the Roses were particularly quiet. Certainly Shakespeare's record of the savage tournament of the Middle Ages, with the contention at home that brought disaster abroad, cannot be conducted in any muted, throw-away fashion.

Part One, with its cast of thirty-nine, besides 'Lords, Warders, Heralds, Officers, Soldiers, Messengers, Attendants, etc., Sundry Fiends', was the first Shakespeare play I read and the last I heard. To a boy of eight and a half, unaware of 'comets importing change of times and states', Bedford's line at the funeral of Henry V, 'Brandish your crystal tresses in the sky', had had a purely local meaning. Lying awake an hour or so after looking at the play (Shakespeare, a heavy volume, had slipped to the rug from an overcrowded top shelf) I saw as usual the great beam of the Lizard Light piercing my closed green blinds, flashing across the bedroom wall, fading, and again returning until sleep supervened. It was thirty-seven years before I heard the line from the stage of the Old Vic.

Until 1953, indeed, collectors had mourned the play as practically inaccessible. Robert Atkins, warrior of the Vic – a Talbot among directors – had done portions of the trilogy there in 1922, a conflation within two nights. Before this there had been a revival or so with texts much-clipped, Frank Benson's at Stratford in 1906 and, most remarkably, a single Stratford *Part One* (1889) in a confused version by Osmond Tearle, a sturdy provincial manager.[2] Henry Irving lent some properties and costumes from the Lyceum wardrobe. Tearle found that his own Lord Talbot could give a fine lead to the armed skirmishing.

Talbot, 'terror of the French', must always dominate. We hear of him first from a Messenger, one of three who interrupt the funeral service for Henry V in Westminster Abbey; he describes how, because of the cowardice of a certain Sir John Fastolfe, who 'fled, not having struck one stroke', Talbot was taken prisoner when returning from the siege of Orleans. He is ransomed, recaptures Orleans, and later – among the rarest Shakespearian scenes in performance, and a poor one – escapes from a trap set for him by the Countess of Auvergne. Next he re-takes Rouen (again Fastolfe escapes 'to save myself by flight'), is created Earl of Shrewsbury, tears the Garter from Fastolfe's leg in the presence of the King, and arrives 'with trump and drum' before Bordeaux. There he is beleaguered and, eventually a prisoner, dies with his dead son John in his arms:

O thou whose wounds become hard-favoured Death,
Speak to thy father ere thou yield thy breath!
Brave death by speaking, whether he will or no;
Imagine him a Frenchman and thy foe.
Poor boy! he smiles, methinks, as who should say,
Had Death been French, then Death had died today.
Come, come, and lay him in his father's arms.
My spirit can no longer bear these harms.
Soldiers, adieu! I have what I would have,
Now my old arms are young John Talbot's grave. (IV, vii, 23–32)

II

In an earlier scene from Douglas Seale's production (Birmingham Repertory and Old Vic, 1953) the old lion and those about him had remained stock-still in the background while, down on the forestage, Sir William Lucy vainly urged on first York, then Somerset, to send Talbot immediate aid. He is a redoubtably conceived figure[3]: a great general lost because the nobles, preoccupied by the faction-fighting at home, allow the French possessions to crumble:

> Whiles they each other cross,
> Lives, honours, lands, and all, hurry to loss. (IV, iii, 52–3)

The framework of the play is firm enough as Douglas Seale's work on it for Sir Barry Jackson showed. The verse can slide into bathos ('Discourse, I prithee, on this turret's top') and there is some mixed cursing ('Thou bastard of my grandfather!'), but the writing is roughly serviceable. Occasional lines glint, as in Talbot's 'Poor boy' couplet, and so in its direct fashion does much of the plucking of the red and white roses in Temple Gardens:

RICHARD PLANTAGENET:[4] Let him that is a true-born gentleman
And stands upon the honour of his birth,
If he suppose that I have pleaded truth,
From off this brier pluck a white rose
with me.

SOMERSET: Let him that is no coward nor no
flatterer,
But dare maintain the party of the
truth,
Pluck a red rose from off this thorn
with me . . . (II, iv, 27–33)

For the rest, we have the beginnings of the young King Henry VI and of Margaret of Anjou, who one day will be the English Queen (Peggy Ashcroft used a lisping French accent at the dawn of her celebrated progress through *The Wars of the Roses:* Stratford 1963). Here also is Shakespeare's – and the historian Raphael Holinshed's – idea of Joan of Arc, the 'holy maid': her valour aside, she is in open league with the powers of darkness, 'sundry fiends'. Bernard Shaw who, in his preface to *Saint Joan,* called it a 'scurrilous' portrait, observed, as we do, that the part opens in the heroic manner, and that Shakespeare let it dwindle into savagery, 'almost as if the cast had rebelled against any attempt to glorify the enemy of England'. Joan is shown through the eyes of the French and the English. She must be taken as her actress[5] presents her, though nothing can mitigate the raging desperation of a last scene in which she is the

Joan Elizabethans expected, the harlot and sorceress. At her first appearance[6] she has the play's most familiar lines:

Glory is like a circle in the water,
Which never ceaseth to enlarge itself
Till by broad spreading it disperse to nought. (I, ii, 133–5)

III

The trilogy returned to the theatre, at Birmingham, through the zest and confidence of Sir Barry Jackson. Disregarding academic warnings, and there were plenty, Jackson saw no reason why this war correspondence, designed for the stage, should not succeed on the stage. He had in Douglas Seale a director who knew what a straight, clear thrust could mean to any crowded chronicle. Beginning with *Part Two* in the spring of 1951, Birmingham went on to *Part Three* in the following year, and during the summer of 1953 achieved *Part One:* an achievement indeed. The entire trilogy then came to the Old Vic. It began with the disembodied speaking of the last Chorus of *Henry V* ('Henry the Sixth, in infant bands crowned King') while the barons stood silent in the Abbey about the dead King's bier. The Countess of Auvergne episode, in which, charmingly, she calls Talbot 'a weak and writhled shrimp', was cut; and so was the entire passage for Mortimer, Earl of March, in the Tower of London. On the eve of death ('the dusky torch of Mortimer') he makes a genealogical statement of thirty-two lines: 'Death approach not, ere my tale be done.' But the production retained, excitingly, all that mattered, with the full variety of clamours: in the first act alone, armed battle, civil brawl, friendly combat, hand-to-hand encounter in arms, alarums, excursions and sudden devastating casualty from a heavy gun.[7]

Since the Jackson-Seale revivals, the most expansive production of the trilogy has been in John Barton's arrangement of *The Wars of the Roses* (Stratford, 1963 and 1964). This ingenious text contained instalments entitled, confusingly, *Henry VI* and *Edward IV*, and ended with *Richard III:* a masque of kings, set in a world steel-environed, that until the last play moved in fierce and free assurance.[8] With cutting, patching, and rewriting – Mr Barton was expert in his bridge passages – it became a narrative coherent and logically organised. Even so, one could not accept, by any means, that the *Henry VI* plays, 'immensely diffuse and uneven in quality, were not viable as they stand'. Jackson and Seale had proved that they were.

NOTES

1 In 1977 Terry Hands directed them at Stratford-upon-Avon.
2 Three or four actors in the cast were described simply as 'An Amateur' or 'Amateurs'. Tearle was resolved to draw the line.
3 *The Times*, reviewing Frank Benson's Talbot at Stratford in 1906, said that he was 'a rugged dog of war, bent in the shoulders, all but shuffling in his walk, lean, grim, and graceless'.
4 Afterwards Richard, Duke of York.
5 Professor Arthur Colby Sprague discusses Joan in his description of a 1959 production *(Shakespeare's Histories: Plays for the Stage*, 1964, pp. 114–16) when the little Hovenden Theatre Club in London essayed *1 Henry VI* with thirteen players: one doubled John with John Talbot.
6 In this scene Alencon says of the English: 'They want their porridge and their fat bull beeves.' See the Constable of France on 'barley-broth' (*Henry V*, III, v, 19) and 'great meals of beef' (*Henry V*, III, vii, 149–50).
7 Martin Holmes, whose list this is in *Shakespeare and His Players* (1972, pp. 120–1) adds: 'An Elizabethan audience coming to the play for the first time, may well have paused for breath at this moment, and wondered if, and how, the author was going to keep up his excitement. He does it without repeating his effects.'
8 *The Wars of the Roses*, published by the BBC, 1970.

King Henry VI, Part Two
(1590–1)

In the second, and much finer part of *Henry VI*, with well over fifty characters, we reach the core of the faction-fighting and what Hazlitt called 'the bear-garden in uproar', – high holiday for an Elizabethan audience. Here Margaret of Anjou, French tigress for the pale religious King, is sharpening her claws. The Duchess of Gloucester, 'presumptuous dame', moves in penitential progress before her exile. Humphrey of Gloucester is murdered. Margaret and Suffolk (after his banishment) have their love scene, with Suffolk's curse on his enemies which must be among the most sibilant passages in the Folio:

> Their sweetest shade a grove of cypress trees!
> Their chiefest prospect murd'ring basilisks!
> Their softest touch as smart as lizards' stings!
> Their music frightful as the serpent's hiss . . . (III, ii, 323–6)

Jack Cade of Ashford is in brutal rebellion. Death presses upon death; clamour overrides clamour; throughout, King Henry, a forlorn figure, is seeking peace amid the clash of arms and the pelting verse. The play is in angry surge from its opening, in which Suffolk, royal proxy, brings Margaret to London, down to the Yorkist victory at St Albans, the Wars of the Roses in dreadful flower, and the Duke of York's salute to Salisbury:

> Of Salisbury, who can report of him,
> The winter lion, who in rage forgets
> Aged contusions and all brush of time
> And, like a gallant in the brow of youth,
> Repairs him with occasion? This happy day

Is not itself, nor have we won one foot,
  If Salisbury be lost.   (V, iii, 1–7)
(He is not.)

Part Two concentrates on the fall of Humphrey of Gloucester, Lord
Protector,[1] and the rise of Richard Plantagenet, Duke of York. Like
the other sections of the trilogy, it needs the clarifying animation of
performance. On the page it can jangle; upon the stage it has a constant
drive. Queen Margaret announces herself in her angry speech to the
new-made Duke of Suffolk, who is far more to her taste than the
gentle King:

Not all these lords do vex me half so much
As that proud dame, the Lord Protector's wife.
She sweeps it through the court with troops of ladies,
More like an empress than Duke Humphrey's wife.
Strangers in court do take her for the Queen.
She bears a duke's revenues on her back,
And in her heart she scorns our poverty;
Shall I not live to be aveng'd on her?
Contemptuous base-born callet as she is . . . . (I, iii, 73–81)

Revenge comes. Margaret makes an excuse to strike 'the callet' in open
court ('I cry your mercy, madam; was it you?'). There follow the
spirit-raising scene[2] when the Duchess, turning to sorcery, is trapped
and captured, and her public humiliation, barefoot in a white sheet
and carrying a taper. All of this is pictorially theatrical as Frank
Benson recognised. Daringly, he chose the play for Stratford in 1899,
but, though it was acclaimed at the Shakespeare Memorial where
people by then expected a rarity, the provinces in general never took
to *Henry VI* – any Part, any battle. In fact, when *Part Two* was
announced, someone invariably refused to see the middle of a play with
neither beginning nor end: the oldest jokes have a habit of coming
true in the theatre, as Barry Jackson realised when he revived *Part
Two* in Birmingham more than half a century later.

Benson, whose reasons could be highly individual, probably chose
to appear as Cardinal Beaufort at Stratford because he knew so well
the Beaufort tomb in Winchester Cathedral. He acted in full scale the
brief and terrible scene of the Cardinal's death and the cry from a
conscience tortured by the thought of Gloucester's murder:

Bring me unto my trial when you will.
Died he not in his bed? Where should he die?
Can I make men live, whe're they will or no?

O, torture me no more! I will confess.
Alive again? Then show me where he is;
I'll give a thousand pound to look on him.
He hath no eyes, the dust hath blinded them.
Comb down his hair; look, look! it stands upright,
Like lime-twigs set to catch my winged soul! (III, iii, 8–16)

The figure of the limed twig occurs thrice in *Part Two*: once when
Suffolk says to the Queen of Dame Eleanor: 'Madam, myself have
lim'd a bush for her'; once when the Duchess, at her penance, cries
to her husband:

For Suffolk – he that can do all in all
With her that hateth thee and hates us all –
And York, and impious Beaufort, that false priest,
Have all lim'd bushes to betray thy wings. (II, iv, 51–4)

and then, a third time, at Beaufort's death.³ (It would reappear
during the King's prayer in *Hamlet*: 'O bosom black as death!/O
limèd soul, that, struggling to be free,/Art more engaged').

Benson again presented *Part Two* during his 'Week of Kings' at
Stratford in 1901 and 1906, half a dozen histories in what W. B. Yeats
(1901) called 'a strange procession of kings and queens, of warring
nobles, of insurgent crowds, and people of the gutter'. Swans listened
to torrential iambics; the town teemed with Murderers and Citizens.

II

The 'strange procession' of *Part Two* can find an urgent life in the
theatre, particularly the King, sad symbol on the throne of England,
who asks only for unbroken peace ('Was never subject long'd to be a
King/As I do long and wish to be a subject'); Humphrey of
Gloucester, honest man destroyed; Richard of York in relentless
conquest; Beaufort; amorous Suffolk. Gloucester evokes a few of them
after his arrest for treason at the Bury St Edmunds council:

Beaufort's red sparkling eyes blab his heart's malice,
And Suffolk's cloudy brow his stormy hate;
Sharp Buckingham unburdens with his tongue
The envious load that lies upon his heart;
And dogged York, that reaches at the moon,
Whose overweening arm I have pluck'd back,
By false accuse doth level at my life. (III, i, 154–60)

The chronicle moves from death to death: from Gloucester's to
Beaufort's; to Suffolk, beheaded off the coast of France in the ebb
of a scene that begins with the Marlowe-sounding lines spoken by
a Lieutenant:

> The gaudy, blabbing, and remorseful day
> Is crept into the bosom of the sea;
> And now loud-howling wolves arouse the jades
> That drag the tragic melancholy night. (IV, i, 1–4)

And from this to the terrors of the Cade rebellion, a civil war within
a civil war, fomented by York, and led by a Kentishman, John
Cade of Ashford, demagogue, mock-grandee, single-minded ruffian.
Shakespeare, steadfast for 'degree' and public order, dreaded the mob
(as he shows in *Julius Caesar* and *Coriolanus*). Here, uncompromisingly,
he registers the brutality of this rising of 'the filth and scum of Kent':
the murders of the Clerk of Chatham – as horrifying as that
of Cinna the poet elsewhere – the brothers Stafford, and Lord Say
and Sir James Cromer whose pole-borne heads are carried before the
rabble – 'At every corner have them kiss.' At length, and none too
soon, Cade himself is slain by the Kentish squire, Alexander Iden.

Before the end of the play others have fallen, Somerset and the
elder Clifford. It is a long casualty list, and we meet for the first
time a man who will lengthen it. York's son, Richard Plantagenet, is
in the field, greeted by his adversaries as 'Foul stigmatic' and 'Heap
of wrath, foul indigested lump,/As crooked in thy manners as thy
shape!' We shall hear more of him, and of the others that remain alive.
One line from *2 Henry VI* rings in the mind and seems now to speak
for the whole thunderous trilogy; it is, simply, Margaret of Anjou's 'I
stood upon the hatches in the storm.'

NOTES

1 Humphrey, Duke of Gloucester, fourth son of Henry IV, Henry VI's uncle.
2 For this scene ('Here they do the ceremonies belonging, and make the circle')
   Arthur Machen, at the 1901 revival, supplied a Latin incantation. It was, he said,
   so accurate and so potent that he feared the speaker might raise the Devil in earnest.
3 In Douglas Seale's production (Birmingham, 1951; Old Vic, 1953) the scene was
   not played by Beaufort's bedside. He raved on to his death before an altar.

King Henry VI, Part Three
(1590–1)

I

Sean O'Casey, in the second volume of his autobiography, *Pictures in the Hallway*,[1] has a definitive epigraph for any revival of the *Henry VI* trilogy:

'Battles, castles, and marching armies; kings, queens, knights, and esquires in robes today and in armour tomorrow, shouting their soldiers on to the attack, or saying a last lone word before poor life gave out; of mighty men of valour joining this king and ravaging that one; of a king gaining a crown and a king losing it; of kings and knights rushing on their foes and of kings and captains flying from them.'

The young Sean was to have played Henry at a Dublin charity concert in the last scene but one of *3 Henry VI* where the King is murdered by Richard of Gloucester, played by Sean's brother Archie. (Because of the Duke of Clarence's death – the year was 1892 – the concert was abandoned.) An unexpected choice for a duologue; but, in Dublin, Cibber's version of *Richard III*, which began with the murder, was not yet forgotten.

   The final play of the trilogy, all 'battles, castles, and marching men', is at least as theatrically violent as the second. Never was there a more bellicose peerage. Richard, Duke of York, deposes the King and is himself defeated, humiliated, and slain; Warwick the King-maker first establishes Edward of York as Edward IV, then restores Henry VI before he himself is killed. As the chronicle fades, Edward is on the throne, Henry has been murdered, and Richard of Gloucester, Edward's brother, hunchbacked and with a withered arm, is preparing his own path. In the middle of the play, and newly in his Dukedom, he declares himself:

I'll make my heaven to dream upon the crown,
And whiles I live t'account this world but hell,
Until my misshap'd trunk that bears this head
Be round impald with a glorious crown.
And yet I know not how to get the crown,
For many lives stand between me and home;
And I – like one lost in a thorny wood
That rents the thorns and is rent with the thorns,
Seeking a way and straying from the way;
Not knowing how to find the open air,
But toiling desperately to find it out –
Torment myself to catch the English crown;
And from that torment I will free myself
Or hew my way out with a bloody axe.
Why, I can smile, and murder whiles I smile,
And cry 'Content!' to that which grieves my heart,
And wet my cheeks with artificial tears,
And frame my face to all occasions.
I'll drown more sailors than the mermaid shall;
I'll slay more gazers than the basilisk;
I'll play the orator as well as Nestor,
Deceive more slily than Ulysses could,
And, like a Sinon, take another Troy.
I can add colours to the chameleon,
Change shapes with Protheus for advantages,
And set the murderous Machiavel to school.
Can I do this, and cannot get a crown?
Tut, were it off farther off, I'll pluck it down. (III, ii, 168–95)[2]

The line 'Or hew my way out with a bloody axe' is one key to an utterly relentless drama of battle-cries, death-rattling oratory, and shouting defiance, as the long contention of the Roses sways back and forth. It is a youthful, swashing vigour. Somebody is always hurling invective, or becoming a new king of the castle, or hissing into fanged soliloquy. The grimmest scene is the baiting of Richard, Duke of York, forced by Margaret, tigress or she-wolf of France, to wear a paper crown and to have his face wiped with a cloth dipped in his young son's blood:

Come, make him stand upon this molehill here
That raught at mountains with outstretched arms,
Yet parted but the shadow with his hand. (I, iv, 67–9)

To which York replies with a celebrated line, 'O tiger's heart wrapped in a woman's hide!' that the dramatist Robert Greene parodied in his attack on Shakespeare, as 'tiger's heart wrapt in a player's hide'.

II

The mind is filled with echoes and parallels. Richard's cry (he is not yet Gloucester), 'How sweet a thing it is to wear a crown,/Within whose circuit is Elysium/And all that poets feign of bliss and joy', returns us straight to Marlowe and to Tamburlaine's 'The sweet fruition of an earthly crown'; the words 'sunshine day' speak to us of both *Richard II* and *Edward II* ; Margaret's 'Great lords, wise men ne'er sit and wail their loss,/But cheerly seek how to redress their harms' anticipates Carlisle's 'My lord, wise men ne'er sit and wail their woes,/ But presently prevent the ways to wail' *(Richard II)*. During Margaret's speech, just before she is taken prisoner, we remember how once she stood upon the hatches in the storm. She has a long passage of cumulative sea imagery that begins: 'What though the mast be now blown overboard,/The cable broke, the holding-anchor lost' and goes on to

> And what is Edward but a ruthless sea?
> What Clarence but a quicksand of deceit?
> And Richard but a ragged fatal rock? (V, iv, 25–7)

It is sustained and formidably developed rhetoric. Still, I believe that most playgoers, after *3 Henry VI*, will be haunted by one quiet scene like a shepherd's pipe in the midst of a thunderstorm. The King, fitter for monkish tonsure than for crown, is transiently alone upon the field of Towton, sitting on a molehill – is it coincidence that York is forced to stand on one? – and musing: 'This battle fares like to the morning's war,/When dying clouds contend with growing light.' He has a speech that should be heard with Richard of Gloucester's brag – the wistful dream of a man to whom the crown is torment:

> O God! methinks it were a happy life
> To be no better than a homely swain;
> To sit upon a hill, as I do now,
> To carve out dials quaintly, point by point,
> Thereby to see the minutes how they run –
> How many makes the hour full complete,
> How many hours bring about the day,
> How many days will finish up the year,
> How many years a mortal man may live.

When this is known, then to divide the times –
So many hours must I tend my flock;
So many hours must I take my rest;
So many hours must I contemplate;
So many hours must I sport myself;
So many days my ewes have been with young;
So many weeks ere the poor fools will ean;
So many years ere I shall shear the fleece:
So minutes, hours, days, months, and years,
Pass'd over to the end they were created,
Would bring white hairs unto a quiet grave.
Ah, what a life were this! how sweet! how lovely!
Gives not the hawthorn bush a sweeter shade
To shepherds looking on their silly sheep,
Than doth a rich embroider'd canopy
To kings that fear their subjects' treachery?
O yes, it doth; a thousand-fold it doth. (II, v, 21–46)

Presently, when Henry is silent, there enter 'a Son that hath kill'd his Father, at one door; and a Father that hath kill'd his Son, at another door'. The scene rises slowly into a lament in which the King joins, a three-part threnody on the anguish of civil war between kith and kin, that goes on beating in the mind even when dulled a little in the fury of renewed battle and flight.

As the play passes, so does the weary King. Practically at the end, when we hear once more the image of the 'bird that hath been liméd in a bush', Henry is stabbed to death in the Tower. Gloucester is his murderer:

This word 'love', which greybeards call divine,
Be resident in men like one another,
And not in me! I am myself alone. (V, vi, 81–3)

In the last moments of all, as Douglas Seale directed them at Birmingham (1953), Edward IV was on his throne, Richard gave his Judas-kiss to the child Prince of Wales, and the King spoke his final couplet:

Sound drums and trumpets. Farewell, sour annoy!
For here, I hope, begins our lasting joy. (V, vi, 45–6)

Suddenly music, martial and courtly, faded, and lights concentrated upon Richard as he limped downstage, alone, to begin the first soliloquy of the next play, 'Now is the winter of our discontent/Made glorious summer by this sun of York;/And all the clouds that lour'd upon our House/In the deep bosom of the ocean buried.' The sounds of cheering offstage, and a long, swelling clash of bells, blotted out his voice, the scene darkened, and slowly the curtain fell.

NOTES

1 1942. See also O'Casey's play, *Red Roses For Me*, Act I, a variation on his auto-biography.
2 One recalls Laurence Olivier's imperious gesture at 'Set the murderous Machiavel to school' when much of this speech entered the first soliloquy of *Richard III* during the 1944 revival at the New Theatre.

King Richard III
(1592–3)

I

Sir Arthur Quiller-Couch said, not in a Shakespearian context but in his lecture on Jargon: 'In literature, as in life, he makes himself felt who not only calls a spade a spade, but has the pluck to double spades and re-double.' This is what Shakespeare does during the un-abashed villainy of *Richard III*. It is futile to ask whether the cocka-trice, bottled spider, rooting hog and hunchback toad, and whatever else he is called in the play, is true to the Richard of history: enough that it was the Tudor version. A loyal contemporary group exists to show that Richard was in fact a good son, a loving husband, a noble ruler, and the victim of a foul plot.[1] No doubt; but a play I saw twenty years ago, which was designed to prove all this, merely dripped a bucket of whitewash over Richard very slowly, telling us at the same time that blood boiled, events took shape, webs were woven, secrets were hidden in hearts, hands called to helms, matters broached, and bitter cups drained to dregs.

Shakespearians, for the theatre's sake, hold without argument to the Richard of the chronicle that owes much to those other chroniclers, Holinshed and Hall. The Red King has always been a prized acting part either in the Folio text or in one by Colley Cibber (1700) which governed the stage for so long that some would have been puzzled to say where Shakespeare ended and Cibber's stagily complex mosaic began. It is improbable that new playgoers will hear again the notorious phrases or claptraps, 'Off with his head – so much for Buckingham!', 'A weak invention of the enemy', 'Perish the thought!', and

> Conscience avaunt, Richard's himself again:
> Hark! the shrill trumpet sounds, to horse, away.
> My soul's in arms and eager for the fray.

If they do, they have listened, unaware, to collectors' gold. Besides the great names, Cooke, Kemble, Kean, Macready, Irving and the rest, the least probable actors, tempted by the man's flamboyance, have wanted to fly at Richard. They have thought of it less as 'the continuation of a historic and dynastic development' than as a melodrama of the blood royal. Turned simply to a transpontine storm, it can be tiresome. It can be similarly tiresome if a Richard resolves to be only a macabre Punch figure, alert for the easy laugh. This is the mask without the mind. When the brains are out, a part should die, and there an end. Not so here: it is possible with Richard to ruffle only the surface of the character and yet to give a performance that manages to slip through, a fussy blend of Punch and Quilp, a strutting wicked uncle affair, a Crookback from a child's history book, gloating among the trumpets. Such a bluff as this should be treasonable: the play is melodrama, but it is not enough to present Richard as an animated oleograph, a benefit night Crummles to whom we cry: 'Begin, murderer, leave thy damnable faces, and begin.'

A Richard must expose the man's brain. It was the marriage of intellect and dramatic assurance, forked-lightning bravura and icy reason, that so distinguished Laurence Olivier in the autumn of 1944. One must always judge this famous portrait from its first presentation with the Old Vic company, and not from the film with its more resolutely composite text – 'interpolations by David Garrick, Colley Cibber, etc.' – that arrived a decade later, though that too had its flame. From the first, on the London night (13 September 1944) at what was then the New Theatre, the actor bore Richard forward: evilly debonair, pale of cheek, his hair black and lank, and his gait like a limping panther. He preserved the man's pride – this Plantagenet was from the aëry in the cedar's top – he had a glittering, chilling irony, in rage he could startle ('Out on you, owls! Nothing but songs of death!'), and his silences, malign or mocking, were infinitely laden. Richard distilled his own darkness; and I cannot return to the play now without picturing Olivier, a cauldron-figure crowned and sceptred, as he brooded on the throne, ignoring the urgency of Buckingham. He spoke in his searing voice:

> Richmond! When last I was at Exeter,
> The mayor in courtesy show'd me the castle
> And call'd it Rougemont, at which name I started,
> Because a bard of Ireland told me once
> I should not live long after I saw Richmond. (IV, ii, 107–11)

The name 'Richmond' hissed and fell like molten metal.

II

In the theatre it was once the Cibber fashion to begin with the murder of Henry VI (*3 Henry VI*, V, vi): a mistake, for the entry of 'Richard Duke of Gloucester, *solus*' is a major theatrical effect that should not be sacrificed. The actor is the raven poised above the Royal House:

> And therefore, since I cannot prove a lover
> To entertain these fair well-spoken days,
> I am determined to prove a villain
> And hate the idle pleasures of these days.
> Plots have I laid, inductions dangerous,
> By drunken prophecies, libels, and dreams,
> To set my brother Clarence and the King
> In deadly hate the one against the other;
> And if King Edward be as true and just
> As I am subtle, false, and treacherous,
> This day should Clarence closely be mew'd up. (I, i, 28–38)

Immediately we have Richard's dissimulation with his brother, and what has been called the masochistic wooing of Lady Anne above the coffin of her father-in-law, Henry VI. On the ensanguined path to Bosworth and retribution, Richard is at first a man who puts off care as his villainy mounts; then, weighted by sceptre and crown, he is assailed by clustering doubts. Extraordinary in diablerie and bravado, the part demands an extraordinary performance. We ask if Richard strikes fear when, after stripping his withered arm, he dooms Hastings –

> Thou art a traitor.
> Off with his head! Now by Saint Paul I swear
> I will not dine until I see the same. (III, iv, 77–9)

– or, as bad tidings swell, whether we shiver with those round him at the cry, 'Is the chair empty? Is the sword unsway'd?' Do we hear the molten metal at the name 'Richmond'? Does the weary 'There is no creature loves me' stir our pity?[2] We can say that, if it does, this is a performance for the records. Richard has so much else. There is the wooing, its ardour and confident arrogance even when his breast is bared to receive the sword. There is the meeting with the Princes before they enter the Tower: a scene that inferior child actors can shatter ('little prating York' needs quick intelligence). There is the deception of the Lord Mayor and Aldermen, Buckingham eloquent

below, and Richard, meek aloft 'between two Bishops', ready to cap
Buckingham's 'Zounds, I'll entreat no more' with the chiding 'O, do
not swear, my lord!'

During the second half cunning turns to demonic despotism: the
aside to Catesby:[3] 'I say again, give out/That Anne, my queen, is
sick and like to die'. (IV, ii, 58–9); the sudden dismissal of
Buckingham; the moment when the wrath of the royal women is
drowned by trumpet and drum ('Let not the heavens hear these tell-
tale women/Rail on the Lord's anointed'); and the night and morning
sequence at Bosworth. The tents of Richard and the avenging
Richmond (not much like the man we know as Henry VII)[4] are set
on opposite sides of the stage. There circle round them, sometimes to
a low drum-beat, sometimes to wailing music, the ghosts in grey procession. 'Despair and die!' they murmur to Richard, and to
Richmond, 'Live and flourish!' Trembling, the King starts from his
dream into the soliloquy that must be the crown of any performance:

> Give me another horse. Bind up my wounds.
> Have mercy, Jesu! Soft! I did but dream.
> O coward conscience, how dost thou afflict me!
> The lights burn blue. It is now dead midnight.
> Cold fearful drops stand on my trembling flesh.
> What do I fear? Myself? There's none else by.
> Richard loves Richard; that is, I am I.
> Is there a murderer here? No – yes, I am.
> Then fly. What, from myself? Great reason why –
> Lest I revenge. What, myself upon myself?
> Alack, I love myself. Wherefore? For any good
> That I myself have done unto myself?
> O, no! Alas, I rather hate myself
> For hateful deeds committed by myself!
> I am a villain; yet I lie, I am not.
> Fool, of thyself speak well. Fool, do not flatter.
> My conscience hath a thousand several tongues,
> And every tongue brings in a several tale,
> And every tale condemns me for a villain. (V, iii, 177–95)

After this, to the rival orations, the battle, the strangled shout 'A
horse! A horse! my kingdom for a horse!' and the last fight with
Richmond. 'God and your arms be prais'd, victorious friends;/The
day is ours, the bloody dog is dead.'

III

Richard is supreme. In a full text, which we get very seldom, he speaks 1,164 lines, after Hamlet the longest part in Shakespeare; Buckingham is next with 361; the Queens, Elizabeth and Margaret, follow. These demand for their invective the declamatory voices that are now so rare: it has been said that all such women should be spoken by the shade of Genevieve Ward. Dame Peggy Ashcroft, in our time, brought Margaret commandingly through the whole tetralogy, from the young French Princess of *1 Henry VI*. Though I felt differently once, the part in *Richard III* should not be clipped: it suffers if we find the old Queen only near the beginning of the play and not in the antiphonal cursing. Dame Edith Evans, who had been Margaret to Baliol Holloway's Richard at the Vic in 1925, led the tirades at Stratford in 1961, her voice reminding one critic of the sound of bare branches in a winter wind.

After Richard, from the play's long cast, we may pause first at George, Duke of Clarence: his intensely pictorial dream is not in the Cibber version (where, like Margaret, he does not appear), and it has often been cut from later revivals. We have heard it spoken by such actors as Sir John Gielgud (in the Olivier film) and Alec Clunes (Old Vic, 1936), each of them with the range for

> Methought I saw a thousand fearful wrecks,
> A thousand men that fishes gnaw'd upon,
> Wedges of gold, great anchors, heaps of pearl,
> Inestimable stones, unvalued jewels,
> All scatt'red in the bottom of the sea. (I, iv, 24–8)

and

> Then came wand'ring by
> A shadow like an angel, with bright hair
> Dabbled in blood, and he shriek'd out aloud
> 'Clarence is come – false, fleeting, perjur'd Clarence,
> That stabb'd me in the field by Tewkesbury. (I, iv, 52–6)

Tyrrel's narrative of the death of the Princes has also lines we watch for:

> 'O, thus' quoth Dighton 'lay the gentle babes' –
> 'Thus, thus,' quoth Forrest 'girdling one another
> Within their alabaster innocent arms.
> Their lips were four red roses on a stalk,
> And in their summer beauty kiss'd each other. (IV, iii, 9–13)

From a cast of nearly forty (and extras) one name is missing: the harlot, Jane Shore, has no entrance, though she is spoken of more than once. Directors, putting Shakespeare right, now seem eager to include her in the scene when Hastings is awakened on the morning of his death.

We return to Olivier's rightly honoured Richard. I think of his insolent relish at 'set the murderous Machiavel to school' (from the *3 Henry VI* soliloquy) meshed with the first speech of *Richard III;* the imperatively regal gesture to Buckingham in the very birth of majesty; the wistfully despairing 'Not shine today!' as the King studied the morning sky over Bosworth; the doom in the distorted face; and the last spasm of the death agony at Richmond's[5] feet. Other expert performances in our period have been those of Baliol Holloway who, as the critic Herbert Farjeon said, acted to his finger-nails; Donald Wolfit, more melodramatic than the rest; Ian Holm (at Stratford), smaller in scale than the others, a psychopath playing the power game; and, at St George's, Islington, in 1976, Alan Badel, who had all the deadly menace for the scene with Buckingham which is among the touchstones of the part:

BUCKINGHAM: My lord—
KING RICHARD: Ay, what's o'clock?
BUCKINGHAM: I am thus bold to put your Grace in mind
               Of what you promis'd me.
KING RICHARD: Well, but what's o'clock?
BUCKINGHAM: Upon the stroke of ten.
KING RICHARD: Well, let it strike.
BUCKINGHAM: Why let it strike?
KING RICHARD: Because that like a Jack thou keep'st the stroke
               Between thy begging and my meditation.
               I am not in the giving vein today.
BUCKINGHAM: May it please you to resolve me in my suit.
KING RICHARD: Thou troublest me; I am not in the vein.
               (Exeunt all but Buckingham)
BUCKINGHAM: And is it thus? . . . (IV, ii, 112–24)

It is. This is a test for the Buckingham as well as for his King.

NOTES

1 Members of this fellowship might say, with the Gaoler in *Cymbeline:* 'I would we were all of one mind, and that mind good.'
2 Richard has Catesby; Macbeth, who talks of 'curses, not loud but deep', has Seyton.

3 When John Wood, as an amateur, played Richard for the Oxford University Dramatic Society, the Queen was allowed to overhear her husband's order.

4 In the first-night programme at the New Theatre (1944) he was described, re-markably, as 'later King Edward VII'.

5 In *3 Henry VI*, IV, vi, Henry, Earl of Richmond, appears as a youth whom the King addresses as 'England's hope', saying to those around: 'This pretty lad will prove our country's bliss. . . . His head by nature fram'd to wear a crown.'

Titus Andronicus
(1593–4)

I

This 'most lamentable Romaine tragedy of *Titus Andronicus*' is a ferocious revenge play, with Rome a 'wilderness of tigers' – material for every Elizabethan who expected the playhouse trumpets to be joyful harbingers of blood and death. Undisguisedly, it is what the Empress's Moorish paramour, Aaron, describes at his capture: a thing of

> Murders, rapes, and massacres,
> Acts of black night, abominable deeds,
> Complots of mischief, treason, villainies. (V, i, 63–5)

Influenced by the claustrophobic excesses of the Roman dramatist Seneca, it was among the stock dramas of its time, the early 1590s. Afterwards, during a long period of roughly 250 years after 1725 (when the work of a tenth-rate Restoration botcher, Edward Ravenscroft, faded from the stage), few people had a chance to shiver at *Titus*, even in perversion. Surprisingly, the Negro actor, Ira Aldridge, using Ravenscroft's muddle, turned up as Aaron at the Britannia Theatre, Hoxton (never a fashionable address) in the 1850s. Robert Atkins, who would try anything, did the play without reserve in a scarlet-and-black setting at the Old Vic in 1923; but it was not until the 1950s that it seized attention in a world inured to its 'acts of black night'. We had successively – after an odd compression at the end of a little theatre's Guignol bill – an amateur revival in the East End with Japanese décor, a full-length radio broadcast,[1] a Marlowe Society production at Cambridge that showed humanity and retribution balancing sadism and terror, and finally, on a hot August night in 1955, Peter Brook's triumph at Stratford-upon-Avon.

There the bloodstained thumb at length left its print on the page.
We responded to strong, uncomplicated emotions – violence, hatred,
cruelty, fear – presented without any thick impasto in (Brook's words)
'a form that became unrealistic, transcended the anecdote, and, for
each audience, was quite abstract and thus totally real'. Nothing
has yet matched this; but the play does return, though not often.
Titus has thirteen violent deaths of one kind and another, and more
to come. The later Elizabethans did not mind. Accepting any form
of violence, they never thought it bizarre to stand about the bear-pit
on Bankside while lute music drifted over the Thames. They saw
nothing strange when Marcus Andronicus, instead of swiftly bringing a surgeon to his niece, the ravished and mutilated Lavinia,
addressed her in a run of classical conceits. The late A. V. Cookman,
drama critic of *The Times*, used to insist on the theory noted in his
review[2] of Brook's production. The atrocities, he said, were surely
meant to illustrate 'that familiar Elizabethan metaphor in which dis-
ruption of the body politic is imaged in dismemberment of individual
men and women'. (So, too, in the early history plays.) I still recall
Cookman, silver-haired and urbane, debating this at a Stratford
hotel until four in the morning after the Brook revival, while he was
opposed, no less urgently, by another playgoer who held that
Shakespeare's only thought was to write a roaring melodrama, or
what Herbert Farjeon, at the Old Vic in 1923, called 'a stark piece
of stage frightfulness'.[3]

II

The bare plot is melodramatic enough, simply one revenge pressing
upon another. Tamora, Queen of the Goths, made Empress of Rome
in an extraordinary reversal after her defeat and capture, brings
brutal disaster upon Titus and his family; in return, he kills two of
her sons, has the heads baked in a pie which he serves to her at a
gruesome feast, and then stabs her. (The end of Marlowe's *The Jew
of Malta* is comparably lurid.) At the last – I quote John
Masefield – 'the survivors – about half the original cast – move off,
as they say, to order well the State'.[4]

Verbally, it is often crude, in spite of fevered gusts of rhetoric and
a passage such as this for Marcus when Lavinia appears with her
hands cut off:

O, had the monster seen those lily hands
Tremble like aspen-leaves upon a lute
And make the silken strings delight to kiss them,
He would not then have touched them for his life! (II, iv, 44–7)

Logan Pearsall Smith, rapidly dismissive of the tragedy as a whole, confessed that he had overlooked these lines.

In performance, if a cast can go straight into the attack, and the director does not meet crudity with crudity, which does happen, *Titus Andronicus* can still possess the stage. Its narrative is not to be searched critically. Why in the world does Tamora, who has been cunning enough, evolve that last ridiculous plan? Yet any competent revival must strengthen the view that whatever Shakespeare wrote, must be expressed in the theatre, however dubious it may seem in the study. Act it first; analyse it afterwards. A director must be careful with *Titus*. Even in these days when hell has opened, he must contrive, if not to rationalise, at least to excuse some of the sanguinary invention. He should spare us too much insistence on the recipe for something (as a Cornishman, I object) that is called a 'pasty' and usually mispronounced. He must spare us a too ludicrous huddle of deaths, that rapid skittle game, and avoid repetitive dagger-play. Brook proved that it does not harm *Titus* to temper the more violent shocks, such as Lavinia's entry after her ordeal in the wood. One thing that must always startle is the chopping of Titus's hand; I imagine that this strikes as sharply as it ever did.

The beginning, like the end, needs infinite care. Our imaginations have to be trapped at once. I have seen this managed in two ways. Brook created a shadowed, brooding city, a world remote, almost lunar, where processions coiled and green-habited priests moved in a hieratic solemnity. At the Birmingham Repertory Theatre (1963) Ronald Eyre raised his curtain upon utter darkness from which Rome, its warring lords, its tribunes, its insignia, and its fettered Goths, slowly emerged, balefully lit. Another English director tried the everything-on-a-staircase method defined in the rhyme of the grand old Duke of York: 'When they were up they were up, and when they were down they were down.' It can be fidgety, and *Titus* is not meant for fidgets.

III

There are two ample major parts. Others fill out the plot: Tamora ('I'll find a day to massacre them all,/And raze their faction, and their family'); Saturninus, a potential Neronic voluptuary; the tortured Lavinia; the classically-minded Marcus; Bassianus in his pit; and a pair of horrific brothers. Aaron, the Moor 'beloved of Tamora', is an incarnation of gloating villainy, with some passages of protective affection for his black child that such actors as George Hayes, Anthony Quayle, and Derek Jacobi[5] have left in our minds:

Look how the black slave smiles upon the father,
As who should say 'Old lad, I am thine own.' (IV, ii, 120–1)

the later 'My son and I will have the wind of you' (he has someone
now to be proud of, someone who is on his side); and the sustained:

Now to the Goths, as swift as swallow flies,
There to dispose this treasure in mine arms,
And secretly to greet the Empress' friends.
Come on, you thick-lipp'd slave, I'll bear you hence;
For it is you that puts us to our shifts.
I'll make you feed on berries and on roots,
And feed on curds and whey, and suck the goat,
And cabin in a cave, and bring you up
To be a warrior and command a camp. (IV, ii, 173–81)

Otherwise, he is past redemption and revels in it:

Even now I curse the day – and yet, I think,
Few come within the compass of my curse –
Wherein I did not some notorious ill. . . . (V, i, 125–7)

I have done a thousand dreadful things
As willingly as one would kill a fly;
And nothing grieves me heartily indeed
But that I cannot do ten thousand more. (V, i, 141–4)

Titus Andronicus must govern the play. He is a warrior desperately
tired; a veteran on the edge of the gulf (an early trace of Lear); and a
man in whose rage we can feel the storm wind of the equinox. Lear is
identified with the storm in his mind, Titus with the sea which is his
constant image. At the play's height, after the loss of his hand, he cries:

If there were reason for these miseries,
Then into limits could I bind my woes.
When heaven doth weep, doth not the earth o'erflow?
If the winds rage, doth not the sea wax mad,
Threat'ning the welkin with his big-swol'n face?
And wilt thou have a reason for this coil?
I am the sea; hark how her sighs do blow.
She is the weeping welkin, I the earth:
Then must my sea be moved with her sighs;
Then must my earth with her continual tears
Become a deluge, overflow'd and drown'd . . . (III, i, 220–30)

There Laurence Olivier (Stratford, 1955) expanded the part in a splendour of heroic acting, the kind of acting, more than life-size, that *Titus* must have if it is to live. Anything less than mastery in direction and performance, and we find ourselves noting what we should not – the tactful change of conversation (Titus has just killed his son) when Marcus observes:

> My lord – to step out of these dreary dumps
> How comes it that the subtle Queen of Goths
> Is of a sudden thus advanc'd in Rome? (I, i, 391–3)

the wicked brother's 'I'll broach the tadpole on my rapier's point', and that query to Aaron:

> Say, wall-ey'd slave, whither wouldst thou convey
> This growing image of thy fiend-like face? (V, i, 44–5)

which is simply an Elizabethan synonym for holding the baby. Too bad; but we must listen also for some powerfully evocative lines: these, which may remind us of a passage[6] from *I Henry VI*, for one of the savage Goths, Demetrius:

> She is a woman, therefore may be woo'd;
> She is a woman, therefore may be won;
> She is Lavinia, therefore must be lov'd; (II, i, 83–5)

the hunting scene in the forest ('The hunt is up, the morn is bright and grey,/The fields are fragrant, and the woods are green') which looks forward, curiously, to a passage in *A Midsummer Night's Dream;* Tamora's speech to Aaron in the forest depths:

> Wherefore look'st thou sad
> When everything doth make a gleeful boast?
> The birds chant melody on every bush;
> The snake lies rolled in the cheerful sun;
> The green leaves quiver with the cooling wind
> And make a chequer'd shadow on the ground.
> Under their sweet shade, Aaron, let us sit,
> And whilst the babbling echo mocks the hounds,
> Replying shrilly to the well-tun'd horns,
> As if a double hunt were heard at once,
> Let us sit down and mark their yellowing noise . . . (II, iii, 10–20)

and the later rapid change for the benefit of her sons:

A barren detested vale you see it is,
The trees, though summer, yet forlorn and lean . . .
Here never shines the sun, here nothing breeds. (II, iii, 93–6)

Then, too, Marcus's 'aspen-leaves' speech, though it is most awkwardly placed and often cut; Titus's

What fool hath added water to the sea,
Or brought a fagot to bright-burning Troy? (III, i, 68–9)

all of his sea-imagery; and the order to young Lucius after Lavinia has written in the sand, with her staff, the names of her ravishers:

And come, I will go get a leaf of brass,
And with a gad of steel will write these words,
And lay it by; the angry northern wind
Will blow these sands like Sibyl's leaves abroad. (IV, i, 103–6)

and his earlier lines:

Behold our cheeks
How they are stain'd, like meadows not yet dry
With miry slime left on them by a flood . . . (III, i, 124–6)

IV

Here, I suppose, it is tempting, though thoroughly dangerous, to think of the Avon meadows in early spring. Over and over, in the plays, we have to stop ourselves from localising an image. Though much obviously derives from Warwickshire, we cannot grab at every pictorial reference – at, say, Celia's lines in *As You Like It*:

West of this place, down in the neighbour bottom,
The rank of osiers by the murmuring stream
Left on your right hand, brings you to the place (IV, iii, 77–9)

as a direction to Anne Hathaway's cottage. In *Coriolanus* a Messenger exclaims, after Volumnia's return to Rome:

Ne'er through an arch so hurried the blown tide
As the recomforted through th'gates (V, iv, 46–7)

and we ask instinctively, which arch? Can it be Clopton Bridge?

There are other bridges, other ranks of osiers, other 'miry meadows'. In *Titus* a phrase for Demetrius,

> What, hast thou not full often struck a doe,
> And borne her cleanly by the keeper's nose? (II, i, 93–4)

is not necessarily a gloss on the legend of the young Shakespeare and the Charlecote deer.

For a good many collectors, *Titus Andronicus* may still be the last play of all: distant, desolate beach, ensanguined tide. They should not despair. I remember, in 1955, coming into the Stratford night not as if we had dug up a mandrake but as if we had been in the presence of high tragedy. It was strange, remembering how embarrassed, even facetious, the audience had been before curtain-rise. Ivor Brown spoke for the majority[7] when he called this revival 'a masterpiece of salvage, a display of extreme cunning in the art of covering up . . . There had to be a positive development of the play's merits as well as a cloaking and evasion of its faults . . . The audience was coaxed into believing that this was a worthy play about a man both sinned against and sinning.'

True, much must depend on the coaxing quality of later directors. Elizabethans had no need to be coaxed. We know that *Titus*, at the Rose, took as much as three pounds eight shillings at one performance and forty shillings at each of two others – the sums at that time were considerable – and the play was still being reprinted in quarto after twenty years. Not with unanimous enthusiasm: 'He that will swear *Jeronimo*[8] or *Andronicus* are the best plays yet shall pass unexcepted at here, as a man whose judgment shows it is constant and hath stood still these five and twenty or thirty years.' The speaker was Ben Jonson,[9] but, doubtless to his irritation, nobody marked him.

NOTES

1 With Wilfrid Walter and George Hayes, who thirty years earlier had acted Titus and Aaron for Atkins at the Vic.
2 *The Times*, 17 August 1955.
3 *The Shakespearean Scene* (1949), p. 114.
4 *William Shakespeare* (1964 edition).
5 At, respectively, the Old Vic (1923; also on radio, 1953), Stratford (1955), and the Birmingham Repertory (1963).
6 In the scene with Margaret of Anjou:
   SUFFOLK *(aside)*: She's beautiful, and therefore to be woo'd;
                   She is a woman, therefore to be won. (V, iii, 78–9)
7 *The Shakespeare Memorial Theatre 1954–56*.
8 Thomas Kyd's *The Spanish Tragedy*.
9 In the Induction to *Bartholomew Fair*, 1614.

The Comedy of Errors
(before 1594)

I

We can be sure of one thing: we shall not again see *The Comedy of Errors* as an undoubtedly charming but anonymous 'American lady well-known in artistic circles, who has music in her pen as in her voice,' – the words are those of Clement Scott, the drama critic – described it in *The Theatre* (London, April 1887). She was writing of a revival at the Star Theatre, New York, in 1885:

'The incident of the shipwreck was a loop through which was drawn a scenic prologue entitled 'The Wreck of the Trireme,' as Egeon so graphically describes in his speech before the tribunal of the Duke in Scene I: 'For ere the ships could meet by twice five leagues/We were encounter'd by a mighty rock' . . . As the curtain rose, a darkness rested on the scene. Soon a faint gleam of rosy dawn broke over it, deepening and brightening, revealing the sea rearing its white-capped waves against a mighty rock and dashing the helpless rock with its cruel crest. Nothing more exquisite in stage mechanism could be imagined.'

('Exquisite' is an agreeable word). Later, so it seems, the comedy vanished in a pageant of the priests and priestesses of Diana of the Ephesians, with vestals and acolytes, Ionian flautists, Egyptian harpers, curators of the temple, heralds, and Praetorian guards. As for the villa of the courtesan Phryne, introduced by the speech of Antipholus of Ephesus, 'Since my own doors refuse to entertain me,/ I'll knock elsewhere, to see if they'll disdain me'. (III, i, 120–1), this was a place of tinted marble columns, canopies of embroidered and spangled lace, lamps of perfumed oil, genuine Negroes 'selected for their symmetry of outline', palms, brilliant flowers, sumptuous couches, singing slaves, and Bacchantes. Among all this 'the action of the play stood out clearly defined.'

Alarming: we shake our heads. But in 1976, at Stratford-upon-Avon (I am condensing a review[1]) Ephesus was a disreputable modern town of tourist shops, whorish girls leaning from balconies in silky dressing-gowns, the Dromios as red-nosed clowns with baggy jeans and braces, an Adriana with 'a liking for the revealing dress and the bottle', Antipholus of Ephesus a man of 'a lean gum-chewing sleaziness', a comically vast dictator (Solinus), and nine new songs.

Alarming, once more. But there it is: *The Comedy of Errors* has become a directors' palimpsest. Usually it is a boiling-kettle romp; frequently, the libretto for a musical play (*The Boys from Syracuse* was only one). Without music it is simply an uninhibited farce – in spite of a growing academic resolve, expressed most reasonably by Dr Stanley Wells[2], to suggest that it is more serious than a glib piece of theatrical craft. 'The play ends', he says, 'not in the chaos characteristic of some types of farce, but in a re-establishment of order and harmony, accompanied by an assertion and demonstration of humane values such as are associated with the most romantic of romantic comedies.' This would baffle many directors: we shall be lucky indeed now to find the last scene played with true gravity.

II

Briefly, here is the work of a young but already acutely professional technician. It may be asking too much to presume (as a former actor, Hesketh Pearson, thought) that an early speech of Antipholus of Syracuse refers to Shakespeare on tour in the year 1592:

> Within this hour it will be dinner-time;
> Till that, I'll view the manners of the town,
> Peruse the traders, gaze upon the buildings,
> And then return and sleep within mine inn;
> For with long travel I am stiff and weary. (I, ii, 11–15)

It is quite enough that he is a professional, humanising the Plautine mechanics of (in the main) the *Menaechmi* in his version of 'one day's error'. Humanising certainly, but making his task harder by doubling the identical twins and their identical masters who wander at cross purposes through the Ephesian streets. The shortest of the plays (1777 lines), it used often to pad out a theatre evening. I have known it acted with *The Two Gentlemen of Verona* and *Titus Andronicus*, each unsparingly cut; early in the 1920s an English provincial actor-manager would put it on as a disorganised skirmish, its Dromios in black-face (how could one of them talk of being 'pinched black and blue'?) before a portentous revival of *The Bells*. Today we shall either see it on its own and in a permanent setting (free from marble columns and sumptuous couches), or, most likely, as a musical free-for-all.

However it is done, it has to be brief, for a director who slows down 'the flashing to-and-fro of identical dragon-flies' (Edward Dowden's phrase) does so at his peril. Dramatists have always loved identical twins. The young Shakespeare establishes his two pairs in a city reputed to be a place of magic, of cozenage, sorcerers, soul-killing witches, cheaters, prating mountebanks, and various 'liberties of sin', where anything can happen, and does. But Ephesus was also the home of the cult of Diana, goddess of childbirth; and we can suppose, too, if we wish, that Shakespeare is remembering Paul's discussion of Christian marriage in the epistle to the Ephesians: 'Wives, submit yourselves unto your own husbands, as to the Lord.'

The comedy of losing and finding begins in the early hours of an Ephesian morning with a long speech, difficult to fit into any burlesque, by old Egeon, merchant of Syracuse, who used – as far back as Kemble – to be brought on in chains. His exposition is so serious that many directors, afraid to trust an audience intolerant of the long narrative, have turned him into a bore, an ancient with nothing else to fill eternity. It is easy enough; an experienced actor can drag a laugh from a misplaced pause. But Egeon, even when treated seriously, was often consigned to the dullest of character men, gnawing and quavering through the hundred-odd lines. As a deliberately comic and falsifying method grew more popular, it was not hard for a director to find appropriate emphases for a yawning Duke:

Well, Syracusian, say *in brief* the cause
Why thou departed'st from thy native home. (1, i, 29 – 30)

Facile; but is this what Shakespeare desired? The too anxious director shuts his mind to probability. Such a piece as the *Errors* is all the better for rising naturally from a basically grave situation. Egeon's life is endangered. For five years he has sought the twin son and slave who went out in search of their lost brothers; now, unwittingly, he is in a town at enmity with Syracuse, and he must die unless by the evening he can pay his ransom of a thousand marks. In the first lines of his speech he is sure (though we do not believe him) that his plight is hopeless:

Proceed, Solinus, to procure my fall.
And by the doom of death end woes and all. (I, i, 1–2)

This opening is packed, and its treatment will give a good idea of the way in which the comedy will go: whether the later quibble-loaded text, the tangle of crooked answers and cross-questions, will be taken as nonsense unabashed, or whether the director will allow any kind of plausible humanity to aerate it. The Duke is a key. We must listen anxiously to that early

> Do me the favour to dilate at full
> What have befall'n of them and thee till now. (I, i, 123–4)

III

The 'errors', which must be observed in the theatre, begin with the mistaking of Dromio of Ephesus for his brother of Syracuse. We yield then to a dramatist's licence and accept that A and B and C and D look precisely like each other and (with no excuse at all) wear precisely the same clothes. There is little poetry until the beginning of the second act when Adriana and Luciana move into early Shakespearian lyric rhyme. A later scene, when Adriana, quite seriously, addresses the wrong Antipholus, is another theatrical temptation. It can be rattled through, or taken with the pleasant mock gravity of Clifford Williams's production at Stratford-upon-Avon (1962). There, after a good-looking young woman had addressed Antipholus of Syracuse in thirty-seven lines of impassioned blank verse, informing him, among other matters, that she was his wife and 'possessed with an adulterate blot', the actor answered in the mildest bewilderment: 'Plead you to *me*, fair dame?'

The best way with the *Errors* is to play it lightly, not to batter at the clowning, and not to undervalue that sudden lyrical blossoming for Luciana and Antipholus of Syracuse in the third act, and such lines as 'It is thyself, mine own self's better part;/Mine eye's clear eye, my dear heart's dearer heart' (III, ii, 61–2) that can point towards the verse of *Romeo and Juliet*. We are in the director's hands. The night can be a hullabaloo, a gallop, a joke imposed upon a joke (Komisarjevsky at Stratford-upon-Avon, 1938; Ephesus sprouting in pink bowlers; the set dominated by an enormous clock), or it can move without strain, in the haze of a dream where the irrational is rational. I repeat, Solinus, Duke of Ephesus, may give an immediate clue. He can be sympathetic and authoritative, or he can be the tormented victim of one of Shakespeare's most arduous listening parts. People are continually trying to tell him things: veteran merchants who have lost their families, wives who are raging against their husbands, husbands who are raging at practically everything. 'Why what an intricate

impeach is this!' the Duke exclaims towards the end of the comedy.
And, again: 'I think you are all mated, or stark mad.'

The main people in the intricacy are firmly imagined. Antipholus
of Ephesus is a baffled spaniel goaded to a wrath that reminds us
he has taken 'deep scars in the Duke's wars'. Antipholus of Syracuse
is a blandly sententious young man surprised to be offered a wife, a
house, a gold chain, and a few other bounties. Adriana, nagging and
jealous, and the sadder Luciana speak for themselves. Disciplined
high spirits, without farcical gagging, can ease the burden of the
clowns: the Dromios should be, but seldom are, agile *commedia dell'arte*
virtuosi. Three characters, Luce, Pinch, and the Courtesan, are often
fooled to rags. Luce, or Nell, is Adriana's kitchenmaid: ever careless
with names, Shakespeare does not mind that there is also a Luciana in
the cast; for that matter, he does not explain why the brothers
Antipholus and Dromio should be identical in name as in everything
else. Though Luce has only eight lines, Dromio of Syracuse's protracted
map description ('She is spherical, like a globe. I could find out
countries in her') is a direct invitation to the lowest comedy.

The Courtesan, an opulent peony, is also troublesome. It is wrong
to equate her with a comic prostitute, but I do remember a certain
illegitimate fun with her aspirates ('Hie home to my house'), and
more than one actress has enjoyed the last 'Sir, I must have that
diamond from you' when she invariably addresses the wrong person.
As for Doctor Pinch, 'a hungry lean-fac'd villain . . . a needy, hollow-
eye'd, sharp-looking wretch', with only four more lines than Luce,
he can be grotesquely forced while he yodels incantations and dodges
fire-crackers, a shoddy stand-in for Mephistopheles. His 'cure' for
Antipholus of Ephesus, when he invokes Satan to yield and proposes
that man and master shall be 'bound, and laid in some dark room', looks
forward to another outbreak of the Elizabethan sense of humour, the
Twelfth Night conspirators' way with Malvolio: 'Tis not for gravity to
play at cherry-pit with Satan . . . Come, we'll have him in a dark
room and bound.'

IV

There are few lines to wait for in a piece where narrative is all. Still,
we do not forget the repeated images in speeches by Antipholus of
Syracuse and Adriana. In the first act Antipholus is soliloquising:

> I to the world am like a drop of water
> That in the ocean seeks another drop,
> Who, falling there to find his fellow forth,
> Unseen, inquisitive, confounds himself. (I, ii, 35–8)

In the second act he is adjured by Adriana, who thinks he is her husband:

> Ah, do not tear away thyself from me;
> For know, my love, as easy mayst thou fall
> A drop of water in the breaking gulf,
> And take unmingled thence that drop again
> Without addition or diminishing,
> As take from me thyself, and not me too.   (II, ii, 123–8)

In the very ebb of the comedy we meet the Abbess, a part that, again, rests on a director's whim, and whose revelation as wife and mother is Shakespeare's final surprise: more often than not it rouses needless laughter. Her final lines are:

> Go to a gossips' feast, and go with me;
> After so long grief, such nativity!   (V, i, 404–5)

Though very often in performance the last word becomes 'festivity', the line, as Professor C. J. Sisson has said,[3] is 'the closest possible echo of the words of the Abbess immediately preceding':

> Thirty-three years have I but gone in travail
> Of you, my sons, and till this present hour
> My heavy burden ne'er delivered.

Nativity must suggest not only birth but also Christmas, the Feast of the Nativity as Elizabethans commonly spoke of it. Moreover, it 'includes the notion of *festivity*', and it could be a reference to the Christmas feast when *The Comedy of Errors* was acted at Gray's Inn during 1594. This, we gather, whatever the play was like (without tinted marble or a single 'zappy song'), was not entirely successful as a social evening.

NOTES

1 *Plays and Players*, December 1976
2 New Penguin edition (London, 1972).
3 *New Readings in Shakespeare*, (Cambridge, 1956), vol. 1, pp. 97–8.

The Taming of the Shrew (1593–4)

I

After nearly four centuries few directors of *The Taming of the Shrew* are ready to trust Shakespeare. Though we gather that he wrote a brisk farcical comedy, this seems to be too obvious. I have known the Induction to be cut (very often), and the play to be either shifted into mild naturalism because the director had ideas about psychology, or else wildly and unremittingly fantasticated. One anxious thinker even rewrote and heightened it as a Guignol-drama of a woman's cruel subjection. Today, it is true, Katharina's last speech, without certain tactful emphases, can be embarrassing. Most actresses survive by making it clear to the audience, if not to everyone on the stage, that now Kate has gone so far the wisest thing is to humour the man. He knows; and so does she.

'Simplification', a current vogue word, can shock innovators. But there are times when Shakespeare is telling a plain tale plainly. We cannot be over-subtle about the material of the *Shrew*, an anecdote of the Paduan marriage market, acted at speed, by a group of pomping folk, to amuse a fuddled tinker. The theme is announced, before the main comedy begins, in a line for Bartholomew the page, who is disguised as Christopher Sly's wife: 'I am your wife in all obedience.' Frequently unnoticed, that might be an epigraph for the piece. It is an Elizabethan turn of phrase and mind. Obedience then was a wife's duty, and the night completes its circle when Kate delivers to her sister and the Widow her final homily:

Thy husband is thy lord, thy life, thy keeper,
Thy head, thy sovereign; one that cares for thee,
And for thy maintenance commits his body
To painful labour both by sea and land,

To watch the night in storms, the day in cold,
Whilst thou liest warm at home, secure and safe;
And craves no other tribute at thy hands
But love, fair looks, and true obedience –
Too little payment for so great a debt.   (V, ii, 146–54)

In the original production, and to the satisfaction of the audience, she
would probably have meant every word.

Here I am tempted vainly to know what happens afterwards.
Bianca, the younger sister, who until recently was acted as a pallid
sugar-stick, may rise into another pre-taming Kate, with the difference
that she already has an unwary husband. We meet her early when her
wealthy and widowed father, Baptista of Padua, will not let his petted
younger daughter go until the jealous and disappointed 'Katharine
the curst', an 'irksome, brawling scold', has been safely married.
Whereupon Petruchio, a gentleman of Verona, arrives in full surge,
carries off Kate – not entirely against her will – and proceeds to
justify the play's title. Much of the rest is decoration provided by
such characters as Lucentio, Hortensio, and the 'old Italian fox',
Gremio, a pantaloon-figure, who are wooers; and Tranio, Grumio,
and Biondello, who are various types of comic servant. At first the
names can jingle distractingly, for Shakespeare never minded having
a Gremio and a Grumio in the same play. Sometime, no doubt,
we shall have a book on stage staff, the extraordinary succession of
valets, butlers, footmen, cooks, and maidservants that through the
years has helped to dress, polish, and feed the Drama: the *Shrew* alone
supplies the makings of an entire Staff College.

II

Petruchio arrives as frankly a fortune hunter:

I come to wive it wealthily in Padua;
If wealthily, then happily in Padua.   (I, ii, 73–4)

But an alert performance should suggest at once that he and Kate will
be true partners if he can cure her of the sourness, jealousy, and
arrogance for which her father, by favouring Bianca, is as much to
blame, as anybody. Before she enters, Petruchio explains his method:

Say that she rail; why, then I'll tell her plain
She sings as sweetly as a nightingale.
Say that she frown; I'll say she looks as clear

As morning roses newly wash'd with dew.
Say she be mute, and will not speak a word;
Then I'll commend her volubility,
And say she uttereth piercing eloquence.
If she do bid me pack, I'll give her thanks,
As though she bid me stay by her a week;
If she deny to wed, I'll crave the day
When I shall ask the banns, and when be married. (II, i, 169–79)

This is his plan throughout: while behaving to her as badly as she has ever behaved to others, he implies that she is a paragon. Lucentio, meantime, is winning Bianca, apparently with no thought of any future storm.

The *Shrew* is fitted with an Induction, a brief flourish for a broad comedian. Christopher Sly is 'by birth a pedlar, by education a cardmaker,[1] by transmutation a bear-herd, and now by present profession a tinker'. We find him at the beginning of the night, turned out of an alehouse, possibly Marian Hacket's at Wincot, just to the south of Stratford, where he would drink with old John Naps of Greece and Peter Turph and Henry Pimpernell. Found asleep by a mischievous lord, he is persuaded, with the aid of a convenient troupe of strolling players, whose trumpet is heard round the corner, that he is the lord himself, awakened from a dream of fifteen years: 'It will be pastime passing excellent,/If it be husbanded by modesty.' A pointless enough joke, its development gets the comedy going. Unluckily, after allowing Sly, so expansively absurd, a brief irruption at the end of the first act, Shakespeare forgets him: we have to suppose that originally he remained 'aloft', mute and no doubt sleeping, until the afternoon was over. Most modern directors insert a few snatches from a text entitled *The Taming of a Shrew*, once believed to be Shakespeare's source, now more generally regarded as a pirated and damaged version of his play; at the end they deposit Sly outside the alehouse again. Thence, after waking a second time and remembering his 'dream' far more sharply than Nick Bottom does elsewhere, he rushes home to try the taming exercise on his own wife.

The Induction, though we generally get it now, has long been regarded as detachable. As late as 1955 it was cut from an Old Vic production after the opening performance, and Eric Porter's richly relishing tinker went with it. In provincial Shakespeare between the wars Sly was hardly known. Even Bridges-Adams, at Stratford-upon-Avon – in the 1920s he was nicknamed 'Unabridges' – omitted Sly whom he detested. After seeing a Stratford revival in 1953[2] he wrote to Professor Arthur Colby Sprague: 'We wondered whether Petruchio and his Katharine really liked having twenty preoccupied and irrelevant types round them on the stage – to say nothing of a Bed – at that perfectly thrumming moment when they are alone together for the first time. Seemingly they did: spiritless and obedient slaves of the Producer's Theatre.'

Through the years opinions have differed. Benson, even with George Weir in his cast – that great comedian would play Grumio – invariably cut the Induction. The already immense Oscar Asche, in West End management (1904), doubled Sly and Petruchio – good days for the *Shrew* and its company, who ended with real fruit and real wine at Lucentio's lodging. In 1913 John Martin Harvey, who did the Induction complete, had Sly seated permanently in the orchestra (where the conductor would normally be), his back to the audience. At the New Theatre in 1937[3] an Irish Sly, Arthur Sinclair, not only watched everything from his bed at the back of the stage, but also, and obscurely, doubled as the Pedant. Ten years later, again at the New, and for the Old Vic company, Bernard Miles's Sly sat during the night as a muddled cherub aloft. Yet there has remained an underlying notion that the first scene is superflous; at Chichester in 1972 we went straight to Lucentio and Tranio:

> Tranio, since for the great desire I had
> To see fair Padua, nursery of arts,
> I am arriv'd for fruitful Lombardy,
> The pleasant garden of great Italy . . . (I, i, 1–4)

The night seemed uncommonly bare. We must be glad now to hear Sly, in his sudden transformation, swearing still that he is 'old Sly's son of Barton-heath', which is Barton-on-the-Heath (where Shakespeare's aunt, Joan Lambert, lived) to the west of Long Compton. Moreover, the Lord[4] and the Serving-men have some of the play's very little pictorial verse:

LORD: Wilt thou have music? Hark! Apollo plays,
            And twenty cagéd nightingales do sing.
            Or wilt thou sleep? We'll have thee to a couch
            Softer and sweeter than the lustful bed
            On purpose trimm'd up for Semiramis.
            Say thou wilt walk: we will bestrew the ground.
            Or wilt thou ride? Thy horses shall be trapp'd,
            Their harness studded all with gold and pearl.
            Dost thou love hawking? Thou hast hawks will soar
            Above the morning lark. Or wilt thou hunt?
            Thy hounds shall make the welkin answer them
            And fetch shrill echoes from the hollow earth.

1ST SERV.: Say thou wilt course; thy greyhounds are as swift
                As breathed stags; ay, fleeter than the roe.
2ND SERV.: Dost thou love pictures? We will fetch thee straight
                Adonis painted by a running brook,
                And Cytherea all in sedges hid,
                Which seem to move and wanton with her breath
                Even as the waving sedges play wi'th' wind.

                                  (Induction, ii, 33–51)

One charming incidental is for a reader, not a playgoer, and then only if there is a Folio reproduction handy. The second speech for the First Player, 'I think 'twas Soto that your honour means' – he refers to a part he had acted – is attributed to Sincklo: the name of John Sincklo, in Shakespeare's company, whom we have met before (also a Folio error) as a Keeper in *3 Henry VI*.

III

The Induction is soon over. Sly sits to hear what Bartholomew the page, unwillingly beside him and 'dress'd in all suits like a lady', calls 'a kind of history'. In the Folio text, just before Petruchio's entrance, one of the Servants says: 'My Lord, you nod; you do not mind the play.' Sly awakens with a start: 'Yes, by Saint Anne, do I. A good matter, surely: comes there any more of it?' The Page replies: 'My lord, 'tis but begun.' And Sly: 'Tis a very excellent piece of work, madam lady. Would 'twere done.' After the last three words, echoed by so many unwilling playgoers, the direction is simply: 'They sit and mark.' We should hear no more of Sly if it were not for the pirated text – those various interjections and his ultimate removal to be left again by the alehouse. Then, in *A Shrew*, we get the final awakening prefaced by a woefully unpoetic Tapster:

> Now that the darksome night is overpast,
> And drawing day appears in crystal sky,
> Now must I haste abroad.

It is imaginative, after Sly has gone home on his own taming quest, to end upon the dispersal of the Players, the pomping folk, as they move silently off through the dawn.[5]

    One cannot forecast what will happen next to the *Shrew* – Induction, play, or both. At Chichester in 1972 the director appeared to be thinking, alarmingly, of the power-structure in family life, and the night, except for Joan Plowright's performance, drifted glumly away. Still, a general impression lingers that the piece is a romp, though it has been scaled down from such extravagances as those of Tyrone

Guthrie (Old Vic, 1939) in a world pulpy with custard pies, and Petruchio in red, white and blue corsets; and of Michael Benthall (Stratford, 1948) which took us to a Wild West free-for-all. Things have been calmer since then; but the *Shrew* must keep much of the physical knockabout suited to its principal spectator. We have the early rough by-play for Petruchio (his whip cracking reduced lately) and his servant Grumio; Kate's bullying of Bianca, whose hands she has tied; Hortensio, as music-master, entering 'with his head broke' – usually thrust through the lute – after Kate's abortive music lesson; the struggle in the wooing scene; Petruchio carrying Kate off, fighting, before the wedding feast; and so through the tumult of hunger and sleeplessness in the country house. The play rattles on until Kate at length is the compliant wife, and sub-plots are resolved, and all gather – if not to the real fruit and wine of Asche's day – at Lucentio's banquet.

Speech is unfailingly swift, as in Petruchio's

> I tell you 'tis incredible to believe
> How much she loves me – O, the kindest Kate!
> She hung about my neck, and kiss on kiss
> She vied so fast, protesting oath on oath,
> That in a twink she won me to her love. (II. i, 298–302)

and in the cascade for Biondello as Petruchio rides up for the wedding. The Benson company turned this to an endurance test in which the actor would take as few breaths as possible. With its race of sibilants it is still one of the night's exhibition-pieces:

> Why, Petruchio is coming – in a new hat and an old jerkin; a pair of old breeches thrice turn'd; a pair of boots that have been candle-cases, one buckled, another lac'd; an old rusty sword ta'en out of the town armoury, with a broken hilt, and chapeless; with two broken points; his horse hipp'd, with an old mothy saddle and stirrups of no kindred; besides, possess'd with the glanders and like to mose[6] in the chine, troubled with the lampass, infected with the fashions, full of windgalls, sped with spavins, rayed with the yellows, past cure of the fives, stark spoil'd with the staggers, begnawn with the bots, sway'd in the back and shoulder-shotten, nearlegg'd before, and with a half-cheek'd bit, and a head-stall of sheep's leather which, being restrain'd to keep him from stumbling, hath been often burst, and now repaired with knots; one girth six times piec'd, and a woman's crupper of velure, which hath two letters for her name fairly set down in studs, and here and there piec'd with pack-thread ... (III, ii, 41–59)

It is worth quoting: without a crib all that most listeners will make of it is that Petruchio's horse looks even odder than its master. Grumio has a shorter but equally breathless description in the next act when he tries, peevishly, to tell the interrupting Curtis (sometimes a woman) what occurred on the ride to the country. To which Curtis has the answer: 'By this reck'ning he is more shrew than she.'

IV

There are few traditions now in so elastic a comedy. We expect Petruchio, after the frenzy of the Wooing, to isolate the phrase. 'And therefore, setting all this chat aside . . .' The pantaloon Gremio[7] has two main chances. One is in the bargaining for Bianca's hand when his every offer is doubled by Tranio in Lucentio's clothes: 'These I will assure her,/And twice as much whate'er thou off'rest next.' The other is when he returns from church to report the wedding: 'Such a mad marriage never was before.' At Petruchio's house, though we never see 'my spaniel Troilus', I remember Grumio, at the New Theatre (1937), filling the gap with a not very successful bark. The Tailor used to be a stammerer, something now blessedly out of fashion. Kate is beginning to yield when the Tailor has left; we do not see her fully transformed until the journey home when Petruchio obliges her to call the sun the moon and to embrace old Vincentio as 'young budding virgin, fair and fresh and sweet'. After she has said:

Pardon, old father, my mistaking eyes,
That have been so bedazzled with – (IV, v, 44-5)

most Kates will pause and look to Petruchio for assent before adding 'the sun'. All is ready for the settlement and for Kate's last full-dress speech which can say a good deal between the lines:

Such duty as the subject owes the prince,
Even such a woman oweth to her husband. (V, ii, 155-6)

Petruchio and Kate have a rewarding theatrical game, but few players in our time except Alfred Lunt and Lynn Fontanne have made any durable mark. If we wish to see Kate as the Elizabethans probably thought of her – though I doubt whether a boy 'actress' looked like this – you will find her slightly larger than life size in the Royal Shakespeare Picture Gallery at Stratford-upon-Avon. There, in her portrait, the late nineteenth-century American Katharina, Ada Rehan, stands with folded arms and upflung head, her eyes blazing defiance.[8] We must wonder how this fury subdued herself for the benefit of Bianca and Hortensio's Widow:

> I am asham'd that women are so simple
> To offer war where they should kneel for peace;
> Or seek for rule, supremacy, and sway,
> When they are bound to serve, love, and obey. (V, ii, 161–4)

Here we have to return to a phrase early in the Induction. The *Shrew* is a comedy that its players must take firmly in charge. It is 'sport in hand' where, without going over the moon, the players' cunning can 'assist us much'. What they must not do is to tame their audience: that was not Shakespeare's idea, and from the first it will be fatal.

NOTES

1 He means that he made the iron-toothed instruments that were used for combing wool fibres.

2 George Devine's revival, with Marius Goring and Yvonne Mitchell. See *A Bridges-Adams Letter Book*, edited by Robert Speaight (1971).

3 In this production the usually glorious Edith Evans depended on her mannerisms. Leslie Banks was Petruchio.

4 Memorably spoken by the young Ian Richardson at Stratford in 1960.

5 'They are for the road again, packing up their gear, and with a redistribution of relationships discoverable as Hortensio, it may be, now accompanies Katharine the curst, and Petruchio is paired with Bianca . . .' Arthur Colby Sprague in *Shakespeare's Plays Today* (1970), p. 54.

6 The word is thought to be corrupt. This may or may not help.

7 G. R. Hibbard suggests in his New Penguin edition (1968) that Sincklo might have played the part in the original production.

8 She appeared as Kate for a single night at the old Stratford Memorial Theatre in August 1888. The portrait is by Eliot Gregory.

The Two Gentlemen of Verona (1594)

The two gentlemen are the wildly magnanimous Valentine and (his name is significant) the inconstant and treacherous Proteus. It is Proteus who says at the end of the first act:

O, how this spring of love resembleth
The uncertain glory of an April day,
Which now shows all the beauty of the sun,
And by and by a cloud takes all away! (I, iii, 84–7)

Here, in thirty words, is the youthfully variable comedy. A few years on, Shakespeare would have known precisely what to do with a romantic anecdote that seemed to be worth adapting. Now he is putting down pell-mell everything as it occurs to him, the beauties and the absurdities; and there are so many absurdities, especially in the last act, that some critics speculate on tinkering by another hand. That need not concern us, for what may be puzzling in a text slips by on the stage: I remember the happy astonishment with which an Old Vic audience in 1952 received Denis Carey's production, a Renaissance masque before a mistily shining set of filigreed pillars fit for a mistily shining romance. Not many at this revival asked whether Milan had an Emperor or a Duke, why Valentine travelled by ship from Verona, and why people were uncertain of their own town ('Welcome to Padua!' says Speed irrelevantly in Milan).

The play derived from a tale by a Portuguese writer. But Italy was fashionable, so Shakespeare put down a few Italian names, Verona, Milan, Mantua, and went on from there. A court of some kind, imperial or ducal; a romantic coil; rings and letters – always important properties – ladders of cord, star-crossed lovers, a girl as an ardent boy (acted by a boy, anyway), a serenade ordered by a coxcomb just as an aubade would be ordered fifteen years or so later. Then a final scene in a forest, and everyone disposed of: 'One feast, one house, one mutual happiness.'

It is wrong to brush the dew from this comedy: Shakespeare at large in his early morning among words and ideas that will recur or be reworked in the strengthening day. We have the impression of a young and rapid writer talking to himself as the stage waits. Again and again, among its clouding plots, the piece sparkles into lyric:

> I as rich in having such a jewel
> As twenty seas, if all their sand were pearl,
> The water nectar, and the rocks pure gold. (II, iv, 165–7)

> The current that with gentle murmur glides,
> Thou know'st, being stopp'd, impatiently doth rage;
> But when his fair course is not hindered,
> He makes sweet music with th'enamell'd stones,
> Giving a gentle kiss to every sedge
> He overtaketh in his pilgrimage;
> And so by many winding nooks he strays,
> With willing sport, to the wild ocean. (II, vii, 25–32)

(Everyone cries 'Shakespeare's Avon,' and, for once, why not?)

> To die is to be banish'd from myself,
> And Silvia is myself; banish'd from her
> Is self from self, a deadly banishment.
> What light is light, if Silvia be not seen?
> What joy is joy, if Silvia be not by?
> Unless it be to think that she is by,
> And feed upon the shadow of perfection.
> Except I be by Silvia in the night,
> There is no music in the nightingale;
> Unless I look on Silvia in the day,
> There is no day for me to look upon. (III, i, 171–81)

(That is Valentine after being banished by the Duke. One day Romeo will put it better, but it is a start).

> Say that upon the altar of her beauty
> You sacrifice your tears, your sighs, your heart;
> Write till your ink be dry, and with your tears
> Moist it again, and frame some feeling line

That may discover such integrity;
For Orpheus' lute was strung with poet's sinews
Whose golden touch could soften steel and stones,
Make tigers tame, and huge leviathans
Forsake unsounded deeps to dance on sands. (III, ii, 73–81)

That is Proteus – an unpleasant young man whose lips could be royally touched – instructing the coxcomb Thurio how to woo. He tells him to 'visit by night your lady's chamber window/With some sweet consort'; and from this rises one of Shakespeare's loveliest songs:

Who is Silvia? What is she,
    That all our swains commend her?
Holy, fair, and wise is she;
    The heaven such grace did lend her,
That she might admired be. (IV, ii, 38–42)

II

In the study *The Two Gentlemen* can be faint, subdued. We must hear it spoken to know how 'thick the bursts come crowding through the leaves' as Shakespeare prepares for the future. From a pale Romeo mood he shifts to the word spinning of *Love's Labour's Lost,* and we come next upon Julia and Lucetta, mistress and confidante, as they foreshadow, roughly, the uncreated Portia and Nerissa:

JULIA :   Of all the fair resort of gentlemen
            That every day with parle encounter me,
            In thy opinion which is worthiest love?
LUCETTA :   Please you, repeat their names; I'll show my mind
            According to my shallow simple skill.
JULIA :   What think'st thou of the fair Sir Eglamour?
LUCETTA :   As of a knight well-spoken, neat, and fine;
            But were I you, he never should be mine.
JULIA :   What think'st thou of the rich Mercatio?
LUCETTA :   Well of his wealth; but of himself, so so. (I, ii, 4–12)

and so on. What is this but a first venture at the scene in *The Merchant of Venice* where the maid becomes questioner? In the second act we look forward again:

Even as one heat another heat expels
Or as one nail by strength drives out another,

So the remembrance of my former love
Is by a newer object quite forgotten. (II, iv, 188–91)

The idea will recur in *Romeo and Juliet* (and, years later, in
Coriolanus). Both Valentine and Romeo have a ladder of cords;
Valentine's banishment speech becomes more poignant in Romeo's

> Heaven is here
> Where Juliet lives, and every cat, and dog,
> And little mouse, every unworthy thing,
> Live here in heaven and may look on her;
> But Romeo may not. (III, iii, 29–33)

The future is in phrase on phrase ('honour's pawn' for one), cadence
upon cadence, jest on jest; names, even, that will soon be familiar:

> 'Tis true; for Friar Lawrence met them both
> As he in penance wander'd through the forest. (V, i, 37–8)

In the theatre all this charming apprentice-work used to be
disregarded, though John Philip Kemble did rearrange it (Covent
Garden, 1808); and Macready (Drury Lane, 1841) decided after long
debate that to act 'the unimportant part of Valentine' could hardly
affect his reputation, 'or, at least, not injuriously'. The public remained
unimpressed, even by a new, gold-fringed crimson velvet curtain.
Today, though *The Two Gentlemen* has more chance, few directors
can resist a new frame. Thus it has been decorously mid-Victorian,
or (Old Vic, 1957) transferred to a Snodgrass-and-Winkle world of
swooning young women, *The Keepsake* as required reading, and young
men in caped coats packing their carpet-bags among lushly romantic
verdure. Robin Phillips, at Stratford-upon-Avon (1970), and later at
Stratford, Ontario, saw it as a comedy – located vaguely by a
swimming-pool – of the unpredictable volatility, as well as the predictable fashions, of modern youth.

In any period, the lovers, Valentine and Silvia, Proteus and Julia,
are quickly actable, even if audiences have to remember the White
Queen who could sometimes believe as many as six impossible things
before breakfast. The narrative is a love-knot. Valentine, nobly
faithful to the Duke's daughter, Silvia, is banished for wooing her.
Proteus, having skimmed lightly from Julia who adores him, woos
Silvia himself and fruitlessly. Towards the end they all meet in a forest
near Mantua. Julia, in boy's clothes and under the stock name of
Sebastian, is now – unrecognised, of course – Proteus's page. Valentine,
who has become an outlaw, watches, horrified, from a thicket when
Proteus, who has momentarily rescued Silvia from the other outlaws,

proposes rape. The words 'O heaven!' are the last she utters in the play, and no wonder. The scene goes like this:

PROTEUS   I'll woo you like a soldier, at arms' end,
(to Silvia): And love you 'gainst the nature of love – force ye.
SILVIA: O heaven!
PROTEUS: I'll force thee yield to my desire.
VALENTINE: Ruffian! let go that rude uncivil touch;
           Thou friend of an ill fashion!
PROTEUS: Valentine!
VALENTINE: Thou common friend, that's without faith or love –
           For such is a friend now; treacherous man,
           Thou hast beguil'd my hopes: nought but mine eye
           Could have persuaded me. Now I dare not say
           I have one friend alive: thou wouldst disprove me.
           Who should be trusted, when one's own right hand
           Is perjured to the bosom? Proteus,
           I am sorry I must never trust thee more,
           But count the world a stranger for thy sake.
           The private wound is deepest. O time most accurst!
           'Mongst all foes that a friend should be the worst!
PROTEUS: My shame and guilt confounds me.
           Forgive me, Valentine; if hearty sorrow
           Be a sufficient reason for offence.
           I tender't here; I do as truly suffer
           As e'er I did commit.
VALENTINE: Then I am paid;
           And once again I do receive thee honest.
           Who by repentance is not satisfied
           Is nor of heaven nor of earth, for these are pleas'd;
           By penitence th'Eternal's wrath's appeas'd.
           And, that my love may appear plain and free,
           All that was mine in Silvia I give thee.
JULIA: O me unhappy! (V, iv, 57–84)

Most naturally, Julia swoons; but, a dozen brief speeches later, Proteus is observing: 'What is in Silvia's face but I may spy/More fresh in Julia's with a constant eye?' Somehow, when all of this is acted with resolute White-Queen belief, an audience takes it calmly, even Valentine's preposterous abnegation (which timid directors have cut). It is a final scene that brings a long relaxing laugh: the passage in which Valentine asks the Duke's pardon for the outlaws he has been living with (and who, earlier, have been on the splinter-edge of burlesque):

These banish'd men, that I have kept withal,
Are men endu'd with worthy qualities;
Forgive them what they have committed here,
And let them be recall'd from their exile:
They are reformed, civil, full of good,
And fit for great employment, worthy lord. (V, iv, 152–7)

That may remind us, all too sharply, of the end of *The Pirates of Penzance*: 'They are no members of the common throng;/They are all noblemen who have gone wrong.'

III

The Duke of Milan, who at once pronounces a brisk pardon, is a craftily irascible ruler and parent. Sir Eglamour, 'agent for Silvia in her escape', has only seventeen lines during which he changes, unexplained, from the perfect gentle knight to a runaway: the few words, 'Being nimble-footed, he hath outrun us', have caused directors to be merciless, and at Stratford in 1970 Eglamour became a comic scoutmaster. Valentine's 'clownish servant', Speed, and Launce, 'the like to Proteus', are a couple of insistent drolls. Launce is the broader and better: his soliloquies about his dog Crab prove that the Elizabethans surrendered, as we do, to an animal on the stage. Any Crab in the theatre must be a Sirius and outshine his master; still, as the late Patrick Wymark showed (Stratford, 1960), the monologues – especially the first, helped by its miming – do get an immediate response. Not much can be done with Speed whom Granville-Barker chose, incredibly, to play at the Court in 1904. The man never stops quibbling:

PROTEUS: But what said she?
SPEED (nodding):   Ay.
PROTEUS: Nod-ay. Why, that's 'noddy'.
SPEED: You mistook, sir; I say she did nod; and you ask me if she did nod; and I say 'Ay'.
PROTEUS: And that set together is 'noddy'.
SPEED: Now you have taken the pains to set it together, take it for your pains.
PROTEUS: No, no; you shall have it for bearing the letter.
SPEED: Well, I perceive I must be fain to bear with you.
PROTEUS: Why, sir, how do you bear with me?
SPEED: Marry, sir, the letter, very orderly; having nothing but the word 'noddy' for my pains.

PROTEUS: Beshrew me, but you have a quick wit.

(I, i, 106-19)

Shakespeare thought so; but Speed, for most of us, ceases to be mechanical only when Valentine says to him, 'How know you that I am in love?' and gets the answer:

> Marry, by these special marks: first, you have learn'd, like Sir Proteus, to wreath your arms like a malcontent; to relish a love-song, like a robin redbreast; to walk alone, like one that had the pestilence; to sigh, like a school-boy that had lost his ABC; to weep, like a young wench that had buried her grandam; to fast, like one that takes diet; to watch, like one that fears robbing; to speak puling, like a beggar at Hallowmas. You were wont, when you laughed, to crow like a cock; when you walk'd, to walk like one of the lions; when you fasted, it was presently after dinner; when you look'd sadly, it was for want of money. And now you are metamorphis'd with a mistress, that, when I look on you, I can hardly think you my master. (II, i, 16-28)

Rosalind, as Ganymede, would be varying this one day when she rallied Orlando in Arden. Shakespeare seemed to keep *The Two Gentlemen* affectionately in mind; even as late as *The Tempest* he was using a far from riotous joke that he had tested nearly twenty years before[1].

Postscript: John Philip Kemble, in 1808, could not resist adding a special scene for the Outlaws, unnamed by Shakespeare. Kemble called them, operatically, Ubaldo, Luigi, Carlos, Stephano, Giacomo, Rodolfo, and Valerio. No room, we notice, for Moses, whom Shakespeare, curiously, includes at V, iv, 8: 'But Moses and Valerius follow him.'

NOTES

1 *Two Gentlemen*, I, i, 138–40; *The Tempest*, I, i, 27–32.

Love's Labour's Lost
(1594–5; revised 1597)

This is a court play, a lyric comedy of youth's affectations. Speaking with the voice of 'Love, whose month is ever May', it is a dance of sound, a rally of conceits and silken terms, a flashing of dragonflies in the summer air. It ends, artifice shed, with the country rhymes of the Owl and the Cuckoo. Sir Barry Jackson,[1] who loved the play, would often quote from David Lindsay's fantasy, *A Voyage to Arcturus*: 'It looked as if life-forms were being coined so fast by Nature that there was not physical room for all,' and refer it to *Love's Labour's Lost*. There a young dramatist is seeking while he can to express everything he can, almost as if there will be no theatre after tomorrow.

Enchantment though it is, it seems to come as a surprise. Playgoers move round it cautiously, forgetting that the records are starred with wise revivals. It is, we agree, not for the matter-of-fact who dwell first on plot and who are aggrieved that the sets of wit, the taffeta phrases, do not advance the narrative. This was the spirit of a German pedant who said long ago that the piece was 'excessively jocular'. It is better described in the words of Armado: 'The King would have me present the Princess (sweet chuck) with some delightful ostentation, or show, or pageant, or antic, or firework.' *Love's Labour's Lost* is all these; but we may find that we remember it for its romantic self-deception, the open avowals of love, and the last sudden modulation.

Some will never be satisfied. A few years ago I stood in the Old Vic foyer and heard an elderly man deliver a brief oration to the box office (which remained calm). 'I'm not booking for this,' he proclaimed. 'I have seen it twice, and, believe me, it hasn't a chance.' He was not in the company of the actor, Burbage, who when a play was needed for James I's queen at the Earl of Southampton's house at Christmas 1604-5, said that the 'wytt and mirthe' of the comedy, then ten years old, would please her exceedingly. My angry man would have been much more at ease with Dryden who said it was 'meanly written,' and with Samuel Jonson: 'Some passages which ought not to have been exhibited, as we were told they were, to a maiden queen.' (The dogmatic Doctor did redeem himself with 'many sparks of genius'.) William Hazlitt, who thought rashly that if we were to part with any of the comedies it should be this, also went on to qualify his attack. It is hard to set a stern front against *Love's Labour's Lost;* before long, however we may have fumed, we are at peace in the park of Navarre.

Shakespeare is still a very young man, with a young man's pleasure in the topical joke, the whisking shuttlecock of stage speech, and what Sean O'Casey has called, in another context, 'the lovely confusion of singing of birds, and of blossom and bud'. Beside the man-of-the-world sophistication are the songs of Hiems and of Ver. The play may satirise the French Court; it may gibe at the inflated tropes of what was called Euphuism; but we need not be too laborious about overtones and undertones. Why worry about the puzzle of the fox, the ape, and the humble-bee, or 'the charge-house on the top of the mountain'? It is enough to join a festival of words. Armado, Spanish fantastic, has 'a mint of phrases in his brain'; the peasant, Costard, is overcome by the wonder of 'remuneration'; Holofernes, the schoolmaster, loves the 'elegancy, facility, and golden cadences of poesy'; Sir Nathaniel, the curate, relishes 'a most singular and choice epithet'; and the wit of the Court party jets without pause. The comedy, Granville-Barker says, demands the utmost style in presentation: 'Happy-go-lucky, with the hope of a few guffaws to punctuate it, would never have been the method for this sort of play.'

Mercifully, it has not been the method of our time. Again and again, *Love's Labour's Lost* has been fortunate in its productions: by Bridges-Adams (Stratford, 1925, 1934); Guthrie (Old Vic, 1936; two pavilions, wrought-iron gates, a fountain); Brook (Stratford, 1946); Hugh Hunt (1949); Olivier (National Company, Old Vic, 1968); and several more, including – over forty years – the pastorals in Regent's Park. There have been failures as well: an Old Vic revival (1954) was one, set in movable floppy arches and bits of matted yew, with little sense of the 'wide fields', the coppices, the landscape before which the courtiers tread their measure. More than once, directors have used lighting too low-keyed for a comedy that lives in the sun until that last moment when, ideally, torches are lit and everyone, King to dairymaid, stands against the profound dark blue of a summer night. In costume this should be as far as possible a play for all the flower colours of the parterre.

II

I agree, it is sometimes far from easy, without previous toil, to know what the jokes are about, and when you do know the information can be unprofitable. In performance – and observe the part of the veteran courtier, Boyet – what matter are the speed and the rhythm; the varying of couplets and quatrains and octosyllabics; the dancing patterns, as in this quite simple passage after the Muscovite masque:

ROSALINE: But will you hear? the King is my love sworn.
BEROWNE: And quick Berowne hath plighted faith to me.
KATHARINE: And Longaville was for my service born.
MARIA: Dumain is mine, as sure as bark on tree.
BOYET: Madam, and pretty mistresses, give ear:
             Immediately they will again be here
             In their own shapes; for it can never be
             They will digest this harsh indignity.
PRINCESS: Will they return?
BOYET: They will, they will, God knows,
             And leap for joy, though they are lame with blows:
             Therefore, change favours; and, when they repair,
             Blow like sweet roses in this summer air.
PRINCESS: How blow? how blow? Speak to be understood.
BOYET: Fair ladies mask'd are roses in their bud;
             Dismask'd, their damask sweet commixture shown,
             Are angels vailing clouds, or roses blown.

                                        (V, ii, 282–97)

This is plain enough; but *Love's Labour's Lost* contains passage after passage that, even when the comedy was new, would have needed the quickest apprehension (and found it in the court audiences). Others might have felt like Constable Dull, that early and less assured Dogberry, whose only accomplishments seem to have been the morris dance and the tabor. '*Via*, goodman Dull,' says Holofernes, 'thou hast spoken no word all this while.' And Dull replies: 'Nor understood none neither, sir.'

   The plot, superficially, appears to be the most direct in Shakespeare. Yet when I was adding to a *Lamb's Tales* edition [2] the plays, more than a dozen of them, that Charles and Mary Lamb had omitted, I found it as rich in detail as even the most routine production will show. The spine is a bare statement that the King of Navarre and three courtiers, who have sworn for three years to avoid the society of women and to live in improbable rigour, find when the Princess of France and her ladies arrive that they are at once forsworn. There is far more than this. Besides the romantic evasions and mischievous misunderstandings, we have the grand verbal bravura of Armado, who sees language as a kind of over-flowing knot-garden; and the gloating pedantry of Holofernes, with little Nathaniel – among the most endearing minor figures in Shakespeare – in permanent attendance. Costard, Dull, and the 'country wench', Jaquenetta, speak for the villagers.

The whole invention, verbally intricate and echoing, is dramatically shaped. After the interlude of the Worthies, which can be as comic as the Mechanicals' 'Pyramus and Thisbe' in *A Midsummer Night's Dream*, the night darkens with the entrance of Mercade,[3] the messenger of death. The court is laughing at the proposed fight between Armado and the clown, Costard. All is bustle and noise. Sometimes we hear the galloping of a horse; sometimes not. But out of the dim background a tall figure approaches, in deepest black, and bows to the Princess:

MERCADE: God save you, madam!
PRINCESS: Welcome, Mercade;
But that thou interruptest our merriment.
MERCADE: I am sorry, madam; for the news I bring
Is heavy in my tongue. The King your father –
PRINCESS: Dead, for my life!
MERCADE: Even so; my tale is told. (V, ii, 703–8)

It is. He does not speak again; but his four lines, at the end of this dancing glitter, strike like a knell. After 'my tale is told' there should be a pause, a fall of frost on the summer night; at Stratford (1946) the company remained stricken into absolute stillness, a pause held for over half a minute. I recall, too, how in the following year, at an OUDS production after nightfall in the garden of Merton, we saw Mercade emerging from the distant trees to bring with his tidings of death the realities of life. Robert Speaight[4] had a similar but earlier memory of an OUDS revival in Wadham garden during 1924: 'All of a sudden, out of the deep and very distant shadows, a magnificent figure in black came striding. There was a great sweeping bow – Gyles Isham knew how to bow – and then: "God save you, madam!" '

In the theatre the last few pages linger in an elegiac, twilit wistful-ness. The lovers, raillery over, will not meet again for a twelvemonth and a day; Berowne's part must be 'with all the fierce endeavour of your wit/To enforce the pained impotent to smile'. Even Armado has his task; for Jaquenetta's love he will serve three years at the plough.

Then the villagers arrive to sing (from Warwickshire rather than Navarre) their songs of spring:

> When daisies pied, and violets blue,
> And lady-smocks all silver-white . . .

and of winter:

> When icicles hang by the wall,
> And Dick the shepherd blows his nail . . .

All done, Armado steps forward: 'The words of Mercury are harsh after the songs of Apollo.[5] You that way, – we this way.' The speech has been curiously transferable. Thus Peter Brook gave it to the Princess of France; John Barton, at Stratford in 1965, to Boyet. Bridges-Adams thought that Armado should speak it direct to the audience. Probably there will be other variations.

III

Berowne, who would be on good terms with the later Benedick in *Much Ado About Nothing*, has more character than the rest of the lovers. He seems to be Shakespeare's self-portrait – originally, I believe, the idea was Walter Pater's – and I like to think it might be so. Rosaline speaks in the second act:

> Berowne they call him; but a merrier man,
> Within the limit of becoming mirth,
> I never spent an hour's talk withal.
> His eye begets occasion for his wit,
> For every object that the one doth catch
> The other turns to a mirth-moving jest,
> Which his fair tongue, conceit's expositor,
> Delivers in such apt and gracious words
> That aged ears play truant at his tales,
> And younger hearings are quite ravished;
> So sweet and voluble is his discourse. (II, i, 66–76)

The mercurial rebel among his companions, a 'merry madcap lord', he accepts against his will the catalogue of 'strict observances'. When he is finally trapped, as he has trapped the others, his justification of their behaviour is a marvellous piece of lyrical sophistry. No player can stray timidly round the fringes of such lines as these:

For valour, is not Love a Hercules,
Still climbing trees in the Hesperides?
Subtle as Sphinx; as sweet and musical
As bright Apollo's lute, strung with his hair.
And when Love speaks, the voice of all the gods
Make heaven drowsy with the harmony. (V, iii, 336–41)

His companions, the other *précieux ridicules*, as James Agate called them, are defined less clearly. Ferdinand of Navarre, Longaville, and Dumain are pleasantly affected young men, and much of what they say is interchangeable:[6] here it is left to the actors. Dumain, with his 'On a day – alack the day', is the best poet. The Princess of France, who has a gracious dignity when it is needed, and two of her ladies, Katharine and Maria, are also much alike. Katharine, it is true, has a moment no actress should miss – the memory of her sister killed by love, by the cruelty of Cupid:

ROSALINE :   You'll ne'er be friends with him; 'a kill'd your sister.
KATHARINE : He made her melancholy, sad, and heavy;
             And so she died. Had she been light, like you,
       .   Of such a merry, nimble, stirring spirit,
             She might 'a been a grandam ere she died,
             And so may you; for a light heart lives long.
                                          (V, ii, 12–18)

At once the shadow passes, and they are back to wit-cracking: 'Well bandied both.'

Just as Berowne will lead to Benedick, so Rosaline, chief of the Princess's ladies, shows the way to Beatrice. But, above all else, she is a close picture of the 'Dark Lady,' Shakespeare's obsession, who could have been so many people, and who in Berowne's words is

A whitely wanton with a velvet brow,
With two pitch balls stuck in her face for eyes;
Ay, and, by heaven, one that will do the deed
Though Argus were her eunuch and her guard. (III, i, 186–9)

The others rally him unmercifully:

DUMAIN :   To look like her are chimney-sweepers black.
LONGAVILLE : And since her time are colliers counted bright.
KING :   And Ethiopes of their sweet complexion crack.
DUMAIN :   Dark needs no candles now, for dark is light.
                                          (IV, iii, 264–5)

Black was unfashionable among the late Elizabethans. The Queen herself was red-haired.

IV

No doubt the pedants of *Love's Labour's Lost* have to be an acquired taste, but on acquaintance they blossom. Armado, whose name at that period would have had the right ring, is a shabby grandee, a refined traveller from tawny Spain, with an insatiable love of words. Some major actors have been uncomfortable with him – Baliol Holloway, who played him so precisely in three productions, admitted it[7] – but he can be admirable company if he has for his page Moth[8] a boy actor who suggests that he does know what it is all about: too frequently a poor, gabbling Moth has imperilled Armado's first important scene. The Don is a man who would drift naturally towards Holofernes and Sir Nathaniel, two people, clearly from Stratford-atte-Navarre, who have survived across four hundred years because the mere sound of their absurd conversation is, in itself, witty: a score of actors have heightened it.

Holofernes fixes himself very well in his own words on Armado: 'His humour is lofty, his discourse peremptory . . . his gait majestical, and his general behaviour vain, ridiculous, and thrasonical.' I think of Mark Dignam (New Theatre, 1949; Stratford-upon-Avon, 1956) talking as a wind-blown thorn bush might talk if it had a love of Latin and a wild laugh to punctuate its tags. For me, Nathaniel, with his nineteen speeches, must always be Miles Malleson (New, 1949), the image of Costard's apology for him during the interlude: 'A foolish mild man, an honest man, look you, and soon dash'd. He is a marvellous good neighbour, faith, and a very good bowler: but for Alisander, alas, you see how 'tis, a little o'erparted.' (Directors should be careful of the 'bowling': emphasis on it became tedious in a Regent's Park pastoral, 1976.)[9] Malleson, with kind, anxious eyes in a sketch of a face that appeared to be moulded from jelly, was pathetically anxious to please. Generally, though the mists – in spite of himself – would gather, he wore a look of immense wisdom, for he had to keep up with his companions, even if at heart I think he preferred what Armado described as 'eruptions and sudden breaking-out of mirth'. His walk was a form of merry twitch. It was only when he had to take to poetic declamation in the higher society that he found life troublesome. As for the clownish Costard, seldom a bore and once acted almost definitively by Hay Petrie (Old Vic, 1923), we may think of him for his comparison of 'remuneration' and 'guerdon', his way with *honorificabilitudinatibus* (the stock long word that he drags in rather unpersuasively), and the two lines with an oddly modern sting:

> And his page a t'other side, that handful of wit!
> Ah, heavens, it is a most pathetical nit! (IV, i, 140–1)

The various settings for the play can be summarised as Another Part of the Park. A permanent scene is entirely convenient: Bridges-Adams (Stratford, 1934) had a curve of meadow at the back, with a single immense oak in front of it for Berowe to climb in the revelation scene: 'Like a demi-god here sit I in the sky.' The orchestration of *Love's Labour's Lost* will vary with every new director; those Armado–Moth dialogues are the most teasing. Even such an apparently functional speech as the King's statement of policy (with its exact placing of the name 'Aquitaine', four times repeated) can shine in the theatre. Dead topicalities should not bother us: 'chapmen's tongues', for example, probably a reference to George Chapman, the poet, concerned with the small philosophical society, the School of Night, which Shakespeare may also be mocking. When we are in the theatre's park of Navarre, speculations hardly matter. If the acting rhythms are right, the play will dance itself into memory.

NOTES

1 Founder of the Birmingham Repertory Theatre.
2 Nonesuch (1964)
3 Pronounced Mercadé.
4 *The Property Basket* (1970), p. 70.
5 'Apollo' is possibly a tribute to Christopher Marlowe.
6 When I was writing *Peter Brook* (1971), John Harrison, the actor, remembered the Stratford-upon-Avon *Love's Labour's Lost* (1946): 'Peter knew that though I was playing Longaville, I had a great affection for Dumain's poem, "On a day – alack the day". So he switched the poems.'
7 'I think', he wrote once, 'that I can trace why it was regarded as a good part. Phelps elected to play it in his own production at Sadler's Wells – and he was too much of a gentleman to swap it for Costard on the second night'.
8 Moth, not that it matters, may be a satirical portrait of the novelist, Nashe. Holofernes could be John Florio, compiler of the first English-Italian dictionary.
9 Nathaniel here was that charming actor, Richard Goolden.

King John (*1594–6*)

I

George Rylands has said cogently[1] that *King John* is sculptural, 'constructed out of metal rather than fashioned from material to fall in coloured folds. It is a matter of strains and stresses, not of shading and hue.' In the theatre a splendid play is in shadow. Embarrassed excuses are found for it. One director, John Barton (Stratford-upon-Avon, 1974) even offered a synthesis of the received Folio text; a second-rate piece,[2] strikingly similar in form, which is now held to be Shakespeare's primary source; lines from John Bale's *King Johan*, an early Tudor morality; and many of Mr Barton's own composition ('My uncle John, I fear, plays King o'beasts', and so on). He may have felt happier; but how many Shakespearians did? The chronicle, when reasonably presented, can state its own case. If it has occasional atrocious lines, such as King Philip's meditation on a tear during Constance's agony:

> Even to that drop ten thousand wiry friends
> Do glue themselves in sociable grief,
> Like true, inseparable, faithful loves,
> Sticking together in calamity (III, iv, 64–7)

these can be matched elsewhere in the Folio. A main trouble is that *King John*, drama of thrones, dominations, virtues, princedoms, powers, has no sure focus: it is not a popular play for a star actor. On the battlefield before Angiers, the Bastard says: 'From north to south,/Austria and France shoot in each other's mouth.' In a sense, the Bastard and King John, as acting parts, do likewise.

This has not kept the chronicle from the stage. Hanging beside me is the playbill of William Charles Macready's revival (Theatre

Royal, Drury Lane, December 1842) which deserves to be read for
its list of dramatis personae highly improbable in any current
programme. Thus:

'King John; Prince Henry, his son, afterwards King Henry 3rd;
Arthur, Duke of Bretagne, son of Geffrey, Duke of Bretagne, the
elder brother of King John; William Marshall, Earl of Pembroke;
Geffrey Fitz-peter, Earl of Essex, Chief Justiciary of England;
William Longsword, Earl of Salisbury; Robert Bigot, Earl of Norfolk;
Hubert de Burgh, Chamberlain to the King; William Plantagenet,
Earl of Warrenne; William, Earl of Arundel; Robert, Baron Fitz-
walter; Bohun, Earl of Hereford; Vere, Earl of Oxford; Robert de
Ros, Richard de Percy, Gilbert de Clare; Sheriff of Northampton;
Knights; English Herald; Robert Faulconbridge, son of Sir Robert
Faulconbridge; Philip Faulconbridge, his half-brother, bastard son
to King Richard 1st; James Gurney; Peter of Pomfret, a Prophet;
Archbishops, Bishops, Mitred Abbots, Monks, Esquires.

Philip Augustus, King of France; Lewis the Dauphin; Arch-Duke
of Austria; Giles, Vicomte de Melun; D'Arras; Thibaud, Count de
Blois; Eustace de Neuville; Chatelain de St Omer, Baldwin de
Bretel, Bartholomew de Roye, Ralph de Beaumont; Chatillon, Count
de Nevers, Ambassador from France to King John; French Heralds;
Cardinal Pandulph, the Pope's Legate; Attendants on the Cardinal,
Notaries Apostolicus, Crosier Bearer, Bishops, Monks, Knights
Templars, Gentlemen, Citizens of Angiers, Knights Hospitallers,
Barons, Austrian Knights, Esquires, Trumpeters, Standard Bearers,
Attendants.

Queen Elinor, widow of King Henry 2nd and mother of King
John; The Lady Constance, mother to Arthur; Blanche, daughter
to Alphonso, King of Castile, and niece to King John; Lady
Faulconbridge, mother to the Bastard and Robert Faulconbridge;
Ladies.'

Though we can hardly expect today a cast list of this intricacy,
we understand why *John* has often been treated as a processional
and pageant play. No one will provide, as Herbert Beerbohm Tree
did, an extraneous Runnymede tableau and show a king from the
woodcut of *Little Arthur's History,* flinging himself down to gnaw the
rushes after signing Magna Charta. At present we can be relieved
if anyone finds a complimentary word for the splendid chronicle. It
has suffered because it is apart from the historical cycles, the
tetralogies, dwelling in a crowded antechamber of its own with the
banners and barons, the scenes of ringing contention, the dagger-
stabbing verse (and not a little exhilarating bombast).

II

John himself, crafty but fallible and vacillating, is no psychopath but a politically-minded monarch who might at some time (as Holinshed says rather desperately) have had 'a princelie heart in him'. He does grow into a haunted man, marsh-lit; his death at Swinstead can freeze the mind. Anyone who knows those cold flats of The Wash where John lost 'a great part of his army, with horses and carriages' ('These Lincoln Washes have devouréd them,' says Hubert) will be in tune with the last scenes. Chilling though they are, they end with the play's most quoted utterance, the patriotic affirmation. Some writers dislike the Bastard (illegitimate son of Richard Coeur de Lion) who speaks the lines. Lingering on the 'commodity' speech (II, i, 561–98), they call him a brazen opportunist, which is unfair to a man of common sense and vigorous humour, a blunt patriot as loyal to King John, the symbol of England, as he will be to young Prince Henry: 'Happily may your sweet self put on/The lineal state and glory of the land.' The Bastard's character has developed during the play. Externally and vocally, it is as unwise to make him initially too rustic as it is to change him suddenly into an incarnation of Saint George.

His grandmother, Queen Elinor, discerns in him the very spirit of Plantagenet. Her influence on the play can be under-rated. Very often she is acted as a conventional beldame, but she is more: she must be steadily at John's ear, his prop, his evil inspiration; in Chatillon's words to the King of France, 'the mother-Queen, an Até stirring him to blood and strife'. In France she has a sword at her side. When he learns of her death, John mutters twice in one scene 'My mother dead!' With barely a score of speeches, Elinor must not be a small-part cipher.

Briefly, *John* is a chronicle – direct in action, ample in substance – of greed, ambition, promise-breaking, religious intransigence, a furious and wholly unscrupulous struggle for power among 'the thorns and dangers of this world'. We begin in state ritual with the ambassador of Philip of France demanding the English throne on behalf of John's nephew Arthur, son to Lady Constance. Within a moment, from a matter of kingdoms, we shift to the dispute between two brothers over the Faulconbridge estate, and to the acknowledgement of Philip the Bastard as Coeur de Lion's son, 'Sir Richard and Plantagenet'. 'Go, Faulconbridge,' says King John to Philip's puny brother. 'Now hast thou thy desire;/A landless knight makes thee a landed squire.' Alone, the Bastard has a bluff, self-amused soliloquy before his mother, Lady Faulconbridge, hurries in for the fifteen lines of another tingling minor part: one that Charles Flower, in Stratford's Memorial Theatre edition nearly a century ago, condemned as 'unnecessary as well as disagreeable'. Thence to France and the dynastic quarrels before Angiers that can possess an audience if they are strongly and lucidly performed.

III

Certain things are noticeable. Occasionally, not always, the principal Citizen who addresses the Kings from the walls of Angiers is identified with Hubert, John's later follower and the boy Arthur's warden at Northampton Castle. In the text, after the first inconclusive battle, most of the man's speeches are attributed to 'Hubert' or 'Hub.' (His position as a commoner would explain Lord Bigot's snobbish outburst in Act IV: 'Out, dunghill! Darest thou brave a nobleman?') Well, it may be so; it must rest with any new director to decide whether, originally, it was a mere question of an actor doubling the parts, or whether the Hubert who has made the King a 'voluntary oath', and to whom (III, iii, 19) John 'owes much', is indeed the Citizen of Angiers.

Looking down on the glittering panoply before the walls – and even in our barebones theatre some glitter is forgivable – this Citizen suggests the marriage of Lewis the Dauphin to Blanche of Spain as an expedient for settling the war: a plan that brings from the Bastard the famous 'commodity' speech ('Mad world! Mad Kings!') at the end of the second act. It is a meditation on the value of expediency. 'Commodity', which has changed its meaning, may puzzle a modern audience: no one, not even Professor Dover Wilson and Sir Barry Jackson, objected to the young Peter Brook's addition of five words to the text in the Birmingham Repertory revival of 1945 when the young Paul Scofield spoke the lines. '*Commodity*', Brook explained on that occasion, 'has undergone a complete change of sense. Yet to substitute another word throughout would have been unpardonably irritating. So we have introduced an extra phrase on the first appearance of the word to "plant" its meaning: "That smooth-fac'd gentleman, *Expediency*,/Or, as they say, tickling commodity . . ."' Most other directors have let the audience make what guesses it can.

During the ensuing scene Constance's rage and grief have created an exhibition piece for actresses since the days of Mrs Cibber. (Doubtless Shakespeare's male actor had his hour as well.) The part became known as 'crying Constance'; and though the woman does protest too much, and acting styles have altered, we can feel the throb of tradition when she exclaims, seating herself upon the ground:

> To me, and to the state of my great grief,
> Let kings assemble; for my grief's so great
> That no supporter but the huge firm earth
> Can hold it up. Here I and sorrows sit;
> Here is my throne, bid kings come bow to it. (III, i, 70–4)

On their cue King John and Philip of France arrive. The play's most theatrical entrance is to follow, sixty lines later: that – preceded often by the shadow of a great cross – of Cardinal Pandulph, arrogant casuist moulded from icy silver, who brings with him a threatened curse of Rome. The threat, which disjoins Philip and John after their hands have been clasped, leaves the new-married Blanche of Spain lost between the contenders:

BLANCHE: . . . . Whoever wins, on that side shall I lose;
                Assurèd loss, before the match be play'd.
LEWIS: Lady, with me, with me thy fortune lies.
BLANCHE: There, where my fortune lives, there my life dies.

Here an actress as free and truthful as Doreen Aris (Stratford-upon-Avon, 1957) can seize us: we do not hear of Blanche again.

While the battle rages, with the customary '*Alarums, excursions*', the Bastard should enter, according to text, with the head of the Archduke of Austria. He was the vainglorious figure, not necessarily moronic, who wore the lion's skin about which the Bastard had mocked him ('Doff it for shame,/And hang a calf's-skin on those recreant limbs!') Today complete fidelity is rare. Normal enough to Elizabethans accustomed to those heads spiked on London Bridge, the sight can embarrass a modern audience. Professor Sprague[3] has recorded that, as far back as 1814, John Philip Kemble spoke as a soliloquy Faulconbridge's

> Now, by my life, this day grows wondrous hot;
> Some airy devil hovers in the sky
> And pours down mischief. (III, ii, 1–3)

Whereupon Austria entered, they fought, and the Bastard drove his adversary from the stage, returning at once not with the head but with the lion's skin. 'This', said Professor Sprague, 'not only provides a bit of desirable single combat but also gets rid of a property too often laughed at when it is shown.' Often now the Bastard will bring on the skin at the words 'Austria's head lie there!' In the Stratford production of 1940[4], almost ignored critically because it was during the first spring of the Second World War, Baliol Holloway chose to say 'Austria's *hide* lie there!'

IV

The English have won. Young Arthur is given in charge to Hubert. At the New Theatre (1941; Tyrone Guthrie's revival for the Old Vic) Ann Casson had her wrists chained together and stared at them incredulously: 'O, this will make my mother die with grief!' When Elinor has taken the boy conveniently aside, the King and Hubert have a charged colloquy ('I had a thing to say . . .') in which John approaches stealthily the idea of Arthur's murder. It ends with a deadly, flickering exchange, almost within the scope of a single pentameter:

JOHN:	Death.	
HUBERT:	My lord.	
JOHN:		A grave.
HUBERT:		He shall not live.
JOHN:		Enough.

(III, iii, 65)

Philip of France, seeking an analogy for the result of the battle, talks in the next scene of 'a whole *armado* of convicted sail . . . scattered and disjoined from fellowship'. That would have reminded Elizabethans of the Armada of 1588: though the Bastard is from the early years of the thirteenth century, his mood is that of the sixteenth: he could have sailed with Drake, and we can imagine him on those July days when the crescent of the Armada was in eclipse.

Constance, hysterical after her son's capture, leaves the room to die. Almost at once we are in England, at Northampton Castle, for the Arthurian legend, the scene between Hubert and his charge, ten minutes or so that have defied minority scorn. A threat to eyesight can be the most agonising stage experience, and with a child's voice the agony is heightened. We may find that a girl plays Arthur, as Ann Casson did, but this is gradually becoming outmoded. The chronicle rushes on through baronial broils: Arthur's death on that crude couplet after leaping from the castle walls – 'O me! my uncle's spirit is in these stones./Heaven take my soul, and England keep my bones!' (IV, iii, 9–10), – a line for the Bastard that looks to *Othello* ('Your sword is bright, sir; put it up again'), and the various tumults of the French invasion of England. We have on the way Pembroke's speech with probably the most misquoted line in our literature,[5] 'To gild refinéd gold, to paint the lily', and a passage for Hubert in which his diction ('I saw a smith stand with his hammer, thus/The while his iron did on the anvil cool') hardly seems to my ear to be that of the First Citizen.

At length, under 'the black brow of night' and the blazing torches, we reach the Swinstead orchard where King John lies, poisoned by a monk. His death in gusty fever is prefaced by a magnificent speech which nowadays is often cut or, what is worse, pattered off in a breathless treble. The speaker is the young Prince Henry. Pembroke has said: 'He is more patient/Than when you left him; even now he sung.' And Henry replies:

> 'Tis strange that death should sing.
> I am the cygnet to this pale faint swan
> Who chants a doleful hymn to his own death,
> And from the organ-pipe of frailty sings
> His soul and body to their lasting rest. (V, viii, 20–4)

After a dozen revivals I have yet to hear this fully honoured.

Within a few moments John is dead, a death scene, not too lingering, that William Charles Macready is said to have acted with frightening realism. The Bastard ends with a few famous lines that should not be spoken, as they sometimes are, directly to the audience. Always loyal, he is addressing his new King, among the English peers. It is time to restore the nation's fortunes (which we have known to be symbolised in crumbled pillar and tattered flag[6]), and he cries:

> . . . Come the three corners of the world in arms,
> And we shall shock them. Naught shall make us rue,
> If England to itself do rest but true.

Directors who have lost faith in *King John* might ponder the last phrase instead of the first.

NOTES

1 Introduction to Argo recording of *King John*.
2 *The Troublesome Raigne of King John*.
3 *Shakespeare's Plays Today* (1970), p. 27.
4 Directed by Iden Payne and Andrew Leigh.
5 Its rival is Milton's 'To fresh woods and pastures new.'
6 Stratford-upon-Avon (1948).

King Richard II (1595)

I

'Alack, why am I sent for to a king?' The speaker, in Westminster Hall, is Richard Plantagenet, Richard the Second. King and no king, he is about to be deposed – the self-indulgent, self-destructive weakling, strange offspring of the Black Prince, Mars of men. He has endured his fall before it comes; when it does come he can hardly believe that the angels do not fight on Richard's side. In a Marlovian phrase from another context, he has lived for the sweet fruition of an earthly crown; but for him 'within the hollow crown/That rounds the mortal temples of a king/Keeps Death his court'.[1] The nobles who depose him personify the iron strength of the Middle Ages; he has the poet's imagination and sends its outriders scouring into the future.

'Alack, why am I sent for to a king?' A simple phrase, it has stayed with me in the groundswell of George Hayes's voice since a July afternoon in 1929 when I first met *Richard II* at a matinée in a Stratford-upon-Avon cinema. Stratford was not yet fashionable; very few drama critics came from London for what was then a brief 'festival'. The first Shakespeare Memorial Theatre had been burned three years before; and its director, W. Bridges-Adams, was working on the shallow stage of the local Picture House, a pleasant building with gondolas in moonlight all over its walls. *Richard II* was played much less then. Bridges-Adams had a special instinct for it, and, Hayes, who repeated his Richard when the Stratford company visited the United States, gave a performance ('of incessant sensibility', said the Boston critic, H. T. Parker) that lingers yet, line by line. Here was the conscious artist in words, incompetent in deeds: in Westminster Hall, a missal-figure in black velvet; vocally, a splendour of lyrical grief. Few Richards – perhaps because he was my first – have expressed the entire play so affectingly in those four lines from the Pomfret dungeon:

> And here have I the daintiness of ear,
> To check time broke in a disorder'd string;
> But, for the concord of my state and time,
> Had not an ear to hear my true time broke. (V, v, 45–8)

II

There are two treatments of Richard in our theatre. The actor, Ernest Milton, called them the Montague (for reasons that will appear) and the Capulet. Both are valid, and it is hard to separate them. In one, after being at the heart of the 'rash fierce blaze of riot', an arrogant, neurotic intellectual mocking at life, secure in the consciousness of divine right, and allowing the parasites – 'caterpillars of the common-wealth' – to prey upon his realm, he becomes another man, finding maturity in sorrow and in loss, examining his state, and of his grief – at once its subject and its lord – making shivering music. This Richard stands aside from himself, entranced by the complexity of his own arias. For the other Richard, the music, the profusion of images, are secondary; he suffers deeply every reverse and humiliation. Today in the theatre it often needs the eye and ear of faith to decide which of the men is before us.

Charles Edward Montague, drama critic of the then *Manchester Guardian*, who would have so much effect on the consideration of Richard, saw Frank Benson's performance at Manchester in 1899. He discerned in it the 'capable and faithful artist' in the same skin as the 'incapable and unfaithful king'; and he noted Benson's 'warmed and lighted apprehension' of each new grief: 'He runs out to meet the thought of a lower fall or a new shame as a man might go to his door to see a sunset or a storm.' Possibly, for critics have a way of doing this, Montague read more into the performance than Benson had intended, though the actor was a genuine intellectual (by no means as obsessed with sport as he is alleged to have been – gossip he much disliked). His Richard, crown lost, took comfort from the word. 'Can sick men play so nicely with their names?' he exclaimed over the dying Gaunt. But a time would come when he himself was playing with word and image, and would do so until the end, spinning his metaphysics in the Pomfret dungeon. Benson, the artist, was as affect-ing as any 'unking'd Richard' who today (Capulet-fashion, Ernest Milton said) refuses to luxuriate in his imagination and strides across the play as a suffering egotist.

III

With *Richard II* Shakespeare began his narrative of the curse upon the House of Lancaster, a tetralogy that is a comment upon kingship. Like *1 Henry VI, 3 Henry VI,* and *King John,* the play is entirely in verse. Its note is lyrical; there are no battle alarums, and no conscious humour. The Gardeners, in their stylised metaphor, should not be teased into incongruous comedy;[2] the search for humour at any cost is tiresome.

Richard is in the Plantagenet succession. He is conquered by Henry Bolingbroke ('Henry of Hereford, Lancaster, and Derby'), a man whose silences counterpoint Richard's need to unpack his heart in words. After the first few scenes the narrative is direct; the opening, less so. A stranger may be distracted by the unexplained talk of events before the play began. In the theatre, unless there is some preliminary and superflous dumb-show, modish at present, the night should begin with the King in council, hearing the charge brought by his cousin, John of Gaunt's heir, Henry Bolingbroke, Duke of Hereford (here often pronounced as a disyllable, 'Harford'), against Thomas Mowbray, Duke of Norfolk. The charge, which develops into an interrupted trial-at-arms in the lists at Coventry, allows Richard, at a blow, to dispose – as he thinks – of a dangerous enemy, his cousin (banished for six years) and a dangerous friend and accomplice, Mowbray, banished for life. Mowbray, we gather, is guilty, as an agent, of a murder Richard incited: the death of the king's uncle, Thomas of Woodstock, Duke of Gloucester. We are soon led away from these distant events at Calais. The point made is that Richard is autocratically treacherous, Bolingbroke unflinchingly resolute. Mowbray, the 'contriver', must be merely a sacrifice. Whatever he did before the play, he takes our sympathy, and later he is brought back to our minds in an elegiac passage that reports his death.

The night's first words are Richard's often ironically stressed 'Old John of Gaunt, time-honoured Lancaster.' Bolingbroke's father was fifty-eight. In this play of contending youth he must appear as an aged man whose 'inch of taper' will soon be burnt and done; we are to accept him as 'a prophet new-inspired'. Though Richard seeks to hear Bolingbroke and Mowbray with aloof cynicism ('How high a pitch his resolution soars!'; 'Our doctors say this is no time to bleed'), he should indicate – at Bolingbroke's 'He did plot the Duke of Gloucester's death' – some awareness of personal guilt. Not every actor does; John Neville certainly did at the Old Vic in 1955.

As the scene ends, Richard rises to the regal authority of 'We were not born to sue but to command.' This is the king, secure in the power of which Gaunt speaks ('God's substitute, His deputy anointed in His sight') during an ensuing brief dialogue with the widowed Duchess of Gloucester; she cries to a pacific Gaunt for revenge on her husband's murderer. The scene is a useful pause for Bolingbroke and Mowbray to change into armour for their reappearance in the lists at Coventry – something directors in the actor-managerial period would make an excuse for chivalrous spectacle. Little of that today, though the ritual of the verse can match the sound of the trumpets:

> My name is Thomas Mowbray, Duke of Norfolk;
> Who hither come engagèd by my oath –
> Which God defend a knight should violate! –
> Both to defend my loyalty and truth
> To God, my King, and my succeeding issue,
> Against the Duke of Hereford that appeals me;
> And by the grace of God and this mine arm
> To prove him, in defending of myself,
> A traitor to my God, my King, and me.
> And as I truly fight, defend me heaven! (I, iii, 16–25)

When the King has thrown down his truncheon to stop the fight, before it has begun, the actor, in the decree of banishment – 'Draw near,/And list what with our council we have done. (I, iii, 123–4) – must face a challenge to his breath control as sharp as anything in Shakespeare. Some directors cut a line or two, presumably to stop us from observing Richard's technique rather than the words he utters. Thenceforward, after the scene has closed on Bolingbroke's awkward couplet, 'Where'er I wander, boast of this I can;/Though banish'd, yet a trueborn Englishman' (I, iii, 308–9), the play moves to the 'setting sun' and Gaunt's magnificent paean to England, 'This royal throne of kings': the throne Richard misprizes. A famous set piece, the speech should not be consciously isolated between quotation marks. Thence to the King's impatient comment on his uncle's death, 'So much for that. Now for our Irish wars'; and to the rapid sequence that encompasses the first threatenings of rebellion; news of Bolingbroke's landing at Ravenspurgh (crumbled now) in Holderness, while Richard is in Ireland; the rebel army in Gloucestershire ('these high wild hills and rough uneven ways'); and sentence on Richard's favourites, Bushy and Green, at Bristol Castle. Soon Richard will fall to despair, assert himself for a glittering moment on the battlements at Flint, lose his crown in Westminster Hall, and pass to imprisonment and doom at Pomfret. During the last two-thirds of the play we must accept the change from haughty insolence to a contemplative artist conquering in adversity. It is difficult.

IV

Richard lands from Ireland on the coast of Wales: 'Barkloughly Castle call they this at hand.' Some productions have brought on Lord Berkeley – who has appeared with Bolingbroke a little earlier – but his presence is a complicated error: the name Barkloughly is based on a textual mistake in Holinshed for 'Hartlowli' or Harlech. We have been in Wales two brief scenes before, when a Welsh Captain tells the Earl of Salisbury that many portents (thus 'the bay-trees in our country all are wither'd') show that the King is dead and the Welsh forces must disperse. This Captain, in Shakespeare's mind, might have been Owen Glendower, who will be so prominent in *1 Henry IV*. At least two recent directors have identified him: Richard Cottrell (in the Prospect revival of 1969) and David William for the National company in 1972.[3] Dr Stanley Wells, who considers that the Captain is a purely choric figure, says in the New Penguin edition (1969) that he is 'important rather for his representative quality than for any personal characteristics'; and John Barton, the Stratford director, translated this into stage terms. The speech was 'spoken not by one man but by eight of them: each of the additional seven was given one line. They stood in a row across the stage in a low light and with their backs to the audience. There was an accompaniment of plaintive horn music. Thus all suggestion of individuality was eliminated, and their choric function was made abundantly plain.'[4]

Already in Wales Richard is seeking to blur his fears: 'The breath of worldly men cannot depose/The deputy elected by the Lord.' As the two messengers, Salisbury and Scroop, arrive successively with ill tidings, he surrenders to the melancholy music of 'Let's talk of graves and worms and epitaphs.' The problems here are vocal, 'exquisite cadenzas and variations', says Sir John Gielgud, all to be contained within the framework of the verse. No play has to be so carefully scored by actor and director: bold centre-stage sonorousness will not do. Richard's is always the dominant violoncello voice, though such lines live with us as Scroop's

> An unseasonable stormy day
> Which makes the silver rivers drown their shores,
> As if the world was all dissolved to tears. (III, ii, 106–8)

Salisbury's 'O, call back yesterday, bid time return' (which has had many variants through the centuries, down to the melodrama of *The Silver King*: 'Oh God! Put back Thy universe, and give me yesterday!'); and, at Flint Castle, Bolingbroke's 'The fresh green lap of fair King Richard's land.' Richard then is no longer the man born not to sue but to command; we have already heard the warning crack in the voice at

> I live with bread like you, feel want,
> Taste grief, need *friends*. (III, ii, 175–6)

Upon the castle battlements he utters the last royal declamation, 'We are amaz'd', which must be spoken in the key of the Duke of York's 'Yet looks he like a king.' This is his last desperate appeal to the idea of Divine Right: he is not 'barren and bereft of friends', for

> My master, God omnipotent
> Is mustering in the clouds, on our behalf,
> Armies of pestilence . . . (III, iii, 85–7)

Yet it is the end, and he knows it, when to the few with him on the walls, and hopelessly to himself, he cries 'What must the king do now?' and answers his own questions, longing – and we remember Henry VI – for a hermitage and an almsman's gown. He is still letting his imagination possess him while, 'like glist'ring Phaethon,' he descends to meet the kneeling Bolingbroke:

> Up, cousin, up; your heart is up, I know,
> Thus high at least

– and he points to his crown

> –although your knee be low. (III, iii, 194–5)

It is the strained anguish of defeat. In the final lines,

RICHARD: Set on towards London. Cousin, is it so?
BOLINGBROKE: Yea, my good lord.
RICHARD: Then I must not say no (III, iii, 208–10)

he is echoing a phrase of Lewis the Dauphin in *King John*: 'If you say ay, the king will not say no.'

V

Transiently we are away from Richard. Two Gardeners, overheard by the Queen in the Duke of York's park at Langley, have the exchange that describes England in terms of a garden and reveals that Bolingbroke has 'seized the wasteful king'. Presently we are listening to the Deposition in Westminster Hall: a scene that begins with the tumult, often cut, in which the conspirator, Bagot, accuses the Duke of York's son, Aumerle, of Gloucester's death. It is inessential. Certainly the tossing down of the gages as the nobles stand for or against Aumerle must be watched anxiously: in the theatre it is an almost impossible passage. The text contains seven gages; their effect can be cumulatively absurd as gauntlet after gauntlet is thrown upon a littered stage. In my experience the house has usually begun to laugh at the third, and mirth grows slightly hysterical when one of the lords becomes a gage collector. It is odd why this should defeat an audience; probably it is because repetition of any sort is one of the formulae for laughter in farce. 'Do it once, and all's well; repeat it, and it is near a laugh; repeat it again, and a laugh is certain.'

Before Richard arrives, there are the Bishop of Carlisle's tribute to Mowbray, dead at Venice – in the English theatre, for most of the century, it has been a convention to double the parts – Carlisle's outburst against Bolingbroke, and his instant arrest. At once Richard is brought in:

> Alack, why am I sent for to a king
> Before I have shook off the regal thoughts
> Wherewith I reign'd? (IV, i, 162–4)

We hear the first of the Christ similitudes:

> Did they not sometime cry 'All hail!' to me?
> So Judas did to Christ. (IV, i, 169–70)

Nowadays it is less customary than it was (at Stratford in 1929 and 1933 and in various Old Vic productions) to suggest any physical resemblance. The unwilling surrender of the crown has had an earlier parallel in Marlowe's *Edward II*. With Edward's 'But what are kings when regiment is gone/But perfect shadows in a sunshine day?' goes Richard's 'God save King Henry, unking'd Richard says,/And send him many years of sunshine days!' (IV, i, 220–1) (undreamt-of irony there). After wringing from his renunciation its last drop of pathos, the shattering of the looking-glass he has called for with a theatrical flourish allows Richard once more to seize at an idea:

BOLINGBROKE :   The shadow of your sorrow hath destroy'd
                The shadow of your face.
RICHARD :   Say that again.
                The shadow of my sorrow? Ha! let's see.
                                        (IV, i, 292–4)

It is soon over: he goes out to the parting from his queen. I remember Paul Scofield's pause[5] when, at the command 'Go some of you, convey

him to the Tower', Richard, numbed, felt suddenly the humiliation of
'convey' and pounced upon it in the high scorn of 'O, good! convey!
conveyors are you all!' The farewell to his 'sometimes queen' is interrupted by the arrogance of Northumberland, ordering him to Pomfret,
and it is remembered in the modern theatre for Maurice Evans's
long, flashing upward gesture at

> Northumberland, thou ladder wherewithal
> The mounting Bolingbroke ascends my throne,
> The time shall not be many hours of age
> More than it is, ere foul sin gathering head
> Shall break into corruption. (V, i, 55–9)

VI

Through the years the next passage, York's discovery of the plot to
kill King Henry – for this the shorthand is 'the Aumerle conspiracy' –
has seemed to be an obvious cut. In two decades, from 1934 to 1955,
it was excluded from any English revival, and we have missed it occasionally since; a pity, for it includes York's tale of Bolingbroke and
Richard entering London – a speech Beerbohm Tree translated to
pageantry – and also Bolingbroke's 'Can no man tell me of my unthrifty
son?' which sounds the note of *Henry IV*. The family conflict over
Aumerle's treachery can act well, though York's roaring for his
boots may be too much for a house even when, mercifully, he is not
played for laughs. This is followed by the dangerously consecutive
rush of son, father, and mother into the King's presence.

Hard upon the sinister little scene for Pierce of Exton, who believes
himself to be Richard's appointed murderer, is the long Pomfret
soliloquy, never spoken more cogently than by Alec Guinness when
in 1947 he paced round the New Theatre stage, touching the slender
pillars of the permanent set and defining the limits of his cell; today
it appears necessary for the King to be elaborately tethered. The
entry of the former groom with his story of roan Barbary is a
sympathetic and unlikely decoration, even unlikelier at Stratford-
upon-Avon in 1973 and 1974 where the groom proved to be
Bolingbroke in disguise, one of the less felicitous ideas. Finally to
Pierce of Exton's dramatic arrival at Court with Richard's coffin:

> Herein all breathless lies
> The mightiest of thy greatest enemies,
> Richard of Bordeaux, by me hither brought. (V, vi, 31–3)

his dismissal, and the mourning processional close.

Exton is one of the few minor figures to impress himself. Another, and firmer, is the Bishop of Carlisle, who has his moment in Westminster Hall; and there is a surprising entry among the high, wild hills in Gloucestershire, young Harry Percy – Hotspur-to-be – arriving to tender his service to Bolingbroke. We have known him do it in a thick Border accent. The reply, 'I count myself in nothing else so happy/As in a soul remeb'ring my good friends' (II, iii, 46–7), will be recalled ironically in *Henry IV*.[6] None of the conspirators counts for much in performance. Bushy's comfort to the queen, 'Each substance of a grief hath twenty shadows', is, if we accept the Montague theory, the kind of riddling that would commend the man to Richard. The run of the last couplet, 'Or if it be, 'tis with false sorrow's eye,/ Which for things true weeps things imaginary' (II, ii, 26–7), may remind us of Helena's 'And sleep that sometimes shuts up sorrow's eye' in *A Midsummer Night's Dream*; but it is a speech in which the ear detaches itself from the sense.

The Queen is a gentle wraith, no more. If Aumerle is a youth who appears to be as wavering as his father, we must remember that, sixteen years on, as Duke of York, he falls while leading the vaward at Agincourt. Northumberland is plain bully. He lives with me, ridiculously no doubt, because one of his actors,[7] in the scene with Ross and Willoughby (II, i) forgot who supported Bolingbroke at Port le Blanc in Brittany. One name he grasped; it was a good round name, Francis Quoint, and he repeated it often, with desperate and increasing emphasis. Even those who let Shakespeare's often exciting nominal rolls pass them by, knew that evening that Bolingbroke had one set of allies, the firm of Quoint, Quoint, and Quoint. Edmund of Langley, the Duke of York, is an important and contentious figure: though there is no reason for him to be comic, his vacillation has encouraged actors to snatch at 'Come, cousin, I'll dispose of *you*' (to the Queen in II, iii) and the repeated call for his boots. He can be unsure and fretful: he has also genuine courage and he can be touching. John Gielgud believed[8] that to make York purely farcical weakened the play.

There remains Bolingbroke, the ambiguous, acquisitive strong man who comes so slowly to the idea of kingship. He is revealed most searchingly in his silences; once he has conquered he will let others speak. We remember too how, when Richard at Coventry has lopped four years from his term of banishment, he says quietly: 'How long a time lives in one little word! . . . Such is the breath of kings.'

NOTES

1 *Richard II*, (III, ii, 160–2)
2 In John Barton's 1973 production at Stratford the Gardeners were monks.
3 In 1969 James Lawrenson was 'Owen Glendower, chieftain of the Welshmen'; the 1972 actor was Peter Rocca.
4 Dr Wells's essay on *Richard II* at Stratford in *Furman Studies*, June 1976 (Furman University, Greenville, South Carolina).
5 Lyric, Hammersmith, 1952
6 *Henry V*, IV, iii, 129–30 and IV, vi, 6–32.
7 Stratford-upon-Avon, 1933.
8 *Stage Directions*, 1963

Romeo and Juliet
(1595–6)

I

This lyric tragedy of the warring houses of Verona, a tragedy of
impetuous youth, of premonition and mischance, doom hanging in
the stars, can be 'a feasting presence full of light': sun and moon,
starlight and torchlight. The theatre must keep it in its true latitude,
a play from the south, no hint of our northern skies. It must be acted
swiftly:

> This bud of love, by summer's ripening breath,
> May prove a beauteous flow'r when next we meet. (II; ii, 121–2)

On Shakespeare's stage it would have been taken straight through
without a break. The more rapidly it moves now, the less we ask
about its plot devices, its various vials, or a carefree young dramatist's 'house where the infectious pestilence did reign':

FRIAR LAWRENCE: Who bare my letter, then, to Romeo?
FRIAR JOHN: I could not send it – here it is again –
                 Nor get a messenger to bring it thee,
                 So fearful were they of infection.
FRIAR LAWRENCE: Unhappy fortune! By my brotherhood,
                 The letter was not nice, but full of charge
                 Of dear import; and the neglecting it
                 May do much danger. (V, ii, 13–20)

On nights when all is going well, these things are trivial.[1] We cannot
bother about them during what Shaw – reasonable about Shakespeare
for once – called 'an irresistibly impetuous march of music':

JULIET: My bounty is as boundless as the sea,
My love as deep: the more I give to thee,
The more I have, for both are infinite. (II, ii, 133–5)

and

ROMEO: Look, love, what envious streaks
Do lace the severing clouds in yonder east;
Night's candles are burnt out, and jocund day
Stands tiptoe on the misty mountain tops. (III, v, 7–10)

Yet there have to be occasions, and particularly here, when things do not go well. Everyone, familiar with the play or not, has a personal idea of the lovers; and if it is not realised, the night at first must falter. Moreover, Romeo and Juliet have found, in another sense, what it is to be star-crossed. Their names have been cheapened, punned upon, pushed into the world's 'epic love stories', dragged through the thorn-brakes of minor fiction. Much has to be forgotten before a *Romeo* begins.

II

It begins with Chorus. One has known him to be the Prince of Verona, or the Friar, or Benvolio. He has also been, ridiculously, a young man in jeans.[2] The earlier of his two sonnets is the better. It compresses the plot into eleven lines; it contains the famous phrase about the 'star-crossed lovers'[3], and it tells us what is flatly impossible today, without wholesale cuts, that the tragedy will take two hours. Once the brawl between the factions is over, and Romeo has entered, still lovesick for Rosaline – his 'O me! what fray was here?' may be prompted by a sword left behind – the march of music is unceasing: its arias, such as the Queen Mab speech (which would have perilously delayed the masquers), its duets (as in the Balcony scene), and its intricately composed finales.

Romeo's part is longer than Juliet's by eighty lines. Each is demanding, but particularly hers. According to the text, she is not yet fourteen. She 'hangs upon the cheek of night/as a rich jewel in an Ethiop's ear'. 'So light a foot/Will ne'er wear out the everlasting flint.' She must express the impatience of 'Love's heralds should be thoughts', the exaltation of 'Gallop apace', followed by overmastering grief, and then the fear and resolution of what in the theatre is the Potion Speech. For a young actress Juliet is as terrifying as it is marvellous:

O, she is lame! Love's heralds should be thoughts,
Which ten times faster glide than the sun's beams
Driving back shadows over louring hills;
Therefore do nimble-pinion'd doves draw Love,
And therefore hath the wind-swift Cupid wings. (II, v, 4–8)

Give me my Romeo; and, when he shall die
Take him and cut him out in little stars,
And he will make the face of heaven so fine
That all the world will be in love with night,
And pay no worship to the garish sun. (III, ii, 21–5)

and in the Potion Speech:

O, if I wake, shall I not be distraught,
Environèd with all these hideous fears,
And madly play with my forefathers' joints,
And pluck the mangled Tybalt from his shroud,
And in this rage, with some great kinsman's bone,
As with a club, dash out my desp'rate brains?
O, look! methinks I see my cousin's ghost
Seeking out Romeo, that did spit his body
Upon a rapier's point. Stay, Tybalt, stay.
Romeo, I come. This do I drink to thee. (IV, iii, 49–58)

Romeo, too, must encompass lyric passion (the 'white wonder of dear Juliet's hand'), ecstasy ('Ah, Juliet, if the measure of thy joy/Be heap'd like mine . . .'), fury, despair, hysteria in the Friar's cell. He is 'fortune's fool'. He receives the news of Juliet's presumed death with the single line: 'Is it e'en so? Then I *defy* you, stars', which some Romeos have cried to heaven, and others have spoken with a toneless resolve. Throughout, he is a passionate young Italian of the Renaissance, not a conscientious Shakespearian with a tenor voice and a northern cast of mind. It is a test for an actor; and yet we remember a Juliet first.

Shakespeare's company would have been grateful for their parts. None is really negligible: we might miss even Lady Montague's three lines. Mercutio is an inflammable Veronese gallant, a poet and swordsman who jests in the bitter realisation of death. Capulet is the irascible heavy father, fussily in command of his house; his wife, not yet thirty ('I was your mother', she says to Juliet, 'much upon these years/That you are now a maid') is a cold personage for whom love is a business matter and from whom her daughter cannot expect sympathy. Tybalt is a flash of rage, Benvolio (Romeo's cousin) a gentle, pacific figure who disappears midway, and Paris a likeable, personable young man who has the misfortune to be Romeo's rival: he should not be under-cast.

Friar Lawrence, arguably a better botanist than conspirator, need not be monotonous. He is frequently permitted to dither about, whereas such actors as Sir Lewis Casson (Old Vic, 1952) and Joseph O'Conor (St George's, 1976) have explained what he should be in strength and sense. 'He should twist that dagger out of Romeo's hand', said Bridges-Adams, 'with the hard sinews begotten of hard living.'[4] The Apothecary of Mantua, who is described so sharply before he enters, has to restrain himself from bettering the description:

> I do remember an apothecary,
> And hereabouts 'a dwells, which late I noted
> In tatt'red weeds, with overwhelming brows,
> Culling of simples. Meagre were his looks;
> Sharp misery had worn him to the bones. (V, i, 37–41)

Alec Guinness, as a young man (1935) was the likeliest I have seen, and he did not at once produce a dram of poison from his 'tatt'red weeds' as if he had been expecting a customer.

The Nurse can vary extraordinarily according to her actress. How old is she? Though she need not be more than fifty, she has the consequential garrulity of age, she is rheumatic, and she repeats her joke in the third scene ('It stinted, and said "Ay" ') until we scream for release. We can assume that Shakespeare wrote the part with an elderly woman in mind (played, of course, by a man) and did not fret himself about the arithmetic. Dame Edith Evans, who played the Nurse at the New Theatre in 1935 (and rather less excitingly at Stratford in 1961), was a massive crone with a life beyond the theatre. W. A. Darlington in his 1935 notice for the *Daily Telegraph* used the shorthand: 'As earthy as a potato, as slow as a cab-horse, and as cunning as a badger.' Her clumsy totter for help after finding Juliet's body is fixed in the mind, with its accompanying jangle of terrified speech:

> Alas, alas! – Help, help! my lady's dead!
> O, well-a-day, that ever I was born!
> Some aqua-vitae, ho! – My lord, my lady! (IV, v, 14–16)

Where, in that squawk of agony, could one have recognised the elegance of Millamant, the spring of Rosalind? Elsewhere she discovered a voice that Cornishmen would call 'cloggy', caked with the earth of all the counties. This was superb; but again and again a Nurse has been a dreary bit of too professional bravura, wheezed to death by a character actress with a voice like a rusty rip-saw. In recent years Angelica, for that is her name – the single mention of it is at IV, iv, 5 – has grown pleasantly younger: we have welcomed the unstrained performances of Elizabeth Spriggs at Stratford (1967), Rosemary Leach at St George's (1976), and the resolutely genteel Helen Lindsay (in modern dress, Young Vic, 1977).

One speechless character who will arrive or not at a director's whim – she shares the uncertainty with Jane Shore of *Richard III* and Kate Keepdown of *Measure for Measure* – is Romeo's first love, Rosaline, a Capulet niece (and Juliet's cousin), the 'pale, hard-hearted wench' of the bright forehead and the scarlet lip. She appeared at the banquet in Irving's Lyceum production (1882). Clement Scott wrote:[5]

'The gaudy peacocks just removed from the banquet table, the minstrels' gallery crowded with musicians, the sedilia of blue and silver, on which sat the black-haired, pale-faced Rosaline, the trees of azalea, the overhanging drapery of silver brocade, the pages, and the dancers, so distracted the attention that the play was for the moment lost. It seemed impossible to get action with all this magnificence.'[6]

III

One of a director's first puzzles is the Queen Mab speech, a self-indulgent interpolation, curiously placed. A mere noisy Mercutio can be a disaster; my happiest recollection is of Paul Scofield (Stratford, 1947) stretched upon the stage in the torchlight, his caped cloak flung round him, his arm raised, and his eyes intent as he let the speech flower into the silence of the grotesquely-visaged masquers. Next, how to isolate the rapt meeting of the lovers, the world forgot? Again I think of Stratford in 1947 and Peter Brook's sudden clearance of the stage. This was an exhilarating night that opened upon a sun-scorched market place bare of scenery except for a toy cincture of crenellated walls, and backed by the indigo expanse that Brook called 'a great tent of Mediterranean blue'.

At Capulet's feast now we usually have his line from the Quarto, 'Ah, youth's a jolly thing.' At the opening of the balcony scene Romeo's 'He jests at scars that never felt a wound' is the second line of a couplet: Benvolio has just left the stage with ' 'Tis in vain/ To seek him here that means not to be found.' The balcony, one feels, must be for Juliet alone; to have it put to lesser use, as inevitably it must be in any permanent set, can oddly imperil illusion. I have known a Juliet to balance herself on the narrowest splinter, though my first (Geneviève Townsend of the Benson company) was allowed to hang upon the cheek of night in a huge sculptured bath-tub, slung aloft apparently in the middle of a forest and illuminated by an immoderate moon. Any lovers' resolve to touch hands can turn to a gymnastic display disliked by Bridges-Adams; at Stratford in the 1920s he avoided inessential movement and trusted the verse. One of the final problems is how to suggest the tomb of the Capulets, the vault that Juliet's beauty makes 'a feasting presence full of light'; Benson, opening it down stage and no doubt remembering Irving, to whom he once played Paris, would be more strenuous with his mattock and wrenching-iron than most later Romeos.

Today the last recapitulation is cut more discreetly than it used to be, and sometimes we get it in full. That is important, for the play is also about the ending of a feud – a matter only hinted at in years when the scene was kept to a brief general assembly, the speaking of perhaps a score of lines after Juliet's 'This is thy sheath; there rust, and let me die.' The last narrative and the close of a long strife can be deeply satisfying, yet it took several productions before I heard even that Lady Montague was dead:

PRINCE: Come, Montague, for thou art early up
           To see thy son and heir more early down.

(Incongruous wordplay that the young Shakespeare could not resist.)

MONTAGUE : Alas, my liege, my wife is dead tonight;
           Grief of my son's exile hath stopp'd her breath.
           What further woe conspires against mine age?
                                            (V, iii, 207–11)

Other favourite cuts have removed a few of the puns and quibbles, Juliet's outburst after 'Hath Romeo slain himself?':

> Say thou but 'I',
And that bare vowel I shall poison more
Than the death-darting eye of cockatrice.
I am not I if there be such an 'I';
Or those eyes shut that makes thee answer 'I'.
If he be slain, say 'I'; or if not, 'No';
Brief sounds determine of my weal or woe. (III, ii, 45–51)

and Romeo's 'This may flies do when I from this must fly' at
the heart of a passionate speech. Regularly we would lose the
entrance of Peter, the Nurse's conventionally comic servant, and
the three Musicians, the consort of recorders, after Juliet's supposed
death:

PETER: Musicians, O, musicians, 'Heart's ease,' 'Heart's
                ease'! O, an you will have me live, play 'Heart's
                ease.'
IST MUSICIAN: Why 'Heart's ease'?
PETER: O, musicians, because my heart itself plays 'My
                heart is full of woe.' O, play me some merry dump
                to comfort me. (IV, v, 100–5)

The Musicians are one of Shakespeare's trios. The number rings
through the plays: Three Favourites, Three Conspirators, Three
Citizens, Three Murderers, Three Witches, Three Strangers, Three
Sisters, Three Servants, Three Bandits. In *Romeo and Juliet* now the
Three Musicians, Simon Catling, Hugh Rebeck, and James
Soundpost, are settling into the cast.

NOTES

1 Even so, there were murmurs at Stratford in 1947 when Brook cut the expository
  passage in which Friar Lawrence explains to Juliet the working of the potion.
2 Stratford-upon-Avon, 1976.
3 'From forth the fatal loins of these two foes/A pair of star-cross'd lovers take their
  life;/Whose misadventur'd piteous overthrows/Doth with their death bury their
  parents' strife.'
4 *A Bridges-Adams Letter Book* (1971).
5 See *From 'The Bells' to 'King Arthur'* (1897), pp. 234–5.
6 Irving's five-act version was in twenty-two scenes. They included 'Loggia of
  Capulet's House', 'Verona: The Cloisters', and 'A Secret Place in the Monastery'.
  Juliet's balcony was 'the marble terrace of an ancient palace . . . [its] roof
  supported by solid pillars', a 'cool and overhanging temple' surrounded by 'the
  richest foliage – real trees'.

A Midsummer Night's Dream (1595–6)

I

Elizabethan England was well forested. Certainly its dramatists never thought twice about using a wood or grove or brake: a tree-bossed parkland, as in *Love's Labour's Lost*; a minor Italian Sherwood as a haunt for those eccentric outlaws in *The Two Gentlemen of Verona*; the middle of Windsor Forest, with Herne's Oak itself, for *The Merry Wives*. In *As You Like It* Shakespeare furnished a palpably Warwickshire Arden with some improbable assets; Gaultree (or Galtres), north of York, is the scene of that hateful treachery in *2 Henry IV*; and in a 'chase' in the North of England (*3 Henry VI*, III, i) two Keepers, with crossbows, capture the King. Tamora, in *Titus Andronicus*, evokes a forest where, when Aaron is with her, 'every thing doth make a gleeful boast', but which changes conveniently, in the passage with her sons, to a 'barren detested vale'. Timon has his wood near Athens, home of roots and gold. But most Shakespearian audiences are happiest, I think, with that other wood, a mile without the town (Athens-by-Arden), in *A Midsummer Night's Dream*: a place of oaks and hawthorn-brakes; a bank for the wild thyme; oxlips and violets, eglantine and musk-roses; the faint primrose beds of spring; ivy-ringed elms, clinging honeysuckle, hedgehogs and glow-worms and spotted snakes. Several provincial theatres would keep a Woodland Set in store for the use of visiting companies; and, as often as not, the play was *A Midsummer Night's Dream*.

The tripartite fantasy, popularly 'the *Dream*', has suffered from an excess of gauze and butter muslin. Kipling's Puck[1] objected to 'little buzzflies with butterfly wings and gauze petticoats and shining stars in their hair', a 'painty-winged, wand-waving set of impostors'. Agreed; but for a long time this was the popular view, carried over from the nineteenth century, of Peaseblossom, Cobweb, Moth,

and Mustardseed, and the rest of the fairy court. When Tyrone
Guthrie (Old Vic, 1937) put on the *Dream*, delightedly, as an album
of Victoriana, with rose-wreaths, flying fairies, and posing sylphides,
opinion that had been lured away from the butterfly wings gratefully
returned. Moreover, Guthrie strengthened the belief from which we
are not wholly free, even now, that this is the libretto for an opera
(sustained Wedding March and all) by Mendelssohn. Though it is
rare today for an Oberon to sing 'I know a bank', Phyllis Neilson-
Terry – as her mother, Julia Neilson, had been at Her Majesty's in
1900 – was in song at Regent's Park as late as 1937. On the same
stage in 1940 Jean Forbes-Robertson was repeating her Puck.
Luckily, the intermittent practice of casting actresses in these parts
has been abandoned. Shaw said of Augustin Daly in 1895: 'A female
Oberon and a Puck who behaves like a page-boy earnestly training
himself for the post of footman recommend themselves to him because
they totally destroy the naturalness of the representation, and so
accord with his conception of the Shakespearian dramas as the most
artificial of all forms of stage entertainment.'[2]

The treatment of the fantasy during the last century and a quarter
is an index to the theatre's changing method. I have not yet seen anything, though Peter Hall came near to it at the Aldwych, London,
in 1963, like Quiller-Couch's idea of an Elizabethan hall, enormous
staircase, recessed Wood, a blaze for the Interlude, then final flickers
on the hearth, and a last thin chorus scarcely more audible than the
dropping embers. Charles Kean, we know, had a good time at the
mid-nineteenth-century Princess's, with the Parthenon, the
Erichtheum, and the temple of Theseus on show; 'innumerable
fairy legions . . . light and brilliant as gossamer'; and a 9-year-old
child, Ellen Terry, as the 'merry goblin' Puck, who was belted and
garlanded with flowers. Young Frank Benson, on tour and in
London (1889), included scampering coveys of elves and fairies, a
protracted fight between a spider and a wasp, and the entire
apparatus of moonbeams and mist. Daly (London, 1895) fitted the
fairies with 'portable batteries and incandescent lights which they
switched on and off from time to time like children with a new
toy';[3] and Beerbohm Tree (1900) had a wood of cushioned moss,
bluebell thickets, and scurrying rabbits; with coryphées in muslin,
and the Oberon of Julia Neilson resembling 'some gorgeous bird'.
It was not until the spring of 1914 that Harley Granville-Barker,
at the Savoy, made the first strong break with the Decorated
manner, replacing Mendelssohn by English folk tunes, stylising a
Wood of draped curtains lighted in various tones of greens and blues
and violets and purples, over which hung an immense terracotta
floral wreath, and presenting marionette-moving fairies in gold and

bronze, their hands and faces gilded like Cambodian idols. A decade later, at Drury Lane, Basil Dean returned more or less to Tree's full-scale method but without rabbits. He did allow laughter at the expense of the romantic lovers. Afterwards, except for Guthrie's operatic fairies among the emerald canvas, and an occasional recession to rose leaves and ballet, the *Dream* turned away from the nineteenth century. In 1929, at the Vic, Harcourt Williams saw it as a Jacobean masque with a high mid-stage mound difficult to negotiate in stiff skirts. Later there were the patrician courtliness of Bridges-Adams's Stratford productions, spacious midsummer pastorals in Regent's Park (Oberon seldom in song), and Guthrie's severe 1951 revival. Ceasing to be an antiquarian, he set on the Vic stage a silver-threaded circlet of bamboo, looking in deep-sea lighting like a haunted grove, and with a Greek landscape behind it.

There was a resolve to see the play freshly. Peter Hall would do so at the Aldwych in 1963 when Tudor mansion melted to glimmering Wood. Finally, during the late summer of 1970, Peter Brook, at Stratford-upon-Avon, using his own forms of magic, enclosed the *Dream* in a white-walled, bevelled cube; the stage became a Wood when Puck and Oberon swung on trapezes, and coils and tendrils of helical steel wire were tossed out on fishing-rods from a catwalk. Many people agreed that they had never heard the verse better spoken.[4] Robert Speaight said (in the *Tablet*): 'Mr Brook takes his cue from nothing but his own artistic conscience, and from no one but Shakespeare himself.'

II

Once a director reaches for a play that to the moon in wavering morrice moves, almost anything can happen. Brook's excitingly personal response is unlikely to recur. New playgoers may be easiest at first with a June-night pastoral; but *A Midsummer Night's Dream* rarely falters if its director can preserve the quality of sheer happiness. Some critics imagine, though we have no proof, that it was written for a wedding; an epithalamic vision that ends with a blessing upon the house. The paths of Romantics, Immortals, and Mechanicals are carefully entwined. All quarrels, lovers' skirmish, Oberon's anger, clowns' amiable squabbling, are transient under the moon. Dissension by day is settled after the racing and chasing by night. As the lovers wake, vaguely remembering 'things small and undistinguishable/Like far-off mountains turnèd into clouds' (IV, i, 184-5), the play, in effect, is over. We are left with Bottom to wake also from his extraordinary dream – maybe finding a few wisps of hay in his pouch,[5] and the Mechanicals all set for their chaotic interlude of Pyramus and Thisby, other lovers moving tragically beneath an inconstant moon.

The play is possessed by the moon. Theseus names it in his first speech, 'Four happy days bring in another moon' (actually two days will be enough), and Hippolyta responds with her 'silver bow new-bent in heaven'. Egeus complains that Lysander has serenaded Hermia by moonlight. Lysander and Hermia propose to fly 'when Phoebe doth behold/Her silver visage in the watery glass'; the Mechanicals arrange to rehearse, 'most obscenely and courageously', by moonlight; Oberon's greeting to his queen is 'Ill met by moonlight, proud Titania' (we seldom have the Folio pronunciation, Tytania). The moon is the governess of floods; Oberon remembers Cupid flying between the cold moon and the earth; the clowns decide that, because Pyramus and Thisby meet by moonlight, someone must come in 'to disfigure, or to present, the person of Moonshine'. So, in the end, to the interlude itself which is as mooncast as the Athenian wood.

As late as the 1920s the lovers, Lysander and Hermia, Helena and Demetrius, were being acted as straight romantics. Gradually, players and directors began to explore these scenes in detail; it was soon clear enough that comedy would take over. Audrey Carten (Royal Court, 1920) and Edith Evans (Drury Lane, 1924) were among the first Helenas of a new order. I have no idea what Victorians would have made of Coral Browne (Old Vic, 1957) when she spoke:

> We, Hermia, like two artificial gods,
> Have with our needles created both one flower,
> Both on one sampler, sitting on one cushion,
> Both warbling of one song, both in one key;
> As if our hands, our sides, voices, and minds,
> Had been incorporate. (III, ii, 203–8)

Granville-Barker, in 1914, held that Shakespeare clearly meant the passage to be spoken 'with a meticulous regard to its every beauty'. At the Vic, Coral Browne, a soulful, questing creature, bewildered by the complexity of life and love, was not noticeably reverent. When she recalled how she and Hermia sat 'both warbling of one song, both in one key', the last four words startled her. 'Both in *one* key,' she exclaimed, her eyes wide in new and unbelievable discovery. Helena now is the first comedienne; Hermia, compact and fiery, might have been created by the small boy who was Moth, and who could presently be the Illyrian Maria.[6] Lysander is as volatile as Demetrius is resolute. The Romantics and, especially, the

Immortals must not be ill-spoken. Oberon, as 'dulcet and har-
monious' as the singing mermaid he saw on a dolphin's back, cannot afford to look (as I have known him) like a Second Murderer.
Titania must move in silver from her entrance with the aria of

> These are the forgeries of jealousy;
> And never, since the middle summer's spring,
> Met we on hill, in dale, forest, or mead,
> By paved fountain, or by rushy brook,
> Or in the beachèd margent of the sea,
> To dance our ringlets to the whistling wind,
> But with thy brawls thou hast disturb'd our sport . . . (II, i, 81–7)

I remember how, in the Haymarket revival of 1945, Peggy
Ashcroft's hands seemed to ripple and shimmer at 'Pale in her anger,
washes all the air'. Titania should have, too, her 'Indian boy'. As
Professor Sprague has said,[7] this contention over the boy profoundly
affects not only the fairy monarchs, but through Puck's mistake the
four Athenian lovers and also Nick Bottom as well. Puck tells the
Fairy at the beginning of the second act why Oberon is so
angered with Titania:

> Because that she as her attendant hath
> A lovely boy stolen from an Indian king.
> She never had so sweet a changeling;
> And jealous Oberon would have the child
> Knight of his train . . . (II, i, 21–5)

We are shown how Titania refuses to yield, how Oberon revenges
himself with the love charm, and how, infatuated with Nick Bottom,
she lets the boy go. Though he has appeared from time to time
during the last hundred and thirty years or so, he has been tan-
talisingly intermittent; in any revival we must watch for him, though
he is unlikely to be described – as he was at the Theatre Royal,
Newcastle (1847) – as a 'sable pledge of hope'.[8]

III

At curtain-rise – a phrase that for the moment still exists – we
should observe the treatment of Hippolyta, the Amazonian queen
who is to be Theseus's bride. There have been several notions of
her: tall and coffee-coloured; aloofly disdainful; urgently in love;
scuffling with Theseus on the ground; or, just as implausibly

(Old Vic, 1960), ironic and in manacles. Then, is Egeus, the heavy father, a comic figure when he enters, 'full of vexation . . . with complaint/Against my child, my daughter Hermia'? With Robert Atkins in Regent's Park during the 1930s he was wholly straight-forward. At Stratford he has often been a testy little tyrant, flicking over his tablets as he reads from them the list of Lysander's love tokens: 'bracelets of thy hair, rings, gawds, conceits,/Knacks, trifles, nosegays – ' a pause; then in contemptuous italics, *'sweetmeats!'*

(I, i, 33-4).

When Theseus warns Hermia that if she refuses to wed Demetrius, she must either 'die the death' or 'abjure for ever the society of men', he can be unbendingly stern or touched with gentle amuse-ment at a fractious and single-minded child. She and Lysander, left alone, are so deeply in love that no production will search for laughter. Yet Lysander has one problem: he speaks of his 'widow aunt, a dowager', and for some reason any aunt in the theatre has comic overtones. The arrival of Helena, tall, fair, and wistful in the sighing music of her couplets, used to be dramatic; it is now the entry of a comedienne ready for the ten monosyllables of 'He will not know what all but he do know.'

After the Romantics, the Mechanicals, the six handicraft-men of Athens – actually from Snitterfield or Wilmcote – who will play in an interlude 'before the Duke and Duchess on his wedding-day at night'. Shakespeare is here the amused professional who must have known something of amateurs. Clearly he is fond of Quince, the carpenter, fussy, conscientious, and (we suppose) elderly; Bottom, the weaver, omniscient leading man; Starveling, the tailor, bound by unexplained tradition to be deaf, crumbling, and teasy; Flute, the bellows-mender, young and timid; Snug, the joiner, and Snout, the tinker, both solid citizens. Snout, who does not care a tinker's curse for acting, will not let anyone outdo him. Snug, slowest of all, has 'the lion's part . . . nothing but roaring'. (A recent Quince, telling him he could 'do it extempore', added 'off the cuff', but this is not in the received text.) We must not ask what happened to the parts of Thisby's mother, Pyramus's father, and Thisby's father, which were to be played by Starveling, Snout, and Quince himself. Shakespeare forgot them between carpenter's shop and Duke's Oak, and so should we.

The First Player is, of course, Nick Bottom, monstrously com-placent, uncrushable ass. Naturally he will wear the ass's head which (as fixed by Puck) used to be full-size, no nonsense about it: one fashion now is for a skeleton head so that we see the actor's face and he need not always be fumbling for the strings that work ears and jaw. Puck is better as a mischievous boy than an indulgently whimsical grotesque. I remember how, at Oberon's 'About the wood go faster than the wind/and Helena of Athens look thou find', Leslie French[9] would answer with a spoilt-child intonation, 'I go, I go – *look* how I go!' The fairies have appeared as anything between the tripping-hither, tripping-thither creatures of *Iolanthe* and the hearty young men (reaction against butter muslin) of Peter Brook. Granville-Barker's 'ormolu fairies, looking as if they had been detached from some fantastic, bristling old clock' (the phrase is Desmond MacCarthy's[10]) sound rather too much, though we can agree with Masefield[11] that 'something eastern, strange, spiced, and gilded should be in their costumes and comings'.

IV

For directors the final interlude, 'palpable-gross play', of Pyramus and Thisby seems to be inexhaustible in device (there is a danger of overcharging it). I doubt whether any two productions have been identical, but certain things are common to all. Quince, mild and flustered stage manager, is lost in the punctuation of his prologue. Snout, as Wall, tries to find an assonance between 'sinister' and 'whisisper'; he forgets to make the essential 'chink' with his fingers until Bottom snarls 'O sweet and lovely wall', and becomes heavily ironical in 'Thanks, courteous wall: Jove shield thee well for this.' Flute-Thisby's falsetto drops regularly to a baritone growl. Snug raises his lion's mask with a benign smile after 'When Lion rough in wildest rage doth roar' (the roar is a trilling purr). Starveling, as Moonshine, is testy and squeaking. Both Bottom and Flute, at 'old Ninny's tomb', get a sharp whisper, 'Ninus, man!' from Quince. Usually Flute will rhyme 'dumb' and 'tum' and 'word' and 'sword'.

These are more or less routine matters. There has been much-else in different productions, generally when Bottom, in a selection of beards, has taken charge of the whole affair. But I think, looking back, of Randle Ayrton, who acted Quince at Stratford-upon-Avon for Bridges-Adams (1932), and who would emphasise his repetitions of 'bloody' by hurrying over them in a gulping whisper. Guthrie, at the Vic (1951), pointed the lines,

PYRAMUS: And like Limander am I trusty still.
THISBY: And I like Helen, till the Fates me kill. (V, i, 194–5)

as a direct salute to Lysander and Helena, though Shakespeare was contemplating Hero and Leander.

One thing. Many people who usually avoid Shakespeare applaud

the nonsense of the Interlude, whereas playgoers used to the business
do grow dubious. Is it all needed? I doubt whether Shakespeare,
relishing amateurs though he did, intended his Mechanicals,
Athenian by name, Warwickshire in spirit, to be as much of a Gang
Show as they are today. While we observe the old ideas and note
the new, we may also remember Theseus's rebuke to Philostrate:

> I will hear that play;
> For never anything can be amiss
> When simpleness and duty tender it. (V, i, 81–4)

Peter Brook realised this. His courtiers were compassionate, not
condescending. Like Granville-Barker, Brook preferred to see the
Mechanicals as a group of charming earnestness, reasonable human
beings, no repository for a hundred gags, the myriad accretions of
the years; no piping treble for Flute, no careful mispronunciation.
In Court the audience was so carried away by the 'lamentable
comedy' that it joined in song with the actors.

At a customary performance, before the clopping of the Bergo-
mask dance at the close, Quince will sometimes stand aside,
obviously hurt at the Duke's light-hearted reception of the tragedy.
Theseus (who has certainly contradicted himself) hastens to put it
right with 'Very notably discharged!' and a matching purse of
gold. On to the twelve strokes of midnight and the fairies' epilogue.
The song employed to 'bless this place' has disappeared. Granville-
Barker would fill the gap with 'Roses, their sharp spines being
gone' from *The Two Noble Kinsmen;* other directors have preferred a
protracted setting of 'Hand in hand with fairy grace/Will we sing
and bless this place' followed by Oberon's spoken couplets.

Puck, in his last two lines, 'Give me your hands if we be friends/
And Robin shall restore amends', is inviting applause. Peter
Brook[12] interpreted the first words literally: his Puck (John Kane)
jumped from the stage and came through the house, shaking hands
left and right, the rest of the company at his heels. That was, and is,
a fitting end to *A Midsummer Night's Dream:* all, on stage and off, must
be at peace beneath the visiting moon.

NOTES

1 *Puck of Pook's Hill.*
2 Shaw, *Our Theatres in the Nineties*, vol. 1, p. 178.
3 ibid.
4 Theseus and Hippolyta doubled with Oberon and Titania, possibly their other
   selves released in dream and night. Frank Dunlop used a similar doubling
   (Edinburgh Festival; Saville, London; 1967).

5　The business is attributed to George Rodger Weir, for a quarter of a century Frank Benson's principal comedian. See Arthur Colby Sprague's *Shakespeare and the Actors* (1945).

6　John Masefield in *William Shakespeare*.

7　*Shakespeare's Plays Today* (1970).

8　I am indebted for this playbill phrase to Miss Kathleen Barker.

9　Old Vic, 1929 (to John Gielgud's Oberon) and Open Air Theatre on many occasions.

10　Reprinted in *Theatre* (1954).

11　*William Shakespeare* (1964 edition): 'These fairies . . . are not those known in Europe; they are linked with antiquity and romance; with the Amazons and with India.'

12　Stratford-upon-Avon, 1970; New York, 1971.

The Merchant of Venice (1596–7)

I

Although we go to any revival of *The Merchant of Venice* in quest of the golden fleece, we do not always have Jason's luck. The romantic comedy with a dramatic core, a 'fairy-tale' according to Granville-Barker, has a trick of eluding its directors, especially if they have hinted, as so often, that because the gloriously theatrical play bores them, it must equally bore its audiences. Like Antonio, this trial by casket and trial without jury has been a 'tainted wether of the flock'. Actors faced with it have been known to sigh in rash-embraced despair; directors search for ways to enliven Venice and Belmont, Gobbos and caskets (gold, silver, and base lead), and we are invited to believe that only elaborate or eccentric decoration will save an audience from the gulfs of sleep. It is, reputedly, for school parties, for sad matinées, for ghosts who whisper: 'It wearies me; you say it wearies you.' That, shortly, is absurd. I doubt whether the most peevish spectator at the dimmest production has escaped the sudden tingling when, in the strict court of Venice, Shylock raises his knife to Antonio's breast and Portia cries: 'Tarry a little; there is something else.' There is a great deal else. I was lucky enough not to have been put off by the shoddiness of outmoded touring productions. In Dogberry's words those managements used to 'bestow all their tediousness' upon the first scene. Antonio, a moping owl ('In sooth, I know not why I am so sad') would be staring across a canvas parapet. By him two of the callowest actors available would grapple with Solanio and Salerio (in stage jargon 'the Salads'). These – and we return to Granville-Barker – are 'magnificent young men of high-flowing speech'. It is their task to represent

Venice, to talk of 'the argosies, with portly sail' and 'the pageants of the sea':

> My wind, cooling my broth,
> Would blow me to an ague when I thought
> What harm a wind too great might do at sea.
> I should not see the sandy hour-glass run
> But I should think of shallows and of flats,
> And see my wealthy Andrew dock'd in sand,
> Vailing her high top lower than her ribs
> To kiss her burial. (I, i, 22–9)

Lordly language; and it would invariably be gabbled by some young man without panache or presence. When he and his confederate had left the stage – I would dread their reappearances and the imitation of Shylock that modulated to 'Let good Antonio look he keep his day' – on would come Gratiano, crying 'Let me play the fool' and doing so almost literally; little in the theatre can be so grating as false merriment.

This, though Shylock and Portia had still to arrive, would have been enough to disenchant many young playgoers who had parsed and analysed the comedy, and learned its 'quality of mercy' speech, until they were sick of it. Even now, *The Merchant of Venice* has to struggle, though less against incompetence than a director's perverse experiment. Never mind. Once we have surrendered to the play, it keeps us unquestioning: 'For Portia's world to us is Colchos' strond,[1]/And we the Jasons come in quest of it.'

That is Portia's world of the caskets. There is also the sternly dramatic Venice of Shylock and the 'merry bond'. They do not come fully together until the Trial. The one link at first is Antonio's borrowing of three thousand ducats from Shylock so that Bassanio can woo the heiress of Belmont. Ships are lost; the money cannot be repaid, and Shylock claims the forfeit of the bond (a pound of Antonio's flesh 'to be cut off and taken/In what part of your body pleaseth me'). Some managers, to avoid the trouble of set changing during the years of realism, would – disastrously – play all the Venetian scenes in a group, followed by all the Belmont scenes; round the night off with the Trial; and omit Shakespeare's tranquil coda under the stars at Belmont. Nobody would attempt that now. The last time I experienced it was at Frank Benson's farewell in what was still the Shakespeare Memorial Theatre at Stratford, on Whit Monday, 1932. That afternoon, when Shylock had walked slowly from the court, the curtain dropped; none would have wished otherwise.

II

For many the play must be *The Jew of Venice,* for Shylock has always been at stage centre. His name, a transliteration of the Hebrew 'shalach', or 'cormorant', says clearly how Elizabethan audiences were supposed to regard him. His relentless insistence on the terms of his bond makes him the villain of a fantastic anecdote. How much sympathy can he have? (Certainly, when Jessica and Lorenzo sit at Belmont discussing the power of music, we may forget too hastily their share in Shylock's fate, and that unpleasant transaction in Genoa[2]). Through the generations Shylock has passed from early low comedy to the ferocity of Macklin, Kean's desperate restraint, Macready's latent nobility, Irving's aristocratic foreigner destroyed by prejudice (he interpolated the Jew's return to his empty house after Jessica's elopement), Tree's histrionic hysteria, Gielgud's version of Granville-Barker's 'sordid little outsider, passionate, resentful, writhing under his wrongs – which are real – and the contempt of the Venetians', and Olivier's prosperous private banker in an 1890s setting,[3] uneasily sociable until, his racial and family pride really touched, he becomes a man of granite with a revengeful devil beneath it. Other Shylocks have varied between the 'impenetrable cur' and the man who, but for an accident of birth, might have been a magnifico of Venice.

However he is treated, he rules the Venetian scene as Portia rules her country estate. While the tale of the bond hardens into realism, the Belmont story is progressively more fantastic. Then they meet. We are aware that Shylock must be defeated; but the Trial scene has renewed its suspense across nearly four hundred years. Shakespeare is arrogant in his demands on our belief, and we continue to acquiesce. During the trial, while a savage revenge recoils on its planner, we have no time to ask whether Portia's adviser has briefed her with the quibble about 'no jot of blood', or whether – as some actresses have tried hopefully to suggest – she hits upon a solution in the ebb of the twelfth hour.

III

It may be enough to say that the shape of *The Merchant of Venice* and the anti-Semitism of the age dictated Shylock's behaviour: he had to be a villain. Now and then, unwillingly, we can bear with him, as Shakespeare does; but there is no room at all for sympathy when he crushes every plea. The last exit from the court is immensely theatrical. It cannot obliterate our memories:

PORTIA: Therefore, lay bare your bosom.
SHYLOCK: Ay, his breast –
                So says the bond; doth it not, noble judge?
                'Nearest his heart,' those are the very words.
PORTIA: It is so. Are there balance here to weigh
                The flesh?
SHYLOCK: I have them ready.
PORTIA: Have by some surgeon, Shylock, on your charge,
                To stop his wounds, lest he do bleed to death.
SHYLOCK: Is it so nominated in the bond?
PORTIA: It is not so express'd, but what of that?
                'Twere good you do so much for charity.
SHYLOCK: I cannot find it; 'tis not in the bond. (IV, i, 247–57)

Stage Portias, like Olivias in *Twelfth Night*, were once mature and dominating. (Idly we wondered if the old Lord of Belmont had suffered.) They are younger now: Portia is what she should be, 'unschool'd, unpractis'd', but witty, patrician, and ready for adventure. What she said to Bellario, and what he said to her, is not evidence; but I do not believe for a moment that she would have gone to Venice on mere speculation. Shakespeare takes care to ensure that her conduct of the trial – the Doge, in his own court, watching admiringly behind her – will satisfy anyone in its judicious tightening of suspense. Afterwards, relaxing in the moonlight and moonshine of Belmont,[4] and in the formal skirmishing over the rings, she can further cheer Antonio with tidings grandly unexplained. (And why should they be, in a fairy-tale? Shakespeare may remind us, too, of the serial writer solving the insoluble: 'With one bound our hero was free'.) 'Antonio,' says Portia casually, 'you are welcome';

And I have better news in store for you
Than you expect. Unseal this letter soon;
There shall you find three of your argosies
Are richly come to harbour suddenly.
You shall not know by what strange accident
I chancèd on this letter.
ANTONIO: I am dumb.   (V, i, 273–9)

Bassanio will have a great lady for a wife. The kind of man she will have as a husband is in the actor's gift. He may be, like other romantic heroes, a fortune hunter, but Portia finds him irresistible; and, 'unlesson'd girl' though she is, she has seen enough of men to respond when her heart tells her. She does not respond to the Prince of Morocco, who is all sonorous declamation, or to the Prince of

Arragon who, when permitted to appear (for he used to be a cut as familiar as the still rare III, v⁵), has been everything between a fop in the manner of a Spanish Thurio and a calculating old fox in the manner of, say, Gremio. The men may guess badly; they can reward their actors.

We cannot guess ourselves how those caskets will be displayed at Belmont. In my first *Merchant* they were obviously old cigar boxes, indifferently concealed. Most directors and designers work hard on them. I have known them huddled on a table, hidden behind tapestry, arranged on a flowerpot stand, wheeled in on a trolley, held by kneeling servants, disposed about the room, and once, and weirdly, enclosed in what resembled an automatic machine: we waited for Morocco to insert a ducat before the machine worked.

IV

Generally, the people of Belmont and Venice have few complexities. Antonio, 'royal merchant' in the toils, is not just a distillation of melancholy: he is an honest and generous man, not free from the prejudices of the place and time. Gratiano is a young man resolved to be witty; even at the trial he has his 'sole-soul' quibble. We have had lamentably artificial performances. Nerissa may improve him; she is sensible and affectionate. Lorenzo and Jessica live with us for the music of the Belmont night:

> Look how the floor of heaven
> Is thick inlaid with patines of bright gold;
> There's not the smallest orb which thou behold'st
> But in his motion like an angel sings. (V, i, 58–61)

I have never much liked Jessica's method of elopement; though she and Lorenzo are in love, their escapade with stolen money and stolen ring (Shylock's turquoise: 'I had it of Leah when I was a bachelor') cannot be particularly endearing. The Gobbos, father and son, have a little elementary and rather painful clowning. And that is practically all of the cast except for a secondary usurer, Tubal, who is Shylock's one support, and Balthasar, Portia's major-domo, whose measured exit at 'Madam, I go with all convenient speed' (III, iv, 56) is among the perennial jokes of *The Merchant of Venice* in the theatre.

In essence, the play is what Granville-Barker said. One of the rules of a fairy-tale is that the right things happen if we wait for them; directors need not be over-anxious and they should certainly not arrange to prompt Bassanio in his casket scene. Komisarjevsky's singer of 'Tell me where is fancy bred', at Stratford in 1932, heavily stressed the rhymes to 'lead' – 'bred', 'head', and 'nourishéd'. It could not have been sillier, for in this scene, at the very centre of the Belmont story, Bassanio knows, Portia knows, and we know. Then:

> How all the other passions fleet to air,
> As doubtful thoughts, and rash-embrac'd despair,
> And shudd'ring fear, and green-ey'd jealousy!
> O love, be moderate, allay thy ecstasy . . . (III, ii, 108–11)

NOTES

1 strand; shore.
2 Venice to Belmont via Genoa was a roundabout journey.
3 Jonathan Miller's production for the National Theatre, 1970.
4 We hear nothing more of the 'holy hermit' supposed to be with her; Shakespeare enjoys his Old Religious Men.
5 For Jessica, Lorenzo, and Launcelot at Belmont.

King Henry IV, Part One
(1596–7)

I

This, first of the Falstaff plays, the great twin brethren, has for its full title 'The History of Henry IV, with the Battle at Shrewsbury between the King and Lord Henry Percy surnamed Henry Hotspur of the North, with the Humorous Conceits of Sir John Falstaff'. We speak of it naturally as a Falstaff play: if he is at all safely acted, he can minimise others on the stage. If he is not safely acted, at least his spirit – like Caesar's, and he would have appreciated the comparison – is mighty yet. Sometimes it can be a pity when he is so overwhelming that, in effect, the captains and the kings depart. There must be ample room for the civil broils and the warring peers; their scenes are never the wavering of a frayed arras in the wind. Certainly among the humorous conceits, I have often waited anxiously for Henry Hotspur of the North, the light by which the chivalry of England moved. True, Hotspurs at all like Laurence Olivier (New Theatre, 1945) are as rare as a crown on a gorse bush – no mere romantic blazon, but a man hurtling, uncouth, and passionate, he sealed himself upon the mind. Falstaff, it has been primly said, is in the play as the corrupting influence on Prince Hal, the tavern companion whom the Prince must throw off when he reaches the throne and 'Consideration, like an angel' comes 'to whip th'offending Adam out of him'. Yet during *Part One* how many in the theatre are contemplating this? Obviously Falstaff possessed his dramatist: 'Banish plump Jack, and banish all the world.'

Polonius would call the plays historical-comical-tragical. The first scene is historical. I remember Randle Ayrton, at curtain-rise on the opening afternoon of the Royal Shakespeare Theatre at Stratford – it was the Shakespeare Memorial then – standing beneath the scarlet canopy of the King's throne and speaking 'So shaken as we are, so wan with care' as if every word were stamped out with a hot iron. Ayrton's gravelly voice, using his short Cheshire 'a', was entirely personal. No one in my recollection has established Henry more completely than he did when the King, afflicted by burdens of state, the memory of his usurpation, and the behaviour of his son, addressed his councillors. He must be autocratic and melancholy, not the unpredictable hysteric an actor made of him in the Stratford-upon-Avon revival of 1974. At this opening two of the play's themes are announced – Hotspur's courage and his dangerous independence, and the King's grief (suggested already in *Richard II*) at the dissolute behaviour of the Prince:

> Thou mak'st me sad and mak'st me sin
> In envy that my Lord Northumberland
> Should be the father to so blest a son –
> A son who is the theme of honour's tongue;
> Amongst a grove, the very straightest plant;
> Who is sweet Fortune's minion and her pride;
> Whilst I, by looking on the praise of him,
> See riot and dishonour stain the brow
> Of my young Harry. O that it could be prov'd
> That some night-tripping fairy had exchang'd
> In cradle-clothes our children where they lay,
> And call'd mine Percy, his Plantagenet. (I, i, 78–89)

We move immediately to the Prince, in his London lodging, and, in the customary business, waking Falstaff. 'Now, what time of day is it, lad?' Falstaff exclaims, starting up. At once his wit is on fire:

> We that take purses go by the moon and the seven stars, and not by Phoebus, he 'that wand'ring knight so fair.' And, I prithee, sweet wag, when thou art a king, as God save thy Grace – Majesty, I should say; for grace thou wilt have none –
>
> PRINCE: What, none?
> FALSTAFF: No, by my troth; not so much as will serve to be prologue to an egg and butter. (I, ii, 12–20)

II

'When thou art king . . .' Falstaff uses the phrase four times. At the end of the scene the Prince is left alone for the soliloquy that only an actor of hypnotic charm – Alan Howard is one – can excuse in

the theatre. Hal is saying that, while it pleases him, he will behave as
he is doing now. When the time comes, he can change instantly

> And, like bright metal on a sullen ground,
> My reformation, glitt'ring o'er my fault,
> Shall show more goodly and attract more eyes
> Than that which hath no foil to set it off.
> I'll so offend to make offence a skill,
> Redeeming time when men think least I will. (I, ii, 205-10)

I agree that Shakespeare is simply preparing the way for Henry V;
but it is a speech that has to be interpreted as cold-bloodedly
as it sounds, and after this, whenever Falstaff and Hal are on stage
together, it can be difficult to remember that the Prince is more than
a time-server.[1] Shakespeare, making the same point a little later,
has left it to the actor's intonation. In a Boar's Head Tavern charade,
after Falstaff, a cushion on his head, has been imitating the King,
the Prince does so too, and takes delight in calling Falstaff everything from a 'swoll'n parcel of dropsies' to 'that grey iniquity, that
father ruffian, that vanity in years'. Here he is at play, but the
temperature of the scene drops. Falstaff has responded with a set of
variations on his name: 'Sweet Jack Falstaff, kind Jack Falstaff, true
Jack Falstaff, valiant Jack Falstaff', ending with the iterated 'Banish
not him thy Harry's company. Banish plump Jack, and banish all
the world.' To which the Prince answers nothing but 'I do, I *will*';
as it is uttered now with an icy determination, it speaks for the
end of *Part Two*, still far ahead. At that moment there is a knocking
on the door; it is not too fanciful to think of the knocking at the gate
in *Macbeth*. It is only the Sheriff in search of Falstaff and his dubious
company. The Prince turns him away; Falstaff's hour has not yet
come. Meanwhile, on one level of the play, there has been the robbery
at Gadshill and the practical joke upon Falstaff, and, on the other,
Hotspur's arrival at Court to explain why he denies the King his
prisoners. A tempest in himself, he described how, after Holmedon
battle, he is 'pest'red with a popinjay' (the officer for the King); he
defends Mortimer, Earl of March, who has married the daughter of
the Welsh rebel, Owen Glendower; and when the King has gone in
wrath, he, his father and his uncle rehearse the promises Henry had
made when, as Henry Bolingbroke new-landed at Ravenspurgh, he
had been anxious for allies. (Throughout both plays Shakespeare
reverts constantly to *Richard II*). Hotspur blazes into the great cry:

> By heaven, methinks it were an easy leap
> To pluck bright honour from the pale-fac'd moon;

Or dive into the bottom of the deep
Where fathom-line could never touch the ground,
And pluck up drownèd honour by the locks;
So he that doth redeem her thence might wear
Without corrival all her dignities. (I, iii, 201–7)

III

When we see him next he is in Glendower's castle in Wales; the Percy faction, with Glendower and Mortimer, is ready to fight. Now the play's pulse is beating fast. Hotspur is in impatient, tactless ardour; Glendower is in high Welsh pride and (an early Prospero) using his magical arts to summon music from the air; and the scene ends with a Welsh song by Mortimer's wife, banter between Hotspur and his wife, Kate; and Glendower's 'Come, come, Lord Mortimer; you are as slow/As hot Lord Percy is on fire to go.' Then (I think of one particular Stratford revival) the gradual thickening of the dark as Lady Percy and Lady Mortimer are left silent and alone.

The chronicle is back at court for the often ill used duologue in which the King upbraids Hal for his behaviour, 'so common-hackney'd in the eyes of men,/So stale and cheap to vulgar company':

By being seldom seen, I could not stir
But, like a comet, I was wond'red at;
That men would tell their children 'This is he';
Others would say 'Where, which is Bolingbroke?' (III, ii, 46–9)

At last – 'the words must seem wrung from him' says Professor Sprague[2] – the Prince is stirred to the promise of great things ('I shall make this northern youth exchange/His glorious deeds for my indignities'). He is back at the Boar's Head only to warn Falstaff that he has procured for him a 'charge of foot' in the wars ('I would', says Falstaff, 'it had been of horse'). And we are at once on the road to Shrewsbury: the embassies between the rival camps; the comic interpolations of Falstaff who, as we have learned earlier, is a 'coward on instinct'; the battle in which two stars can keep their motion in one sphere; Hotspur's death and Falstaff's ruse; and the King's last couplet: '. . . Since this business so fair is done,/Let us not leave till all our own be won.' That skims over many scenes of Shakespeare's most stirring verse, mingled with Falstaff's sallies and retires on the battlefield which I have occasionally found distracting. For a while we may forget the Prince's double-dealing in the excitement of the battle pieces and in his epitaph for Falstaff when he thinks the knight is dead:

> What, old acquaintance! Could not all this flesh
> Keep in a little life? Poor Jack, farewell!
> I could have better spar'd a better man.
> O, I should have a heavy miss of thee,
> If I were much in love with vanity!
> Death hath not struck so fat a deer today,
> Though many dearer, in this bloody fray. (V, iv, 102–8)

Falstaff was never more alive. He is a coward, a liar, a promise breaker, a glutton, everything the Prince has thrown at him, and more. But he is also Eastcheap's oriflamme and he has a wise, agile mind. George Robey, who gave a debated performance between the wars (His Majesty's, 1935) had a confident sack-and-sugar voice, and he seldom externalised: not great playing but an unexpected piece of bravura. That period's definitive Falstaff was Roy Byford at Stratford; just after the war it was Ralph Richardson – all actors of size and authority with an ear for the closely-textured prose; no rubious buffoonery or working arrangements with the prompter. Falstaff is a quotation dictionary in himself. We remember:

> 'Tis my vocation, Hal; 'tis no sin for a man to labour in his vocation. (I, ii, 101)

> There lives not three good men unhang'd in England, and one of them is fat and grows old. (II, iv, 123–5)

> Well, I'll repent, and that suddenly, while I am in some liking; I shall be out of heart shortly, and then I shall have no strength to repent. (III, iii, 5–7)

> O, I do not like that paying back; 'tis a double labour. (III, iii, 178–9)

> Honour pricks me on. Yea, but how if honour prick me off when I come on? (V, i, 129–30)

> The better part of valour is discretion. (V, iv, 119)

> Lord, Lord, how this world is given to lying. (V, iv, 143)

IV

Since Tree suggested the idea to Matheson Lang in 1914, Hotspur has frequently stammered, though of late he has done without something that could interfere with the cascading speeches and had to be treated with tact. Any stammerer hesitates on his own set of awkward sounds, and it becomes farcical when a player is popping corks at random throughout his speeches. Wilfrid Walter, at Stratford with Bridges-Adams (1932), used the explosive 'p' sound; but Laurence Olivier (New Theatre, 1945) chose the letter 'w'. When Hotspur was beaten to the earth, he died with his last word struggling for utterance. Nothing could more sharply point the text:

> O, I could prophesy,
> But that the earthy and cold hand of death
> Lies on my tongue. No, Percy, thou art dust
> And food for –
> PRINCE: For worms, brave Percy. Fare thee well, great heart!
>
> (V, iv, 83–7)

The stammer, not in Holinshed, derives from Lady Percy's line in *Part Two*: 'Speaking thick, which nature made his blemish'. But there 'thick' is used in the sense of 'thick and fast', pelting speech, so the device has theatrical precedent only.

Olivier and Michael Redgrave (who chose a Northumbrian burr at Stratford in 1951) each enjoyed the Warkworth skirmish with Lady Percy – except for Quickly's babble, the play's only important chance for an actress. She gives as much as she gets. While the scene is still in mind the Prince, at the Boar's Head, parodies its spirit in

'I am not yet of Percy's mind, the Hotspur of the north; he that kills me some six or seven dozen of Scots at a breakfast, washes his hands, and says to his wife "Fie upon this quiet life! I want work!" "O my sweet Harry," says she, "how many hast thou kill'd today?" "Give my roan horse a drench" says he; and answers "Some fourteen," an hour after, "a trifle, a trifle." (II, iv, 99–105)

Hotspur is always on fire to go. He has encouragement at Shrewsbury from the richly-inlaid speeches of Sir Richard Vernon. In the first Vernon describes the Prince as he rose from the ground 'like feathered Mercury' and

> Vaulted with such ease into his seat
> As if an angel dropp'd down from the clouds

To turn and wind a fiery Pegasus,
And witch the world with noble horsemanship. (IV, i, 106–10)

Later he tells Hotspur how the Prince issued his challenge to single
fight:

He gave you all the duties of a man;
Trimm'd up your praises with a princely tongue;
Spoke your deservings like a chronicle;
Making you ever better than his praise,
By still dispraising praise valued with you;
And, which became him like a prince indeed,
He made a blushing cital of himself,
And chid his truant youth with such a grace
As if he mast'red there a double spirit,
Of teaching and of learning instantly. (V, ii, 56–65)

Very little can usefully be taken from the play except the Prince's
deception of the little Boar's Head drawer, Francis ('Anon, anon,
sir!') which has always seemed oddly distasteful; and a brief passage,
looking towards *Part Two*, for the conspiratorial Archbishop of York
and a personage called Sir Michael whose name might test the
memory of the readiest Shakespearian. I have known Falstaff's
address to Bardolph in the third act to be cut; but that is a monstrous
notion. It removes the delighted detail on which Bardolphs down
the years have based their make-up, and no listener can spare 'I
never see thy face but I think upon hell-fire, and Dives that lived
in purple; for there he is in his robes, burning, burning.'

NOTES

1 Professor Arthur Colby Sprague writes *(Shakespeare's Histories: Plays for the Stage,*
1964): 'The famous soliloquy . . . is not, I am convinced, to be translated literally
in terms of character . . . The dramatist is assuring his English audience that this
'wayward young Prince will emerge untarnished as the splendid King Harry of
fame and at the same time is inviting them to detect certain ironies in later scenes
which might otherwise pass unnoticed.'
2 ibid, p. 65.

The Merry Wives of Windsor (1597-8)

I

You might call this a revenge play in the key of farcical comedy: bourgeois Windsor (concealing Shakespeare's own Stratford) opposed to a fat and amorous knight from the environs of the Court. It has been underrated in general criticism, possibly because next to no poetry glimmers among its scuffling, and some of what there is – the Garter speech, agreeably ceremonial but allotted to Quickly, of all people, in the last-act masquing – is often lost from a stage text. Maybe, as Professor Hibbard suggests,[1] Shakespeare put together a comedy for the Garter celebrations of 1597 and expanded and revised it later for the play we have.

Tradition, which need not be invariably wrong, says that Queen Elizabeth ordered Shakespeare to write *The Merry Wives of Windsor* because she wished to see Falstaff in love, and that the dramatist responded within a fortnight. Again, no proof; it is an amiable story, and it pleases the majority of editors (and readers) who hold that, to the great man of the *Henry IV* plays, Falstaff of *The Merry Wives* is a despised poor relation. Certainly, though they have the same name, and the knight of Windsor has other familiar names in his entourage, we cannot believe what we are told.

If the play is supposed to follow the events of *II Henry IV*, we ask what has happened to Quickly. An endearing person, servant to a French doctor, Windsor go-between and breathless babbling gossip, good she-Mercury, she has nothing to do with the hostess of the Boar's Head who, by *Henry V*, had married Pistol (always, I have thought, improbable). Corporal Nym, who does not appear in *Henry IV*, is here, torturing the Jonsonian catchword 'humour' as he does in *Henry V*. Pistol, though he does turn up as 'Hobgoblin' to swell the final act round Herne's Oak, is a poor lath of a character with one good phrase:

Why then the world's my oyster,
Which I with sword will open. (II, ii, 4–5)

Justice Shallow is a thin parody of Falstaff's Cotswold host. All very curious.

Perhaps we should not bother. It is wiser to accept that this is a piece, swiftly run up, in which Shakespeare abandoned chronology, grabbed some names from his stock, and put together a repetitive comedy that can carry a theatre in a full-scale performance. No need to be hyperbolical or hypercritical; it is often what Hugh Evans, the Welsh parson, might have called 'admirable pleasures and very honest knaveries', Country versus Town, and the Country getting all the better of it. One problem in the narrative is also better left to the detectives. Believed to be a 'fossil' from an earlier text, it is a fourth-act reference to a horse-stealing sub-plot and unidentified Germans – a topicality that has bred ingenious theories but means as little to us now as 'Mistress Mall's picture' or the 'lady of the Strachy' in *Twelfth Night*. Normally, it is cut, though one has known Pistol, Nym, and Bardolph to impersonate the Germans; and in 1975, without noticeable success, a London revival used some patching and rewriting.

II

The main narrative of Shakespeare's only bourgeois comedy is, simply, the mocking of Falstaff, guest at the Garter Inn, who tries to make love to both Mistress Ford and Mistress Page. They are wives of wealthy Windsor citizens. Three times they fool him; it says a lot for Shakespeare's high spirits that, unless the acting is glum, we can always return to these mild jokes. The knight is carried away under the washing in a laundry-basket; is disguised – not too surely – as the Old Woman of Brentford ('I like not when a 'oman has a great peard,' murmurs Hugh Evans, the Welshman who makes 'fritters of English'); and at length, one midnight in the glades of Windsor Forest, wears the horns of Herne the Hunter and rattles his chain.

Down the years the piece was acted in an early summer setting. Agreed, one thinks of it in terms of the Host of the Garter's description of Fenton, the romantic lover: 'He speaks holiday; he smells April and May.' But to ignore Shakespeare's pointers is to yield to a false tradition, and this one is undeniably wrong, fortified though it has been by the custom of nineteenth-century and Edwardian revivals, all hollyhocks and roses-round-the-door. More properly, the play is a near-Christmas card: Windsor in a frost-sparkling December. We observe early talk of coursing; Quickly's promise to John Rugby to have 'a posset ... soon at night ... at the latter end of a sea-coal fire'; Pistol's warning to Ford, 'Take heed ere summer comes, or cuckoo-birds do sing'; Master Page's greeting to Parson Hugh in the fields at Frogmore, 'In your doublet and hose this raw rheumatic day!'; Falstaff's 'If I be served such another trick, I'll have my brains ta'en out, and buttered, and give them to a dog for a new-year's gift'; his 'Come, let me pour in some sack to the Thames water; for my belly's as cold as if I had swallow'd snowballs'; Mistress Page remembering the old tale of Herne the Hunter who 'doth all winter-time, at still midnight, walk round about an oak'; and, in her last speech but one:

Good husband, let us everyone go home,
And laugh this sport o'er by a country fire;
Sir John and all. (V, v, 228–30)

(No doubt, if the story of Elizabeth's commission is true, Shakespeare used the season in which he was writing.)

Oscar Asche, the English actor-manager, changed the calendar in 1911 when, too thoroughly, as always with Asche, he covered his London stage, in street and field, with salt four inches deep. The cast wore mufflers and gloves and mittens; every nose was red with cold; and wood fires crackled indoors. This was condemned as perverse. When I met the play in the remoter English provinces a dozen years later, Windsor was scorching under high summer (and a strong light that revealed every crease in the ancient backcloths). Even in 1955, at Stratford-upon-Avon, Glen Byam Shaw, most truthful of directors, was blamed unfairly for his winter setting. Winter or summer, *The Merry Wives* speaks holiday; grief will come only if a performance is frostbitten. On the whole, the play has suffered rather less than others from merely eccentric experiment, though it was a choice for modern dress as early as 1929 (Asche again; Falstaff was natural casting for the largest man in the London theatre). At Stratford-upon-Avon in 1935 Theodore Komisarjevsky, by then a licensed jester, staged it, *opera bouffe* fashion, in a more or less Viennese frame; made up his Falstaff – a shamefaced Roy Byford – in whiskers and scarlet hunting coat, as the Emperor Franz Josef; produced some vociferous choral effects, as at 'Have with you, to see this monster!'; and observed with satisfaction that the result was 'faithful in word and deed to Shakespeare'.

III

Place-names are, conscientiously, from Windsor, yet we get the feeling that to Shakespeare it was all much nearer home. In Parson Hugh Evans and his Latin lesson (alas, another favourite cut) to a boy who is called William, we have surely a memory of Shakespeare's own education, and of Thomas Jenkins of the Stratford Grammar school:

EVANS: What is *lapis*, William?
WILLIAM: A stone.
EVANS: And what is 'a stone,' William?
WILLIAM: A pebble.
EVANS: No; it is *lapis;* I pray you remember in your prain.
WILLIAM: *Lapis.*
EVANS: That is a good William. What is he, William, that does lend articles?
WILLIAM: Articles are borrowed of the pronoun, and be thus declined: *Singulariter, nominativo; hic, haec, hoc.*
EVANS: Nominativo, *hig, hag, hog;* pray you mark: *genitivo, huius* . . . (IV, i, 28–40)

And so on, with Quickly a bewildered listener. George Page's fallow greyhound was outrun on Cotsall (Cotswold). Frank Ford could derive from a notoriously splenetic Stratfordian, Nicholas Barnhurst. Quickly speaks to Simple of 'a great round beard, like a glover's paring-knife': this is near home, indeed.

Falstaff and Ford lead the party. An acknowledged butt, Falstaff keeps a certain verbal gift. I agree that his overwhelming namesake would never have allowed himself to say, 'You have the start of me. I am dejected. I am not able to answer the Welsh flannel.' Still, he does have one or two things that might not be scorned in *Henry IV:*

Think'st thou I'll endanger my soul gratis? (II, ii, 13–14)

She is a region in Guiana, all gold and bounty. I will be cheaters to them both, and they shall be exchequers to me; they shall be my East and West Indies, and I will trade to them both. (I, iii, 65–9)

I cannot cog, and say thou art this and that, like a many of these lisping hawthorn-buds, that come like women in men's apparel, and smell like Bucklersbury in simple time. (III, iii, 58–61)

You may know by my size that I have a kind of alacrity in sinking.
(III, v, 10)

A man of continual dissolution and thaw. (III, v, 101–2)

In the shape of man, Master Brook, I fear not Goliath with a
weaver's beam, because I know also, life is a shuttle. (V, i, 20–2)

A small harvest, I daresay, for a wit of Falstaff's antecedents.
Frank Ford is the man we remember from *The Merry Wives*, the
husband who is Shakespeare's comic view of jealousy ('See the hell
of having a false woman!'), and who utters in his frenzied prose
roughly what Leontes will in still more frenzied verse. Much of it is
a roaring, hat-stamping, scarf-twisting part, but Ford can be most
human in remorse; and the actor has also those scenes as Master Brook –
in today's theatre a swivelling, insecure moustache can be cover
enough – when he visits Falstaff at the Garter. Falstaff needs no
persuasion to 'lay an amiable siege to the honesty of this Ford's wife'.
I have never forgotten, from the English provinces in 1923, Ernest
Milton's Ford-Brook, with eyes like angry currants, and a voice of
magnified gentility, tempting his Falstaff with the slow advances and
withdrawals of the bag of gold, and – when left alone – climbing
the wall in his fury. The most accomplished recent Ford has been
Ian Richardson, who twice at Stratford in the sixties, and again in
1974, delivered the speeches as though he were suddenly bounced off
a trampoline.

There can be no hesitation in *The Merry Wives*. Every part asks for
a strong theatrical thrust. Not that an actor can transform Pistol,
booming in his old jargon; Nym and his 'humours', and Bardolph,
who dwindles to a tapster. Fenton can be a handsome blank (I did
see him glorified by the young Gyles Isham at Stratford in 1931);
Abraham Slender is a minor Sir Andrew, without Andrew's
latent charm; and the Host of the Garter, a bluff 'ranting' personage
who, behind his sonorous synonyms, is more of a character than we
are generally shown. Anne Page may appear to be dim, but she can
say most potently when it is suggested that she should marry the
doctor:

Alas, I had rather be set quick i'th'earth,
And bowl'd to death with turnips. (III, iv, 85–6)

(One can hear the laugh swelling through the afternoon from the
Globe Theatre.)

As for Doctor Caius himself, a rocketing caricature of a Frenchman,

he must be absolutely sincere – in performance a firework of a fellow
who regards the world about him as an exercise in pyrotechnics.
Parson Hugh (like so many in the *Wives*, making an assault on
language) is, of course, a gift to any Welshman, just as he must
have been to the actor in Shakespeare's company who played
Glendower, Fluellen, and probably that Welsh Captain of *Richard II*.

IV

What of the Wives themselves, mischievous matrons of Windsor?
They form a brisk double-act – Mistress Page is the longer of the
parts – nearly always together, never short of an idea, and delighted
by their own charades. Bits of their business continue from revival
to revival. Thus Mistress Page, reading Falstaff's letter, will almost
invariably pause at 'You are merry, so am I; ha . . .' and turn
over for the second 'ha!' with sudden pleased recognition. She,
too, when Falstaff has to escape for the first time, will exclaim in the
most unpersuasive surprise: 'Look! . . . here is a basket!' The Benson
company had a prized tradition for Alice Ford. Dorothy Green, who
acted her so often, told me that, before the buck-basket scene, Falstaff
would always find her asleep. This was because immediately he
entered, and before going on to 'Why now, let me die, for I have
lived long enough', he would be singing the first line of Philip
Sidney's lyric, 'Stella Sleeping'. It begins 'Have I caught my heav'nly
jewel?' Elizabethans were expected to know what follows:

> . . . Teaching sleep most fair to be?
> Now will I teach her that she,
> When she wakes, is too, too cruel.

There is relatively little stock business in *The Merry Wives*. It is
the kind of play that springs to spontaneous life in rehearsal when,
say, Caius finds Peter Simple in the closet ('Dere is some simples in
my closet, dat I vill not for the varld I shall leave behind'); or
Ford, in most profound gloom, cries 'I melancholy? I am not
melancholy'; or Quickly rattles on so fast that Falstaff ('Be brief,
my good she-Mercury!') cannot insert a word; or Falstaff manoeuvres
a vast vessel of sack (something must be in it: mere sound effects will
not do); or doctor and parson prepare, variously, for the duel that
will not be fought; or Ford, followed by his train, clatters through
the house while Falstaff is carried out, heaving, in the basket, or
stumbling over the skirts of the Woman of Brentford.

The last winter-midnight scene, with Falstaff as Herne the

Hunter, and the mock fairies singeing him with their tapers, includes what may be the remnant of a Garter masque. We shall be lucky now if we hear the ceremonial speech, assigned so implausibly to Quickly:

> And nightly, meadow-fairies, look you sing,
> Like to the Garter's compass, in a ring:
> Th'expressure that it bears, green let it be,
> More fertile-fresh than all the field to see;
> And *Honi soit qui mal y pense* write
> In emerald tufts, flow'rs purple, blue and white;
> Like sapphire, pearl, and rich embroidery,
> Buckled below fair knighthood's bending knee:
> Fairies use flow'rs for their charactery. (V, v, 63–71)

At the end of the play we shall get the last lines of either the Folio or the Quarto texts. I must always regret the loss of the Quarto line for Evans, 'I will also dance and eat plums at your weddings', but the final Folio couplet, Ford to Falstaff (sometimes spoken now by Alice Ford), is neater than the Quarto:

> Sir John,
> To Master Brook you yet shall hold your word,
> For he, tonight, shall lie with Mistress Ford. (V, v, 231–2)

NOTES

1 New Penguin edition (1973).

King Henry IV, Part Two
(1598)

I

Henry IV, Part One is complete in itself; but Shakespeare had a lot
more to add, and clearly he could not let Falstaff go after a single
play. (We do not count the pretender of *The Merry Wives*.) 'I'll
purge, and leave sack, and live cleanly, as a gentleman should do,'
he has said at the end of *Part One;* when we come upon him again
there is no visible change. Again he does not arrive until the second
scene. We must begin in the northern castle, the 'worm-eaten
hold of ragged stone' where Northumberland, after a flurry of conflicting messages, learns of Hotspur's death. Rumour, who speaks
the prologue, has been presented in several ways, unhappily
(Stratford, 1964) as a kind of crippled Thersites with a Midland
voice, and, ten years later, by a dozen black-clad and masked
players, chopping up the lines between them. No one was better than
Vivienne Bennett (afterwards Doll) in a splendid flare of speech for
the Old Vic revival of 1935:

> I, from the orient to the drooping west,
> Making the wind my post-horse, still unfold
> The acts commencèd on this ball of earth.
> Upon my tongues continual slanders ride,
> The which in every language I pronounce,
> Stuffing the ears of men with false reports. (3–8)

Rumour is prologue only to the first scene: it does not concern
the remainder of the play. This, more loosely organised than *Part One*,
eventually brings Prince Hal to the throne and Falstaff to despair.
Before this we have Lady Percy's lament for her husband; the richest
tavern scene in dramatic history; the northern rebellion ended by

foul treachery in Gaultree Forest; Falstaff recruiting and relaxing in a Cotswold village; and the weary King's approach to death. A marvellous play, it does not stand easily by itself, as *Part One* does. There is less danger now of having them divorced from each other – at one point *Part Two* was much the rarer – and we can observe the mountain that is Falstaff, base to crest, like the Old Man of Coniston seen across the lake. An actor must preserve the man's physical and intellectual proportions without submitting us to a trial by mannerism.

The scenes of rebellion, though they can act well, are in danger of dragging: Scroop has no Hotspur on his side. At court the King can speak much sombre, burdened verse; the apostrophe to sleep is famous:

> Canst thou, O partial sleep, give thy repose
> To the wet sea-boy in an hour so rude;
> And in the calmest and most stillest night,
> With all appliances and means to boot,
> Deny it to a king? Then, happy low, lie down!
> Uneasy lies the head that wears a crown. (III, i, 26–31)

He has the glorious flash after the northern rebellion fades:

> O Westmoreland, thou art a summer bird,
> Which ever in the haunch of winter sings
> The lifting up of day. (IV, iv, 91–3)

the passage after the Prince, believing him to be dead, has removed the crown and is called back to the bedside:

PRINCE: I never thought to hear you speak again.
KING: Thy wish was father, Harry, to that thought,
        I stay too long by thee, I weary thee.
        Dost thou so hunger for mine empty chair
        That thou wilt needs invest thee with my honours
        Before the hour be ripe? (IV, v, 92–7)

and the last advice from the supple mind that was Bolingbroke's:

>   Therefore, my Harry
> Be it thy course to busy giddy minds
> With foreign quarrels, that action, hence borne out,
> May waste the memory of the former days. (IV, v, 213–16)

All of this must impress; but the great strength of *Part Two* is less in its public life than its private – the tavern and the village. At the Boar's Head the Prince and Poins masquerade as drawers to overhear Falstaff and Doll Tearsheet, the local whore, adenoidal, lachrymose, strident, and flushed with canary. Once she so shocked puritan opinion that as late as 1932, at Stratford, her lines were being doctored. Pistol, too, is at the Boar's Head, Falstaff's wildest follower, who talks in a jargon that is a distant echo of the Marlovian rants:

> Shall packhorses,
> And hollow pamper'd jades of Asia,
> Which cannot go but thirty mile a day,
> Compare with Caesars, and with Cannibals,
> And Troiant Greeks? Nay, rather damn them with
> King Cerberus; and let the welkin roar.
> Shall we fall foul for toys? (II, iv, 154–60)

This horrifies Hostess Quickly who, as always, is in good name and fame with the very best and will have no swaggerers. Falstaff demurs that Pistol is merely a cheater, but the Hostess will not be placated: 'Cheater, call you him? I will bar no honest man my house, nor no cheater; but I do not love swaggering, by my troth. I am the worse when one says "swagger".' Quickly is far livelier than in *Part One*. She should not be a wheezing, rusty ancient, shaking with unpersuasive mirth, but wide-eyed, gullible, and voluble. For me now the Boar's Head Falstaff must be in the image of Ralph Richardson. When he turned aside with the low 'Peace, good Doll! Do not speak like a death's-head; do not bid me remember mine end', we caught suddenly a sight of the abyss. Mortality, behold and fear! We knew the terror of the lengthening shade.

II

This has no terror for little Justice Shallow and his colleague, Justice Silence, in their Cotswold village:

SHALLOW: To see how many of my old acquaintance are dead!
SILENCE: We shall all follow, cousin.
SHALLOW: Certain, 'tis certain; very sure, very sure. Death, as the Psalmist saith, is certain to all; all shall die. How a good yoke of bullocks at Stamford fair? (III, ii, 32–7)

These scenes are exquisite in their autumnal gentleness. Shallow can be like a withered leaf of a man or an animated rubbing from a memorial brass. Age, with its stealing steps, hath clawed him in the clutch. The far world of his youth, as he remembers it, is a fantasy in which 'mad Shallow' was the life of Clement's Inn, and he and little John Doit of Staffordshire and black George Barnes, and Francis Pickbone, and Will Squele, the Cotswold man, rogued and ranged through the night and the sunrise. 'Hem! boys!' the old man quivers and chuckles. Jesu, Jesu, what a fellow he was! – fighting with Sampson Stockfish, a fruiterer, behind Gray's Inn; lying all night in the windmill in Saint George's Field. He is entitled to his memories, this white-bearded shadow that a strong puff of wind could blow into the next county. He is easily over-ridden, given to petty economies, worrying maybe in life, but in the theatre the most endearing company. It is Shallow's evening; what does it matter so long as there are wine and leather-coats in the orchard, and Cousin Silence to jet, surprisingly into song.

Falstaff's visit is a joy to him – the same Falstaff that was page to Thomas Mowbray, Duke of Norfolk ('We have heard the chimes at midnight, Master Shallow'). This is an official visit: the choice of military recruits from the village's curious muster. The most likely can escape service at the cost of a bribe to Bardolph, and the least probable are chosen, such as Francis Feeble, the gallant little women's tailor:

> By my troth, I care not; a man can die but once; we owe God a death. I'll ne'er bear a base mind. An't be my destiny, so; an't be not, so. No man's too good to serve's Prince; and, let it go which way it will, he that dies this year is quit for the next.

> (III, ii, 228–32)

The scene will droop only if the recruits – as they can be – are resolutely overplayed. All will live if Shallow does, prating of the days when Jack Falstaff broke Scoggin's head at the court gate, and he himself was Sir Dagonet in Arthur's show at Mile End Green. A little fellow there had a caliver, 'and 'a would manage you his piece thus; and 'a would about and about, and come you in and come you in. "Rah, tah, tah!" would 'a say; "Bounce!" would 'a say; and away again would 'a go, and again would 'a come.'

Such players as Morland Graham, Olivier, Alan Badel, Roy Dotrice, and George Benson have all given a clear gleam from Shallow's inch of taper. We have to be sorry when Falstaff, left alone, exposes him without mercy: 'Lord, Lord, how subject we old men are to this vice of lying . . . I do remember him at Clement's

Inn, like a man made after supper of a cheese-paring.' It is better to think of Shallow in his own terms; and we are glad to meet him again when, after the northern rebellion and Falstaff's musing on sherris-sack 'which makes the brain apprehensive, quick, forgetive' – like his own – the knight returns hopefully to Gloucestershire. During the sweet o'the night, with Silence muzzily in song, Pistol makes his roaring entry with news that the King is dead:

SHALLOW: I am, sir, under the King, in some authority.
PISTOL: Under which King, Bezonian? Speak, or die.
SHALLOW: Under King Harry.
PISTOL: Harry the Fourth – or Fifth?
SHALLOW: Harry the Fourth.
PISTOL: A foutra for thine office!
          Sir John, thy tender lambkin now is King;
          Harry the Fifth's the man. I speak the truth.

(V, iv, 111–16)

The end is very near. Falstaff and his company – poor Shallow among them – wait for the royal procession from the Abbey. Within minutes all is over; we look back, it seems an age away, to the Prince's 'When this loose behaviour I throw off and pay the debt I never promisèd.' Again I am with Ralph Richardson in 1945 as he stood in puzzled half-appreciation at the start of the royal rebuke. Surely it must be the Boar's Head humour, Hal at his tricks? When the King spoke 'Know the grave doth gape for thee thrice wider than for other men', we had a last hint of the true Falstaff, a kindling of the eye and a swing of the body as he prepared to launch an answering quip. We could see the line coming when, cruelly, it was quenched in 'Reply not to me with a fool-born jest', and the spark died, and Falstaff faded into a man tired and old. The King had killed his heart, and what was left to do?

Much Ado About Nothing (1598–9)

I

Writing in the 1890s, Arthur Bingham Walkley, the drama critic, described *Much Ado About Nothing* as 'a composite picture of the multifarious, seething, fermenting life, the polychromatic phantasmagoria of the Renaissance'.[1] A resonant, mouth-filling sentence; more simply, this is a patrician comedy, mostly in prose, which sights tragedy without reaching it and could have been designed as a treatise on eavesdropping. For the sake of the narrative everyone seems to overhear everyone else.

As in *Twelfth Night,* ruled by the Malvolio sub-plot, Shakespeare, in *Much Ado,* is so in thrall to Benedick and Beatrice, whose 'merry war' is in fact a long subsidiary skirmish, that he lets what should have been the main narrative slide. This is about a young bridegroom Claudio's readiness to believe (at the instigation of a scheming malcontent) that at night he had seen his intended bride, Hero, talk with a ruffian from her chamber window. Actually, he has seen one of Hero's gentlewomen, Margaret, in her mistress's clothes. At the interrupted wedding when Claudio spurns Hero ('Her blush is guiltiness, not modesty'), Margaret is surprisingly absent. If she had been there the plot would have ended. Shakespeare has kept it going with some cunning. The constable, Dogberry, whose watchmen have apprehended two suspicious characters, talks so long and pointlessly to Hero's father, Leonato, in a hurry to get to the wedding, that the old man tells Dogberry to examine the prisoners himself. One of them is the 'ruffian', Borachio; and the scene in the church is over long before his guilt is recognised.

With Margaret's convenient absence the plot can go on breathing. Audiences, in any event, are less concerned with Hero and Claudio than with the high-mettled conduct of Benedick and Beatrice, he

determined to be a bachelor, she a spinster, and each led to imagine
that the other is passionately in love. They are two of the great parts
in Shakespearian comedy, whereas no players have been especially
famed as the more serious pair. Leonard Digges said in a poem of
1640 what the theatre has been saying since:

> Let but Beatrice
> And Benedick be seen, lo! in a trice
> The cockpit, galleries, boxes, all are full

In our own period this has been very much a Stratford-upon-Avon
play. With it the first Shakespeare Memorial Theatre opened on the
rainy night of Shakespeare's birthday in 1879: Barry Sullivan as
Benedick, Helen Faucit – her last appearance on the stage – as
Beatrice. Since then *Much Ado* has been revived nearly forty times
in Stratford (it was the golden jubilee choice in 1929 instead of
Titus Andronicus), and John Gielgud's applauded 1949 production
had two London runs. Gielgud, who acted Benedick himself from
1950, is the high master of the play. His treatment, graceful and
supple, never fought for its effect. Speaking the prose with a silken
rhythm, he would not allow Benedick to dwindle: this was the Prince's
friend, not the Prince's jester.

One passage for Beatrice and Benedick has developed into a trial
of skill. In the middle of the duologue that begins 'Lady Beatrice,
have you wept all this while?', when only the two of them are left in
the church, we have the exchange:

BENEDICK : By my sword, Beatrice, thou lovest me.
BEATRICE : Do not swear, and eat it.
BENEDICK : I will swear by it that you love me; and I will make him
        eat it that says I love not you.
BEATRICE : Will you not eat your word?
BENEDICK : With no sauce that can be devised to it; I protest I love
        thee.
BEATRICE : Why, then, God forgive me!
BENEDICK : What offence, sweet Beatrice?
BEATRICE : You have stayed me in a happy hour; I was about to
        protest I loved you.
BENEDICK : And do it with all thy heart?
BEATRICE : I love you with so much of my heart that none is left to
        protest.
BENEDICK : Come, bid me do anything for thee.
BEATRICE : Kill Claudio.
BENEDICK : Ha! Not for the wide world. (IV, i, 272–288)

Laughter here must be calamitous. It wrecks the emotion of the scene, and Beatrice must struggle to win back the house for 'Is 'a not approved in the height a villain?' If Benedick has been presented insincerely, simply as a figure of artifice, the laugh is sure. I wrote this of the Phoenix Theatre revival, with Gielgud and Diana Wynyard, in 1952:

'I hope all who go will mark how the passage is treated; how it is lifted gradually to 'Come, bid me do anything for thee' from a loyal lover; how Beatrice pauses for a moment in charged silence; how the actress holds this before she replies 'Kill Claudio!' (words forced from her), and how Benedick's 'Not for the wide world!' is quick, low-toned, the almost incredulous exclamation of a man who had not realised how friendship must struggle with love and honour. Once past this line and the scene moves on with urgent sincerity.'

II

Much Ado demands a patrician style as well as high spirits, though not an overplus of these, which can grow as irritating as the mis-judged use of the fan in Restoration comedy. It is natural that two performances definitely recorded during Shakespeare's life were at Court revels. Bernard Shaw, resolved to be perverse, insisted that 'Benedick's pleasantries might pass at a sing-song in a public-house parlour', nowhere else; but in this mood he could be crass, even though we agree that it is not so much what Beatrice and Benedick say as the way they say it that makes them so theatrically enduring. Shakespeare borrowed the Hero–Claudio plot from various sources. Beatrice and Benedick he invented himself (and probably had a rightful pride in creation) as well as Dogberry, Verges, and the most ancient and quiet watchmen who shuffle on direct from High Street and Sheep Street in Elizabethan Stratford.

The comedy sets them in Messina where most of the action is in the house or garden of the Governor, Leonato. We discover, if we do not allow plot details to wash over us – and this can happen in the early minutes of any play – that the Spanish Prince, Don Pedro,[2] having assembled an army to quell his bastard brother's rising in Sicily, is back now, apparently reunited with Don John after a brief campaign. They and other officers are Leonato's guests. All we need to know is that they have returned from the wars. Don John, a minor Iago from a higher stratum of society, and on the stage traditionally in black, foments the plot against Claudio out of both envy – 'That young start-up hath all the glory of my overthrow' – and a restless desire for mischief. It is not until late in the play (though the programme will probably have told us) that he is spoken of as 'John the Bastard'. By that time he has gone. We do not see him again, but the last lines announce that he has been captured and brought back to Messina, and that Benedick – not too seriously, we imagine – will 'devise brave punishments for him'.

It is the sparring between Beatrice's 'Signor Mountanto' and Benedick's 'dear Lady Disdain' that fixes our attention. They begin immediately:

BEATRICE: I wonder that you will still be talking, Signor Benedick; nobody marks you.

BENEDICK: What, my dear Lady Disdain! Are you yet living?

BEATRICE: Is it possible disdain should die while she hath such meet food to feed it as Signior Benedick? Courtesy itself must convert to disdain if you come in her presence.

BENEDICK: Then is courtesy a turncoat. But it is certain I am loved of all ladies, only you excepted; and I would I could find in my heart that I had not a hard heart, for, truly, I love none.

BEATRICE: A dear happiness to women! They would else have been troubled with a pernicious suitor. I thank God, and my cold blood, I am of your humour for that. I had rather hear my dog bark at a crow than a man swear he loves me. (I, i, 101–12)

Nothing, apparently, can shake Beatrice's resolve not to be a wife. The visitors admire her. 'You were born in a merry hour,' says Don Pedro; and Beatrice makes the famous response (which no actress should present reverently on a salver):

No, sure, my lord, my mother cried; but then there was a star danc'd, and under that was I born. (II, i, 301–3)

An amiable conspiracy is improvised to 'bring Signior Benedick and the Lady Beatrice into a mountain of affection th'one with th'other'. Meanwhile Don John's own plot is developing; but we are absorbed in the scene where Benedick, in an orchard arbour, hears his friends talking largely (for his benefit) of Beatrice's love for him. Hard upon this Hero and Ursula play a similar trick on Beatrice: a repetition almost invariably flat in the theatre. In time we listen to it principally

for the superfluous parenthesis in Hero's first speech, Shakespeare in-
dulging himself:

> Tell her I and Ursula
> Walk in the orchard, and our whole discourse
> Is all of her; say that thou overheard'st us;
> And bid her steal into the pleachèd bower,
> Where honeysuckles, ripened by the sun,
> Forbid the sun to enter – like favourites,
> Made proud by princes, that advance their pride
> Against that power that bred it. There will she hide her
> To listen our propose. (III, i, 4–12)

for the lines:

> For look where Beatrice, like a lapwing, runs
> Close by the ground, to hear our conference. (III, i, 24–5)

which give a clear direction to any actress who can obey them; for
Hero's 'Disdain and scorn ride sparkling in her eyes,/Misprising
what they look on'; and for Beatrice's last soliloquy, 'What fire is in
mine ears? Can this be true?'

III

Shakespeare, uncoiling his various plots to the general pleasure,
adds to them the bonus of Dogberry, immensely complacent constable, with the piping little 'headborough', Verges,[3] and the members of the Messina watch. Dogberry is at ease, a man who knows
his own value and prizes his vocabulary, even if he is unsure what
the words mean: 'To babble and talk is most tolerable and not to be
endured'; 'You are thought here to be the most senseless and
fit man for the constable of the watch'; 'you are to comprehend
all vagrom men.' A Dogberry ought to be entirely unselfconscious,
unaware of any solecisms, realising that if everyone else is wrong he
must always be right. Probably the most substantial performances in
our time have been those of Roy Byford (Stratford, 1929) and John
Woodvine (Stratford, 1976), though Mr Woodvine was disguised
unexpectedly – a mild word – as a Babu in post-Mutiny British
India. *Much Ado* has been translated into more periods than most of
the plays; this has worked quite well, whether in the Italy of the
Risorgimento and of the early-nineteenth century, or (an Edinburgh
Festival production) in modern South America. Franco Zeffirelli

(Old Vic, 1964) chose the Sicily of eighty or so years ago – less engaging, for Zeffirelli overlooked the social distinctions that Bridges-Adams would watch so carefully, and which in this comedy of manners are vastly important.

At the same revival there was much talk of a revision of the text to make it more intelligible, to change 'allusions virtually meaningless to a present-day audience'. It was an empty idea; while it is one thing to study a text word by word, it is another to hear it borne along swiftly in the theatre by an intelligent cast. Here simplification becomes vexation. Does it really help for Beatrice to change 'I could not endure a husband with a beard on his face; I had rather lie in the woollen' to the flat 'I had rather sleep with a blanket next my skin'? Similar popularising – though there by an erudite Shakespearian – was attempted in a film of *Hamlet;* it cannot be other than condescending.

IV

Much Ado is, in two senses, a comedy for the listener. We can call the muster-roll of its regiment of eavesdroppers:

ANTONIO (to his brother, Leonato):
> The Prince and Count Claudio, walking in a thick-pleached alley in mine orchard, were thus much overheard by a man of mine . . . (I, ii, 7–9)

BORACHIO (to Don John):
> Being entertain'd for a perfumer as I was smoking a musty room, comes me the Prince and Claudio hand in hand, in sad conference. I whipt me behind the arras... (I, iii, 50–3)

BENEDICK:
> Ha! the Prince and Monsieur Love! I will hide me in the arbour, (Enter Don Pedro, Leonato, and Claudio).
> (II, iii, 31–2)

URSULA (to Hero):
> So angle we for Beatrice; who even now
> Is couchèd in the woodbine coverture. (III, i, 29–30)

2ND WATCHMAN (listening to Borachio and Conrade):
> Some treason, masters; yet stand close. (III, iii, 99)

DON PEDRO (at the wedding):
>   Myself, my brother, and this grieved Count,
>   Did see her, hear her, at that hour last night,
>   Talk with a ruffian at her chamber window. (IV, i, 87–9)

A rare collection for a single play. Of the eavesdroppers – and most of
the cast can be included – Benedick was probably Richard Burbage's
part. (No actor in recorded time can have matched his sequence of
great new characters.) Besides Gielgud, such actors as Michael
Redgrave, Alan Howard, and Donald Sinden have lately been
generals in the merry war, and Diana Wynyard, Peggy Ashcroft,
Elizabeth Spriggs, and Judi Dench have all pointed the wit of
Leonato's niece, 'first woman in our literature, perhaps in the
literature of Europe, who has not only a brain, but delights in the
constant employment of it'.[4] Hear her on marriage:

> Wooing, wedding, and repenting, is as a Scotch jig, a measure,
> and a cinquepace; the first suit is hot and hasty, like a Scotch jig,
> and full as fantastical; the wedding, mannerly modest, as a
> measure, full of state and ancientry; and then comes repentance,
> and, with his bad legs, falls into the cinquepace faster and faster,
> till he sink into his grave. (II, i, 60–7)

Hero, Beatrice's cousin, keeps a pleasantly natural gaiety until her
collapse at the interrupted wedding: something at which her mother
Innogen – who is given an immediate first-scene entry in the Folio,
but who neither speaks then nor is heard of again – would have
had a great deal to say if Shakespeare had allowed her. Leonato is
a dignified paterfamilias given to believing too easily what he is told.
His angry speech in the church, with its chiming on 'mine':

> But mine, and mine I lov'd, and mine I prais'd,
> And mine that I was proud on; mine so much
> That I myself was to myself not mine,
> Valuing of her . . . (IV, i, 136–9)

has been steadily under-rated. I remember a Stratford-upon-Avon
player between the wars, his mind suddenly blank, who condensed
the whole twenty-four lines into this gibberish: 'But she I valued,
she, alas, has fall'n/Into a pit of ink which none may cleanse/From
her foul-salted flesh . . .' – a lapse which went practically unnoticed.
In abridged texts the speech has sometimes vanished entirely after
its opening lines: 'Why, doth not every earthly thing/Cry shame upon
her? Could she here deny/The story that is printed in her blood?'

Don Pedro is a Renaissance nobleman who suffers when the part is transplanted. Like Claudio he acts too hastily. In the theatre he must keep his state, and, as Bridges-Adams has said: 'No one should touch Pedro on the arm, or sit in his presence without his gesture of assent.'[5] Claudio is another of Shakespeare's rather foolish young men of the period – Bertram is another – whom today it is fashionable to excuse. In Leonato's household Margaret is the feather-brain indirectly responsible for Hero's plight, a matter (it seems) that does not worry her in the least. In the second scene of the fifth act she is being pert with Benedick in the orchard; we can assume that Shakespeare cast her for General Utility and left it at that without trying to be persuasive. Outside the household Dogberry and Verges are roaring and piping in a double act that rarely flags. Leonato's 'Drink some wine ere you go' before he hurries off to the wedding used to be the cue for traditional business in which Dogberry would dispose lip-smackingly of both goblets while Verges twittered despairingly beside him.

From any performance memory slips inevitably to Benedick and Beatrice and their cross-fire. Other lines that often steal back are in the scene before daybreak when Claudio lays his elegy upon what he takes to be Hero's tomb. After the dirge has been sung, Don Pedro says quietly:

DON PEDRO: Good morrow, masters; put your torches out:
             The wolves have prey'd; and look, the gentle day
             Before the wheels of Phoebus, round about
             Dapples the drowsy east with spots of grey . . .
CLAUDIO: Good morrow, masters; each his several way.

NOTES

1 *Playhouse Impressions* (1892).
2 He could be hardly less like the other Prince of Arragon in *The Merchant of Venice*.
3 A 'headborough' is 'a parish officer identical in function with the petty constable'.
4 Dover Wilson, *Shakespeare's Happy Comedies* (1962), p. 132.
5 *A Bridges-Adams Letter Book* (1971), p. 74.

As You Like It (1599)

I

'With this *Ganimede* started up, made her readie, and went into the fields with *Aliena;* where unfolding their flocks, they sat them down under an olive tree, both of them amorous, and yet diverslie affected.'

That is from Thomas Lodge's *Rosalynde*, the novel on which Shakespeare based his pastoral comedy. His title could hardly be more casual. Lodge's is right, for the narrative is governed by one woman: Rosalind, in Arden, is the deity on whom the forest airs attend. Cast out by her uncle, the usurping Duke, she goes off to the distant glades where her father, the Banished Duke, is living with his Court. She does not reveal herself to him; she is a shepherd boy, Ganymede, and her cousin Celia, her uncle's daughter, who goes with her, is the shepherdess Aliena. They are (more or less in Lodge's words) diversely amorous.

So, too, are others. Though Jaques, one of the Banished Duke's courtiers, wanders through it sardonically, it is a comedy for youth, fleeting the time as in the golden world. It is also a play of love at first sight, a theme expressed in Phebe's couplet that is among Shakespeare's tributes to Marlowe and must not be thrown away:

Dead shepherd, now I find thy saw of might:
'Who ever lov'd that lov'd not at first sight?' (III, v, 80–1)[1]

The forest lovers are Rosalind (who, for most of the play, is Ganymede) and the admirably single-minded Orlando; Celia and Oliver, an unlikely partnership; and the shepherdess Phebe, whose love for Ganymede is unfortunate: she must content herself with an adoring shepherd, Silvius. We need not add Audrey and Touchstone, for the emotions of that garrulous fellow whom the cousins inflict on the forest – and whom Shakespeare probably wrote for his company's new comedian – are often too wayward to chart. It is vastly important that we should love Rosalind at first sight; if not, Shakespeare is being indifferently served. She must be herself many fathoms deep in love; it is no kind of part for an actress who reads on from the 'swashing and martial outside' and discovers only a trilling swaggerer. We look for the Atalanta-flash and the jetting raillery; we look for wisdom and gentleness, and Rosalind's trick of laughing at herself; most, we look for the quality Edith Evans showed at the Old Vic in 1936. Goddess of a Watteau forest, she made us forget the stylisation round her, and her Boy Blue coat and breeches, when – in sudden rapture uncontrollable – she cried to Celia:

ROSALIND: O coz, coz, coz, my pretty little coz, that thou didst know how many fathom deep I am in love! But it cannot be sounded; my affection hath an unknown bottom, like the Bay of Portugal.

CELIA: Or rather, bottomless; that as fast as you pour affection in, it runs out.

ROSALIND: No; that same wicked bastard of Venus, that was begot of thought, conceiv'd of spleen, and born of madness; that blind rascally boy, that abuses every one's eyes, because his own are out – let him be judge how deep I am in love. I'll tell thee, Aliena, I cannot be out of the sight of Orlando. I'll go find a shadow, and sigh till he come.

CELIA: And I'll sleep. (IV, ii, 184–96)

For a moment Shakespeare may have faltered in affection; in the text he has not decided whether Rosalind or Celia is the taller. Directors can put it tactfully right, and some editions do so, anyway. We ask no questions when Rosalind is a woman who 'by heavenly synod was devised'; whose gaiety is born of truth; and who has that guilty pause when, a shepherd boy, she tells Orlando that she lives 'here in the skirts of the forest, like fringe upon a petticoat'. It is Rosalind who has the joyful fling, 'But what talk we of fathers when there be such a man as Orlando?'; and who stresses so meaningly the repetition, 'And I for no woman', in the chiming quartet:

PHEBE: Good shepherd, tell this youth what 'tis to love.

SILVIUS: It is to be all made of sighs and tears;
And so am I for Phebe.

PHEBE: And I for Ganymede.

ORLANDO: And I for Rosalind.
ROSALIND: And I for no woman.
SILVIUS: It is to be all made of faith and service,
           And so am I for Phebe.
PHEBE: And I for Ganymede.
ORLANDO: And I for Rosalind.
ROSALIND: And I for no woman . . . (V, ii, 76–86)

Really, she lives in three words just after Orlando's dreadful couplet:

> Thus must I from the smoke into the smother;
> From tyrant Duke unto a tyrant brother. (I, ii, 266–7)

Then (and nothing else matters): 'But heavenly Rosalind!'

II

Through five-sixths of the comedy we are in Arden, glade upon glade that programmes, at a time when scenes were listed, would assign obediently to Another Part of the Forest. When I knew Arden first, in a provincial theatre between the wars, any phrase would imply the same old trees, limp cut-outs variously arranged, with intrusive lappets of gauze, against a woodland backdrop creased with age. Those productions are under the blanket of the dark. We are lucky now if we get more than one tree; possibly a low practicable branch for Rosalind and Celia, and a log or so. For Edwardians this would have been a mockery; so would the tubular perspex trees in the National's all-male revival (1967). Oscar Asche, directing in Edwardian London, saw Arden comprehensively as two thousand pots of fern, a batch of moss-grown logs, large clumps of bamboo, and cartloads of leaves from the previous autumn.

Wherever Arden is – the Ardennes or Warwickshire, and we know which was likelier in Shakespeare's mind – it contains, besides its oaks, hawthorns, and osiers, sheep and deer, a palm tree, a lioness, a tuft of olives, a green and gilded snake. If, in our economical theatre, we are granted any suggestion of a forest for these properties, it ought to be one that hints at depth, age, remoteness: 'This desert inaccessible under the shade of melancholy boughs', 'An oak whose antique root peeps out/Under the brook that brawls along this wood', 'An oak whose boughs were moss'd with age,/And high top bald with dry antiquity'. I cannot yet warm to a forest like a sheaf of knitting-needles.

As in *The Merry Wives of Windsor*, we must mark the season. *As You Like It* changes from the glaze of winter (rough weather at the usurping Duke's palace as well as in the Banished Duke's wild wood) to the light of high summer and reconciliation. Sometimes spirits have been dashed when a director, faithful to Shakespeare, has expressed 'the icy fang/And churlish chiding of the winter's wind'; but at heart we know him to be justified. If winter is not harsh in those early scenes, we may feel that the Banished Duke and his followers are suffering no more than they might on a sylvan holiday with a little painting and music thrown in. As it is, the place will soon be unshrivelled.

III

Arden is inhabited by lovers, courtiers, and fools, and an unseen hermit who is valuable for cobbling up the plot. Not content with Duke Frederick's 'old religious man', Shakespeare provides Rosalind with 'an old religious uncle' (also unseen and never alive). The more we consider the forest, the less likely it is to be anywhere. It is as magical as Prospero's island, and both in its frosty coppices and its summer-heavy depths the magician is Rosalind. Apart from her, and from Celia, Orlando, Oliver (who comes late), old Adam (who leaves early), and Touchstone, who is always about, other people of Arden are in two groups. One is of transients: the courtiers, free foresters, apparently pastoral fruitarians, though a deer is killed, and for many Stratford seasons it was traditional to carry across the stage a weather-beaten stuffed stag from Charlecote. The other group is of permanent dwellers: Phebe, the coquettish Dark Lady of Arden, pursued by Silvius, her shepherd; the densely bucolic Audrey who, by stage custom, should go barefooted, and who has ceased to munch her Victorian turnip; William, who does nothing but gape; Corin, wise old shepherd; and Sir Oliver Martext, who for a minute or two is the everlasting comic parson, and who can be doubled with Adam. Beyond Arden is a third group: the usurping Duke, who should rush from a Holbein canvas in a tearing temper; Le Beau, a Boyet-like courtier, who has the agreeably ambiguous farewell to Orlando, 'Hereafter, in a better world than this,/I shall desire more love and knowledge of you' (I, ii, 263–4), and Charles the wrestler, called by Adam 'the bonny prizer of the humorous Duke', who has, quite out of character, the bounty of a few famous lines:

OLIVER : Where will the old Duke live?
CHARLES : They say he is already in the Forest of Arden, and a many merry men with him; and there they live like the old Robin Hood of England. They say many young

gentlemen flock to him every day, and fleet the time
carelessly, as they did in the golden world. (I, i, 105-9)

As You Like It maintains an uncommonly large off-stage cast: the
three brothers whose ribs Charles broke, and the old man, their
father; Hisperia, Celia's gentlewoman, who in some revivals has
been dragged in, speechless; Touchstone's Jane Smile; Corin's late
master, 'of a churlish disposition', and, of course, the Old Religious
Man. At the very end two characters are brought from the fringe.
True, 'a person representing Hymen', for the wedlock-hymn, could
be the singing courtier Amiens, of 'Under the greenwood tree'. But
Jaques de Boys is a newcomer. The 'second son of old Sir Rowland',
who presumably has just left school where report 'spoke goldenly of
his profit', in order to knit up everything in fifteen lines, he represents
Shakespeare at his most hurried, straight-faced, and, as ever, careless
about first names. For an actor it is a tormenting entrance: the
Bensonians, calling it 'the Shilling Speech', would give a shilling to
any young player who, in the day's theatrical jargon, was 'dead-
letter-perfect'. The prize was seldom won.

IV

The brother Dukes, noble and evil (we have seen them doubled)
rarely dismay their actors. Once, in a frequently glum film, Henry
Ainley gave the grand manner, and every full vowel sound, to the
Banished Duke's 'Now, my co-mates and brothers in exile', special
pleading ('I would not change it') for a life that he will be equally
happy to leave. Orlando is straight: a lover and a man, who in no
circumstances must be moony. Whether he penetrates Rosalind's disguise (I think not) must be left to the taste and fancy of a director.[2]
Oliver, who has a life crowded with incident – he is pushed out of
doors and saved from a lioness – has to be two different people:
churlish enough at first for us to loathe him, charming enough for
Celia (who until then has been Rosalind's quietly watchful foil) to
love him at first sight.[3] Adam, loyal and ancient moralist, was acted
in the average touring cast by its youngest member, bent towards a
hoop, his face webbed like Clapham Junction, and his voice a
crackling pipe; this was agreed to be a legitimate interpretation of
'My age is as a lusty winter, frosty but kindly'. Today the man is
fairly hale. One tradition says he might have been among
Shakespeare's own acting parts.

We are left with Jaques (pronounced 'Jake-weez') and Touchstone,
neither of whom is in Lodge's novel. The professional melancholic

with a past – and, apparently, a future with the Old Religious Man – has to deal with the platitudes of the 'Seven Ages' speech, never easy now; Richard Pasco, as an acid eccentric, did freshen them at Stratford in 1973. Jaques would be company for Apemantus of *Timon of Athens:* it has been suggested unkindly that today they would be drama critics. Touchstone, worldly-wise jester whom Jaques encourages, is an acquired taste (probably easier to acquire when Robert Armin acted him for Shakespeare). He pervades the forest, at one moment arguing with Corin ('Truly, thou art damn'd, like an ill-roasted egg, all on one side'); at another, dallying with Audrey, for whom his affection is suspect, and making a fool of William, which is not difficult; and, at another, engaged upon an elaborate jest with Jaques: a protracted and portentous joke about 'the degrees of the lie'. It was inserted, we imagine, simply to let Rosalind have time to change from Ganymede into her woman's dress. I am aware that many playgoers must enjoy Touchstone as much as the Banished Duke (or Duke Senior) and Jaques himself do; yet he can be Arden's hair shirt, the funny man forever talking shop beneath the shade of melancholy boughs. Doubtless, as the Duke says, he 'uses his folly like a stalking-horse, and under the presentation of that he shoots his wit'. To the irreverent his arrows flip from a slack bowstring.

An early eighteenth-century hack, Charles Johnson, who adapted *As You Like It* in a crazy patchwork called *Love in a Forest,* omitted Touchstone, Audrey, William, Corin, Phebe, and Silvius; and Jaques became Celia's lover. Nobody has revived this. John Mason Brown, the American critic, would have approved at least of the new pairing; he has written to the effect that the wedding bells of Arden – if they existed – would ring out over 'a tragic assortment of mismarriages'. Two, we can believe, would endure.

Lastly, I find it oddly hard to remember that, after the Duke's couplet, 'Proceed, proceed. We will begin these rites,/As we do trust they'll end, in true delights' (V, iv, 191–2), and the ensuing country dance, Rosalind will come down stage as 'the lady the epilogue'. Here archness is the danger; but I recall how Edith Evans burnished the speech by turning Rosalind, without pretence, into a Restoration belle and ending the night in a quick blaze of Millamantine sophistication.

NOTES

1 This is from Marlowe's 'Hero and Leander', published in 1598. He died in 1593 during an inn brawl; Touchstone may allude to it at (III, iii, 10): 'It strikes a man more dead than a great reckoning in a little room.'

2 Robert Helpmann thought so at the Old Vic (1953) when John Neville was Orlando and Virginia McKenna his Rosalind.
3 Oliver (IV, iii, 112–14) has the lines: ' . . . under which bush's shade/A lioness, with udders all drawn dry,/Lay couching, head on ground, with cat-like watch.' One night during the early 1940s a Stratford Oliver, to Rosalind and Celia's alarm, substituted 'baroness' for 'lioness'. But, as Sir Barry Jackson observed once, practically anything will pass in blank verse if it is uttered with conviction.

King Henry V (1599)

Elizabethans thought of King Henry the Fifth, in Shakespeare's words on Hotspur, as the light by which the chivalry of England moved. Chorus hails him as 'mirror of all Christian kings' and 'this star of England'. The chronicle is a triumphant battle hymn, a salute to national pride symbolised in the victory of Agincourt; and it is all most exasperating for critics who have found the King to be, variously, 'strutting', 'commonplace', 'blatant', and 'heartless', and the play to be simply 'meretricious'. These are judgements taken from a long period; writers reinforce them now at an hour when unquestioning patriotism is mocked. Still, I continue to hope that in the theatre one can see *Henry V* through Elizabethan eyes without being dismissed as a chauvinist.

Some critics condemn it simply because (they say) it is a glorification of the man who rejected Falstaff. The epilogue of *2 Henry IV* promises that the story will be continued 'with Sir John in it'. But we never see him again. 'The King has kill'd his heart,' exclaims Mistress Quickly, married now to Pistol. And Corporal Nym adds in his own jargon: 'The King hath run bad humours on the knight; that's the even of it.' Soon Quickly reports Falstaff's death in a speech quietly touching: ' 'A made a finer end, and went away as it had been any christom child; 'a parted ev'n just between twelve and one, ev'n at the turning o'th'tide.' So the great man has gone, and at the end of *Henry V*, only Pistol, of his old associates, is left. Bardolph has been hanged in France for stealing a pyx; we gather from the Boy (once Falstaff's page) that Nym has been hanged also; Nell Quickly is dead; and though the thundering histrionic blusterer, resilient after his humiliation by Fluellen, is full of plans for a shady future, he too vanishes entirely into the impenetrable dark.

Indeed, there is little chance for the Irregular Comedians in *Henry V*. With its forty-odd characters, there is little elbow-room for anyone but the King (whose play, overwhelmingly, it is) and Chorus – some fruitful small parts, but Henry over all. Today he is not a stock heroic stereotype but a man aware of his fearful responsibility as when he ponders in the flaking daybreak of Agincourt:

> Upon the King! Let us our lives, our souls,
> Our debts, our careful wives,
> Our children, and our sins, lay on the King!
> We must bear all. (IV, i, 226–9)

The modern Henry thinks through his speeches, argues with himself, never tosses away a line without considering where and how he will toss it, the probable trajectory, the point of impact. We cannot equate him with the Lewis Waller reading: that of an Edwardian romantic-declamatory actor who never merely stepped on the stage but hurtled upon it; an uncomplicated blazon; no worrying about the pale cast of thought. It is the difference between a showy portrait in oils and a precise miniature by Isaac Oliver.

This is by no means incompatible with the theatrical excitement of the play. Alan Howard, in the Royal Shakespeare production of 1974–5, proved to be the definitive new-model Henry, giving to the King his own intelligence, a 'cool and temperate wind of grace'. Say that he was a 'star of England' without being a flaring comet. Henry can speak cruelly as in his threat to the Governor of Harfleur. He can act fiercely as in his reprisal ('The King has caus'd every soldier to cut his prisoner's throat'[1]) when the French have killed the boys left with the luggage in the camp. The order has been represented as wise generalship, for had the battle risen again the prisoners might have imperilled their captors. But in the theatre now we often see Fluellen bearing in his arms the dead Boy (who once was Falstaff's page), a sight that rouses the King to uncontrollable wrath: 'I was not angry since I came to France/Until this instant.'

Elsewhere, Henry's splendid rhetoric in the key of 'Once more unto the breach' (which cannot be muted, and which we are told Waller spoke nobly) must still seize any normal audience; and so must the humility in the little touch of Harry in the night, the discussion round the brazier with the English soldiers, and the soliloquy (so like Henry IV's 'Uneasy lies the head that wears a crown') that grows from it:

> 'Tis not the balm, the sceptre, and the ball,
> The sword, the mace, the crown imperial,

The intertissued robe of gold and pearl,
The farcèd title running fore the king,
The throne he sits on, nor the tide of pomp
That beats upon the high shore of this world –
No, not all these, thrice gorgeous ceremony,
Not all these, laid in bed majestical,
Can sleep so soundly as the wretched slave
Who, with a body fill'd and vacant mind,
Gets him to rest, cramm'd with distressful bread;
Never sees horrid night, the child of hell;
But, like a lackey, from the rise to set
Sweats in the eye of Phoebus, and all night
Sleeps in Elysium; next day, after dawn,
Doth rise and help Hyperion to his horse;
And follows so the ever-running year
With profitable labour, to his grave.
And but for ceremony, such a wretch,
Winding up days with toil and nights with sleep,
Had the fore-hand and vantage of a king. (IV, i, 256–76)

Later, the Crispin speech (With 'We few, we happy few, we band of brothers') is no longer a paladin's static, full-voiced oratory but an almost conversational reply to Westmoreland and those about him in the midst of their preparation. Henry, as presently he tells Mountjoy, is a warrior for the working-day (IV, iii, 109). The more relaxed the performance, the more truthful the play must be, and its kindling power is undiminished.

II

My first *Henry V* was both traditional and capricious, certainly capricious, for the curtain rose not upon Chorus and 'O, for a Muse of fire!', but upon Frank Benson – in his middle sixties and still with the glow of his youthful King – saying from the throne: 'Where is my gracious lord of Canterbury? . . . We would be resolved of some things of weight/That task our thoughts, concerning us and France.' When Canterbury entered he was greeted with the question, 'May I with right and conscience make this claim?' A few minutes and a dozen lines later, he was ordering: 'Call in the messengers sent from the Dauphin', and the play swung into progress, 250 lines already condensed into twenty.

The beginning has often teased directors. Undoubtedly the Archbishop's bald versification of Holinshed must plod:

> Besides, their writers say,
> King Pepin, which deposèd Childeric,
> Did, as heir general, being descended
> Of Blithild, which was daughter to King Clothair,
> Make claim and title to the crown of France. (I, ii, 64–8)

We know, without agreeing, why some directors have turned Canterbury and his exposition of the Salic Law to near-burlesque, with one assured laugh, after fifty lines, at 'So that, as clear as is the summer's sun . . . ' The danger is that, in any wholesale cutting of the first two scenes, we are likely to lose such phrases as 'Consideration like an angel came/And whipp'd th'offending Adam out of him', 'The air, a charter'd libertine, is still', Ely's 'My thrice-puissant liege/Is in the very May-morn of his youth', and even Canterbury's passage on the honey-bees (and 'the singing masons building roofs of gold'). Directors make their own selective cuts; but no one, in my experience, was so firm as Benson. From his beginning as an actor-manager (with one short break later when Chorus was restored) he did without the linking speeches that today are sacrosanct.[2]

It is an agreeable speculation – and it should have pleased the older Benson – that Shakespeare himself, as 'our bending author', was the first Chorus, begging his hearers to 'piece out our imperfections with your thoughts', 'eke out our performance with your mind', and see the 'vasty fields of France' in the wooden O of the theatre on Bankside: a theatre whose stage and pit together might have been the size of a small lawn-tennis court. Down the years the aspect of Chorus has been variable. Garrick wore a full-dress Court suit with ruffles and powdered bag-wig. Mrs Charles Kean, in 1859, was Clio, Muse of History. So was old John Coleman's Miss Leighton (1876) with her 'magnificent contralto voice'. Between the wars Sybil Thorndike and Gwen Ffrangcon-Davies were Elizabethan youths. So many actors have been, Michael Redgrave among them. Once formal, sonorous, detached, Chorus is now a friendly companion, though it is as unnecessary to let an actor roam round in a duffle-coat (Stratford, 1974) as it was to immobilise an actress as Clio.

III

The people of *Henry V* are divided between two nations and two armies. On the English side – where Shakespeare, more or less tactfully, gets in the outlines of a Scot and an Irishman – the most engaging figure is a little dragon of a captain, the volubly well-read

Fluellen. 'There is much care and valour in this Welshman', and he
must never be cheapened as an indeed-look-you vaudeville turn, or
shorn of that unanswerable comparison:

> There is a river in Macedon; and there is also moreover a river at
> Monmouth; it is call'd Wye at Monmouth, but it is out of my
> prains what is the name of the other river; but 'tis all one, 'tis
> alike as my fingers is to my fingers, and there is salmons in both.
> (IV, vii, 26–30)

'Uncle Exeter', elder statesman of the army, lingers with me for the
lift of Neil Porter's voice in the embassy to the French King (Stratford,
1934):

>   That you may know
> 'Tis no sinister nor no awkward claim,
> Pick'd from the worm-holes of long-vanish'd days,
> Nor from the dust of old oblivion rak'd,
> He sends you this most memorable line . . . (II, iv, 84–8)

(Many Shakespearian lines, often unremarkable out of context, live
in the tones of one particular speaker: besides Exeter's, I have
Mercutio's 'When King Cophetua loved the beggar-maid', Lysander's
'To do observance to a morn of May', Juliet's 'sole monarch of
the universal earth', and Hamlet's 'Why, even in that was heaven
ordinant.')

In the night's debate before Agincourt the soldier Williams speaks
against war with an unexampled plain eloquence:

> If the cause be not good, the King himself hath a heavy reckoning
> to make when all those legs and arms and heads, chopp'd off in a
> battle, shall join together at the latter day and cry all 'We died
> at such a place' – some swearing, some crying for a surgeon, some
> upon their wives left poor behind them, some upon the debts they
> owe, some upon their children rawly left. I am afeard there are
> few die well that die in a battle; for how can they charitably
> dispose of anything when blood is their argument? (IV, i, 136–42)

Among the French, directors are wisely restoring King Charles to
sanity (Clement McCallin at Stratford, 1974); it was the convention
for some decades to play him as an old man slightly deranged, an idea
that would blur his muster-roll of the land's nobility:

> Up, Princes, and with spirit of honour edged
> More sharper than your swords, hie to the field:

Charles Delabreth, High Constable of France;
You Dukes of Orleans, Bourbon, and of Berri,
Alencon, Brabant, Bar, and Burgundy . . . (III, v, 38–42)

a speech, with all Shakespeare's delight in the resounding proper name, that is still often cut. King Charles's son, the Dauphin, or 'Dolphin', has appeared as both an arrogant fool, Cloten-fashion, and (Alan Badel at Stratford, 1951) deadly quiet, with a velvet sneer. Montjoy, the herald (frequently the Ambassador of the first act[3]) speaks for the untarnished chivalry of France; and the Duke of Burgundy does so in his final picture of a war-stricken land. It is then, wars over, that Princess Katherine – whom we have heard earlier in the hopeful English lesson with her gentlewoman – receives the King's shy, affectionate, clumsy wooing. The scene needs care: one has known it to be coarsened, but such players – among many – as Laurence Olivier, Alec Clunes, John Neville, Richard Pasco, Ian Holm, and Alan Howard have preserved the charm; and there has usually been a Kate to find the right inflections for 'Your Majestee ave fausse French enough to deceive de most sage damoiselle dat is en France.'

NOTES

1 A sad fate, after all, for Pistol's prisoner, Monsieur le Fer.
2 Except the fifth, 'Vouchsafe to those that have not read the story/That I may prompt them . . .' This contains the reference, highly topical in 1599, to 'the general of our gracious empress' (who was the Earl of Essex, engaged in suppressing rebellion in Ireland).
3 He brings to Henry the Dauphin's chest of tennis-balls. One day, in Henry's reply, we may hope to hear an actor making the Elizabeth effect of the 'Rebound'. The to-and-fro of tennis-ball sounds in 'for many a thousand widows/Shall this his mock mock out of their dear husbands;/Mock mothers from their sons; mock castles down . . .'

Julius Caesar (1599)

I

A critic asserts somewhere that the dramatic conflict of *Julius Caesar* is, above all, one of 'linguistic attitudes'. That is an affirmation from the study, a rather secluded study. The ballad Henry Ainley sang from the stage after the St James's première in 1920 gives a less academic view. Ainley had heard, he said, a carpenter singing in the theatre:

> O Julius Caesar was a N.U.T.
> And a rare old cockalorum:
> Brutus it was that stabbèd him
> In a place that's called the Forum;
> Mark Antony sarcastically
> Said unto him, How dare he?
> And Brutus he died
> Of suicide
> With a sword in his little Mary.

This is an irreverent but roughly accurate précis of the tragedy of Roman revolution and civil war. In any sympathetic revival *Caesar* proclaims itself as high drama: Shakespeare, we assume, worked it up at concentrated speed from North's Plutarch.[1] To ask why it is not called *Marcus Brutus* is a waste of time, for the Elizabethan public knew much more about Caesar. He governs his play; murdered early in the third act, he is mighty to the last moment when Antony is saying of Brutus:

> This was the noblest Roman of them all.
> All the conspirators save only he
> Did that they did in envy of great Caesar. (V, v, 68–70)

In effect, it is a tragedy of two men: Caesar the slain and (among the faction) Brutus the slayer. Two other parts are famous: Mark Antony, which used to be reserved for the actor-manager (a much smaller part than Brutus or Cassius, but with the bonus of the Oration), and Caius Cassius, watchful intriguer whom Brutus calls 'the last of all the Romans', and whose every speech is edged. We might add, too, the Roman crowd which should be thought of as a corporate entity. It impresses us most when it growls and thunders from the shadow; we should not be distracted by anxious individuals reminiscent of Max Beerbohm's *Savonarola :* 'The Piazza is filled entirely from end to end with a vast seething crowd that is drawn entirely from the lower orders . . . There is a sprinkling of wild-eyed and dishevelled women in it . . . Cobblers predominate.' One Stratford director in recent years confined himself thriftily to a file of soldiers holding back a few token plebeians at the side of the stage. It did not work; we felt that we were in some unimportant hole and corner. Frequently now the play is scaled down to a dictator's huddled murder, a grim little revolution and counter-revolution – disappointing because, even if the cold spectacle of an Alma-Tadema Rome is inessential, *Caesar* does need its full size. We can do without the reconstructions that weighed on the spirit like several tons of marble – here the temple of Venus Genetrix, there the temple of Jupiter Capitolium – but we want to be assured that the occasion matches the verse:

> Thou art the ruins of the noblest man
> That ever livèd in the tide of times. (III, i, 257–8)

(Mark Antony speaks, and with no one by to hear him.) At the Old Vic in 1955 Michael Benthall established the first part of the tragedy between the bases of two great pillars that rose out of sight; the later battle scenes were set between the same pillars, cleft and crumbling. I remember also the single star that in Glen Byam Shaw's Stratford production (1957) pricked the flaming sky above the Forum and glittered at last over the plains of Philippi:

> I am constant as the northern star,
> Of whose true-fix'd and resting quality
> There is no fellow in the firmament.
> The skies are painted with unnumb'red sparks,
> They are all fire, and every one doth shine;
> But there's but one in all doth hold his place . . . (III, i, 60–5)

II

Caesar himself deserves, and seldom gets, a major Shakespearian.[2] Most of what he says is arrogant; textually, he can be forbidding, yet we must be able to sense the greatness of a man who bestrode the narrow world like a Colossus, and whose very name is a shout in the air. He is murdered because of the envy of Caius Cassius, that bitter dangerous man, able, when he is moved, to speak like the flood-tide of Tiber:

> Once, upon a raw and gusty day,
> The troubled Tiber chafing with her shores,
> Caesar said to me 'Dar'st thou, Cassius, now
> Leap in with me into this angry flood,
> And swim to yonder point?' Upon the word,
> Accoutred as I was, I plungéd in
> And bade him follow. So indeed he did.
> The torrent roar'd, and we did buffet it
> With lusty sinews, throwing it aside
> And stemming it with hearts of controversy,
> But ere we could arrive the point proposed,
> Caesar cried 'Help me, Cassius, or I sink!'
> I, as Aeneas, our great ancestor,
> Did from the flames of Troy upon his shoulder
> The old Anchises bear, so from the waves of Tiber
> Did I the tired Caesar. (I, ii, 100–15)

Cassius, whose danger Caesar knows, impels Brutus to strike – the idealist, the honest man with himself at war, the liberal intellectual (not free from priggishness), the friend who slays his 'best lover for the good of Rome' – not because Caesar is a tyrant then but because he may become one:

> Fashion it thus – that what he is, augmented,
> Would run to these and these extremities:
> And therefore think him as a serpent's egg,
> Which, hatch'd, would as his kind grow mischievous,
> And kill him in the shell. (II, i, 30–4)

Mark Antony is sincere when he stands over the body of Brutus and utters his epitaph ('Nature might stand up/And say to all the world "This was a man." ') Occasionally we have known that to sound like false panegyric. There was a fashion for actors of a marmoreal aspect; for a Brutus, staring with glazed eyes, who never persuaded us that he stood high in all the people's hearts, that he would have a true and honourable wife, and that, more important, he knew what he had to do other than look stonily Roman to the last. Antony, about the same period, was a romantic hero who treated the Oration as organ music, disregarding the plain needs of a speech intricately composed and laid out. Soldier and reveller, Antony is also an astute tactician. He does not speak right on, but sharpens the lines with every device of the mob orator, the opportunist expertly improvising.

Where Brutus is formal, Antony gives himself to the crowd. Brutus has a prim parenthesis about 'the speech . . . which Mark Antony,/ By *our* permission, is allowed to make'. But Antony, in the middle of the Oration, will say, 'Shall I descend? and will *you* give me leave?' The Oration is a grand performance – Mark Antony's actor is playing an actor – and, when it is complete, the orator does not shrink from his success. It was a bad custom – one met it again and again – to end the Forum scene on the noise of the mob roaring away into the distance, and Antony, posed against a sky in fire, exclaiming:

> Now·let it work. Mischief, thou art afoot,
> Take thou what course thou wilt. (III, ii, 261–2)

But the tale is incomplete without its coda, the entry of Octavius's Servant:

ANTONY: How now, fellow!
SERVANT: Sir, Octavius is already come to Rome.
ANTONY: Where is he?
SERVANT: He and Lepidus are at Caesar's house.
ANTONY: And thither will I straight to visit him.·
           He comes upon a wish. Fortune is merry,
           And in this mood will give us any thing.
SERVANT: I heard him say Brutus and Cassius
           Are rid like madmen through the gates of Rome.
ANTONY: Belike they had some notice of the people
           How I had mov'd them. Bring me to Octavius.
                                        (III, ii, 261–72)

And from this we should go directly to the mob law that hounds Cinna the poet to death.

III

Fortune cannot give Antony everything. Lepidus, third of the new triumvirate, is insignificant, 'a slight, unmeritable man,/Meet to be sent on errands'. Octavius, Caesar's great-nephew, will not be thwarted: icily he commands. In Hugh Hunt's production (Old Vic, 1951), when Antony saluted the body of Brutus as it was borne from the field, Octavius stood by, supercilious and unmoving. In a revival (Old Vic, 1962) by the Greek director, Minos Volanakis, Octavius heard the valediction with a frigid smile. Then he stepped forward, kicking contemptuously aside the sword with which Brutus had stabbed himself: 'Within *my* tent tonight his bones shall lie.'

Of the other characters, Casca is a part Shakespeare left unresolved. Often at first a burly, cynical ruffian, he seems to be the last person to quiver an eyelash when 'the sway of earth shakes like a thing infirm'. Yet he does:

> Never till tonight, never till now,
> Did I go through a tempest dropping fire.
> Either there is a civil strife in heaven,
> Or else the world, too saucy with the gods,
> Incenses them to send destruction. (I, iii, 9–13)

The women's parts are small: Portia (90 lines), Calphurnia (25). Portia adds anxiety and affection to dignity and pride;[3] Calphurnia has one passage of haunted terror at 'the most horrid sights seen by the watch':

> Fierce fiery warriors fight upon the clouds,
> In ranks and squadrons and right form of war,
> Which drizzled blood upon the Capitol;
> The noise of battle hurtled in the air;
> Horses did neigh and dying men did groan,
> And ghosts did shriek and squeal about the streets.
> O Caesar, these things are beyond all use,
> And I do fear them! (II, ii, 18–26)

It is not right to suppose that, after Murder, Oration, and Quarrel, the play tails into a ragged droop of battle pieces (and one entrance for Caesar's ghost – now and then his voice only). The closing sequence can be eerie and doom-cast. Before it we have the Quarrel scene in Brutus's tent at Sardis, which will not succeed if the players are clamped firmly to their seats. It must be acted as we assume it was when Leonard Digges[4] was writing in 1640:

> So have I seen when Caesar would appear,
> And on the stage at half-sword parley were
> Brutus and Cassius – O how the audience
> Were ravished! With what wonder they went thence,

> When some new day they would not brook a line
> Of tedious, though well-laboured, Catiline.

(Ben Jonson would not have been pleased.)

IV

Caesar is a strong-driving play that needs a comparable production – either in togas, preferably, or in the kind of costume that allows the conspirators to enter the orchard with 'their hats pluck'd about their ears'. We have got rid of the painful halts for scene changing,[5] and certain contrived 'curtains', as when Portia would discover in the orchard a document that revealed the plot, and Calphurnia arrived in heavy mourning, at the end of the murder scene, to weep over her husband's body. Today I go to any revival certain that, whatever the production, something must rise from it – optimism that has buoyed me through some idiosyncratic performances: a Brutus who had a confusing habit of addressing other people as 'noble Brutus'; an Antony who orated with his back to the audience; and a corpse of Caesar that more than once changed its position on the bier.

Inevitably, we return to the crowd. Granville-Barker, when he directed for Tree a special performance of the Forum scene in Coronation year (1911), compiled a copious pamphlet[6] that instructed every member of his crowd what to do at any given moment. Roughly: 'X 186 groans heavily and moves upstage, where he joins a doleful group consisting of Xs 48–54 and Zs 201–210.' This would have taken so long to rehearse that Tree told the crowd to do what it liked, with the provision that whenever Antony spoke (and Tree, the actor-manager, was Antony), everyone should listen in silence.

One brief crowd scene that used to be cut – or, shamefully, played as if it were comic – is now as agonising as anything in Shakespeare: the death of Cinna the poet, going about his quiet business in Rome immediately after Antony has inflamed the mob:

FIRST PLEBEIAN: Tear him to pieces; he's a conspirator!
CINNA: I am Cinna the poet, I am Cinna the poet.
4TH PLEBEIAN: Tear him for his bad verses, tear him for his bad verses!
CINNA: I am not Cinna the conspirator.
4TH PLEBEIAN: It is no matter, his name's Cinna; pluck but his name out of his heart, and turn him going.
3RD PLEBEIAN: Tear him, tear him! (III, iii, 28–35)

It is the savagery of the Cade rebellion: lynch-law. Or is it a 'linguistic attitude'?

NOTES

1 Sir Thomas North's translation of Amyot's French version of Plutarch's *Lives of the Noble Grecians and Romans* (1579).
2 Sir John Gielgud played Caesar with remarkable effect at the National Theatre in 1977. I had not felt more strongly the truth of 'always I am Caesar' (I, ii, 212). In some productions the part has been doubled (blurringly, I think) with Octavius.
3 Strangely, several actresses, trapped in the phrase, 'A woman well-reputed, Cato's daughter', have stressed the last word.
4 Digges, poet and linguist, also wrote the First Folio's commendatory verses (1623) that include 'When thy half-sword parleying Romans spake'.
5 Programme for *Julius Caesar* (Alhambra, 1934): Act I, Sc. 1, Rome: A Public Place; Sc. 2, A Street; Sc. 3, Brutus's Orchard *(8 minutes' interval)*. Act II, Sc. 1, Rome: A Room in Caesar's Palace; Sc. 2, A Narrow Street near the Capitol; Sc. 3, The Capitol: The Senate sitting *(10 minutes' interval)*. Act III, Rome: The Forum *(10 minutes' interval)*. Act IV, Sc. 1, The Tent of Brutus near Sardis; Sc. 2, Before the Plains of Philippi; Sc. 3, The Plains; Sc. 4, The Plains.
6 Hesketh Pearson, *The Last Actor-Managers* (1950).

Twelfth Night (1601–2)

I

Illyria is, roughly, the sea-coast of Bohemia, a land beyond the horizon; no one need search for an accurate map-reading. It is, in fact, just the place where one would expect identical twins to be shipwrecked and for each to presume that the other is drowned. Just the place also for the kind of misadventures implied in the title, *Twelfth Night; or, What You Will*, probably a reference to the annual 'feast of fools', the Epiphany saturnalia when the world stood cheerfully on its head and anything could happen. In the theatre we can hope for the comedy to be poised and pavilioned against a sky luminous with summer yet touched with a latent melancholy. There is 'matter for a May morning', but when all is over we remember the sigh, 'Youth's a stuff will not endure.'

I daresay that in performance we get as many variations on this as on any other comedy. Directors, taking the secondary title as a challenge, have manipulated Illyria for their own purposes which are not invariably Shakespeare's. The land has no history; it is high-fantastical, raised suddenly from the Adriatic. We are merely aware that Orsino is a noble Duke in nature as in name; that Olivia's brother has died and she is self-consciously in love with grief; that her late father used to be fond of Feste, the jester, who is less spirited than he was; that Malvolio, the puritanical steward, once fell out with Fabian, a person whose status is arguable, about a bear-baiting; and that Antonio, a daring pirate, boarded the *Tiger* (a favourite Shakespearian ship-name) when the Duke's young nephew Titus lost a leg. Yet, if Illyrian history is meagre, we do know most of the people as well as we know ourselves. Though some, Olivia in particular, have changed key during the years, in general we can quote Feste upon the old hermit of Prague who never saw pen and ink, but who said very wittily to a niece of King Gorboduc, 'That that is, is.' The comedy is Shakespeare in middle life, doing with flexible ease much that he had experimented with when he was green in judgement.

Nothing more, we feel, can happen in Illyria. These people fade from our sight, but they go round like a stage army. No sooner has Viola-Cesario moved off to be Orsino's Duchess and his fancy's queen, than she will find herself again shipwrecked on the coast: 'What country, friends, is this?' Malvolio is forever fooled, Olivia wooed from her sorrows. *Twelfth Night* can defy directors who look urgently for some new thing. Their discoveries, often tiresome, drift away in the morning light. Possibly there have been one or two gains; we can say at least that the play has grown younger and quicker. Its pace had become all too slow, held up by extravagant business – certainly in the so-called Kitchen Scene which appeared now and then to be running on to breakfast and was doomed, in minor revivals to as much elaboration as 'Pyramus and Thisby'. What Granville-Barker called the 'happy ease' of the writing was thickly muffled.

II

It is a comfort to meet a revival that respects its dramatist. Sometimes, transposing the opening scenes, a director will begin with Viola cast up on the shore very well dressed, bone-dry, and accompanied by her luggage. Shakespeare himself prefers Orsino's palace and a famous opening line, 'If music be the food of love, play on.' The Duke proceeds:

> That strain again! It had a dying fall;
> O, it came o'er my ear like the sweet sound
> That breathes upon a bank of violets,
> Stealing and giving odour. (I, i, 4–7)

'Sound' is the Folio reading; occasionally, but rarely, we meet Pope's emendation, 'like the sweet south'. I wish we met it more often.

By the second act we have heard everyone who matters, Orsino, who is in love with love and pining for Olivia, has received the answer – matched to his own histrionics – that, in her brother's memory, she will be veiled and isolated for seven years,

> And water once a day her chamber round
> With eye-offending brine. (I, i, 29–30)

Viola, now in boy's dress as the page Cesario, has taken another message. We have seen the Countess and her household: her steward, the intolerably vain Malvolio (pride is one of the themes); her uncle, Sir Toby, roistering, parasitic, and privileged, for whom 'care's an enemy to life'; her gentlewoman, Maria, who is not her housemaid; her jester, Feste; and her hopeless suitor, Sir Andrew Aguecheek, who is Toby's gull. The first scene of the second act has brought the twin brother Sebastian and his saviour, the piratical Antonio who ought not to be around these Illyrian streets. Thenceforward the play flows on with shining certainty until, in one of Shakespeare's complex estuary-acts, all tributaries are merged.

What of these Illyrians in the theatre – a night that ends with three marriages and two disappointments? First, Orsino should not be turned to laughter or to a man trying to recall the minutes of the last meeting. He may be obsessed, but the obsession is high-romantic. Viola is another example of a boy playing a girl who pretends to be a boy. We do not hear her real name until the fifth act. Always she is Cesario, and it is not until Sebastian's

> Were you a woman, as the rest goes even,
> I should my tears let fall upon your cheek,
> And say 'Thrice welcome, drownèd Viola!' (V, i, 231–3)

that we learn a name so familiar to us that it seems to have echoed through the night. It is spoken twice more. I have known it, horribly, and at Stratford-upon-Avon of all places,[1] to be pronounced 'Vee-*oh*-la'. Strangely, Feste's name is used only once, when Orsino asks for the singer of last night's 'old and antique song'; just as strangely, he is 'about the house'. Curio speaks of him as 'Feste, the jester, my lord, a fool the lady Olivia's father took much delight in'.

Cesario-Viola cannot be a pert masquerader. If she tries too obviously to enlist the audience, the comedy must droop. One exception: the soliloquy, 'Fortune forbid my outside hath not charm'd her', which – with its long vocal scherzo – used to be Edith Evans's delight. Viola is truth itself ('By innocence I swear, and by my youth'); her spirit is in the lines:

> If I did love you in my master's flame,
> With such a suff'ring, such a deadly life,
> In your denial I would find no sense;
> I would not understand it.

OLIVIA: Why, what would you?
VIOLA: Make me a willow cabin at your gate,
           And call upon my soul within the house;

Write loyal cantons of contemned love
And sing them loud even in the dead of night;
Halloo your name to the reverberate hills,
And make the babbling gossip of the air
Cry out 'Olivia!' O, you should not rest
Between the elements of air and earth
But you should pity me! (I, v, 248–60)

We wait to see whether a Viola replies at once to 'What would you?'
or whether, and wrongly, she insulates the speech as if it were in a
glass case by itself.

III

Within twenty years or so, Olivia has much changed. Once she
and Orsino would be in early middle age; formally romanticised, she
sat like a Queen with her court. It was in 1958 that Peter Hall, as a
young director at Stratford-upon-Avon, encouraged Geraldine
McEwan to play a coquettish *poseuse* who seemed to have escaped
from a columbarium for slightly cracked doves. That was an extreme
challenge to tradition; now, more often than not, Olivia is a girl
relentlessly affected. Fashions have veered in Illyria since George Foss,
a veteran director, wrote in *What the Author Meant* (1932): 'Originally
the boy actor cast for Olivia in Shakespeare's day was a very amusing
picture of female vanity, but we can never hope to see the part
played humorously unless, perhaps, at a boy's school.'

We cannot prophesy what her household will be like. Usually it
takes charge of the night because Malvolio, relentlessly tricked, is
given to a star actor. As a rhymer has put it:[2]

> The household turns to mock
> The heedless crowing of its turkey-cock.
> Alas, poor fool! How they must baffle thee,
> Feste, Maria, and the teasing three
> Beyond the high box-hedges as the day
> Moves to meridian in the sun of May!

The Malvolio theme belongs to an under-plot, as Mary Lamb saw
when summarising *Twelfth Night* for *Lamb's Tales*. Remarkably, she
omitted Malvolio, Toby, Andrew, Maria, and Feste. On the stage
the romantic comedy ought to be, but rarely is, as important as the
near-farce, the Illyrian knights' entertainment and the fooling in the
formal garden.

Malvolio, sick with self-love, has arrived in many guises from a sour, rigid elder and a Grey Eminence whose silences are glacial, to a parvenu with aspirate trouble, a supercilious young man seconded from the Illyrian Foreign Office, and – unfortunately – a semi-buffoon. Vain though he is, he should have an honesty that can sway us during his imprisonment: there he is heard, not seen. Sir Toby, explaining that he is 'consanguineous', is a battered gentleman and may look like an older, puffier Drake or a slightly dissipated lion. Sir Andrew is a pliant lack-wit ('By my troth I know not'), a young man – no squeaking – who finds life and love too difficult. 'I had rather than forty shillings . . .' appears to be a catch-phrase for the Andrews and Slenders.[3] Feste, who used to be twirled and jingled into nothing, is now examined more carefully; aware that he is ageing, he needs all his professionalism in a world of folly. Armin, who played him in Shakespeare's company, was a singer: hence the three songs. We must suspend our disbelief at his presence in the Duke's palace when needed.

One or two directors – Hugh Hunt (Old Vic, 1950) was the first, I think – have seen Fabian as a second jester, ready to snatch Feste's place, and always at his heels; at the end Olivia orders Fabian to take Malvolio's letter from Feste and read it aloud himself. The man, an extra conspirator, is a puzzle. Various directors (and there is a whole Fabian Society by now) have cast him as a gardener, a manservant, a blacksmith wiping his hands on his apron, a farmer with plenty of time to spare. Dr Leslie Hotson thought he was 'an Illyrian gentleman-reveller'; to Masefield he was 'a gentleman called Fabian'; to Granville-Barker 'a family retainer of some kind; from his talk he has to do with horses and dogs.' In the fifth scene of the second act he simply arrives without preamble. Probably Shakespeare, wanting another useful character, wrote him in swiftly without 'placing' him. He is worth his niche for the line, 'If this were played upon a stage now, I would condemn it as an improbable fiction' (Shakespeare nodding to the audience).

The unluckiest figure in any modern *Twelfth Night* is Maria, Olivia's gentlewoman, who writes so like her mistress that on any forgotten matter one 'can hardly make distinction of their hands'. In the theatre she is relishingly downgraded. One has known her to wear a housemaid's cap and apron, yet to transform her to a soubrette of the backstairs is palpably wrong. Toby speaks of her as 'my niece's chambermaid', or what the Elizabethans called a 'chamberer', but we cannot take that literally. Miss Muriel St Clare Byrne has said: 'It would have been quite obvious from her dress that she was *not* a chamberer, so I can only suppose it was more or less equivalent to calling someone's private secretary "chief cook and bottle-washer".'[4]

She has the same position in Olivia's house as Nerissa in Portia's, Lucetta in Julia's, and Margaret and Ursula in Leonato's. There are various allusions to her smallness: 'the youngest wren of nine', ironically 'Penthesilea' (the giant Queen of the Amazons), 'your giant', and so on. These were probably written in for the boy player; most of today's Marias obediently conform.

IV

We may find that in performance the play takes a little time to grow. In its third scene, that for Sir Toby, Maria, and Sir Andrew, Shakespeare is toiling. A line for Toby, 'Are they like to take dust, like Mistress Mall's picture?' is a topical joke (whatever it means) as faded as Malvolio's later 'The Lady of the Strachy married the yeoman of the wardrobe' (II, v). Still, the lost jests flit by. The comedy rises in the fifth scene, Viola-Cesario's mission to Olivia, generally established in the garden, though it might well be indoors. At the end we have a favourite jest (remembered from Portia's order to Balthasar). 'Run after that same peevish messenger,' says Olivia. 'Hie thee, Malvolio.' Malvolios cannot run; it is an impossible notion. Laboriously, they try. An ensuing street scene, with Viola pantingly pursued, is watched for Malvolio's method of disposing of the ring. Does he thread it upon his staff to present to Viola? When it is thrown down ('There it lies, in your eye'), does he watch carefully to see where it has gone, as Eric Porter did at the St George's, London, in 1976? It is in her later soliloquy that the girl peers for the first time through her boy's disguise; and she goes out with one of the worst of Shakespeare's couplets,

> O Time, thou must untangle this, not I,
> It is too hard a knot for me t'untie! (II, ii, 38–9)

– something to put with Orlando's 'Now must I from the smoke into the smother.'

The third scene of the second act has long been known, illogically, as the Kitchen Scene. There is no reason for it to be in either the kitchen or cellar; the obvious location is a part of the house from which the noise might wake Olivia. What should be a spontaneous midnight revel must not be anxiously protracted. It is here that Feste sings 'O, mistress mine'; there is an exuberant round, 'the twelfth day of December'; and Malvolio rushes on, carrying a candle. He is traditionally in nightgown with steward's chain, and with curl-papers under his nightcap: a mid-Victorian joke that ceased to be funny as soon as it was evolved. The revellers ought not to tweak his cap or fool with his gown. Verbal attack is enough: 'Dost thou think, because thou art virtuous, there shall be no more cakes and ale? . . . Go, rub your chain with crumbs.' Later, after Maria has devised her plot and gone, and Toby has said admiringly 'A beagle true-bred, and one that adores me', Andrew puts in his unexpected 'I was ador'd once too.' The line, which used to be absurdly simpered, does make a human being of the poor man. So to the Duke's palace, Feste singing 'Come away, death', and the Duke and Cesario-Viola in their colloquy on the love women to men may owe:

VIOLA : In faith, they are as true of heart as we.
My father had a daughter lov'd a man,
As it might be perhaps, were I a woman,
I should your lordship.
ORSINO : And what's her history? (II, iv, 105–9)
VIOLA : A blank, my lord. She never told her love . . .

The Garden Scene, Malvolio reading the letter from the Fortunate-Unhappy while the conspirators, fortified by Fabian, listen to him, is now the core of the comedy. Every line of Malvolio's is celebrated, including a snatch of barely concealed bawdy, often unnoticed. The soliloquy is an exercise in control and selection, for an actor who exaggerates it can destroy Malvolio, and an actor who underplays can turn the May sunshine to a drizzle. Malvolio is real. He does not need to spin solemnly on his toes, at 'If this fall into thy hand, revolve', an Elizabethan usage for 'consider'; he does not need to remove his hat at the two mentions of 'Jove'; but we do expect the bleak and painful wintry grimace at 'I will smile.' Today, though we neither ask for nor get the sort of realistic landscape gardening *Punch* once described as 'swardy', we look for the watchers to be persuasively concealed. There should be some form of box hedge; even in a what-you-will Illyria, it reduces the scene to nonsense if Andrew, Toby, and Fabian appear to be playing round games right under Malvolio's disapproving nose.

V

Early in the third act we find again, in Feste's begging technique, 'I would play Lord Pandarus of Phrygia to bring a Cressida to this Troilus', that the old story was strongly in Shakespeare's mind – here he was remembering the legend that Cressida became a leper and a beggar. Rapidly now the play gathers to a head. Olivia has her confession.

Cesario, by the roses of the spring,
By maidhood, honour, truth, and every thing,
I love thee so that, maugre all thy pride,
Nor wit nor reason can my passion hide . . .   (III, i, 146–9)

a speech (it cannot be pattered through) that, in an unwary revival,
may seem dubious from a girl who has been trilling archly in various
sharps and flats. The first London audiences would have enjoyed
Antonio's direction to Sebastian, 'In the south suburbs at the
Elephant/Is best to lodge; I will bespeak our diet'; Malvolio's cross-
gartering; that popular business, a comic duel; Olivia's mistaken
recognition of Sebastian; and Feste's tedious gagging, as the curate
and himself, outside the dark room where Malvolio is bound. In the
final unravelling Antonio's sometimes optimistic cry to Sebastian:

How have you made division of yourself?
An apple cleft in two is not more twin
Than these two creatures   (V, i, 214–16)

can seldom escape without a laugh. But what follows, at the reunion
of the twins – and any doubling of the parts is disastrous – must
invariably hold a theatre; even Viola's 'My father had a mole upon his
brow' goes by. I think of Peggy Ashcroft at the Old Vic in 1950. When
Sebastian faced his sister, with the incredulous 'What countryman?
What name? What parentage?' there was a charged pause before
Viola, almost in a whisper but one of infinite rapture and astonishment,
answered: 'Of Messaline.' Practically for the first time in my experience, a Viola had got me to believe in her past.

Some critics will not hear of a past or future: to imagine the
characters off stage is unforgivable. Yet, as *Twelfth Night* is ending,
the mind follows Malvolio. Released from imprisonment, he arrives,
desperately bewildered, sometimes blinking from the darkness and
with wisps of straw caught in his cross-gartering, to hear of the May-
morning trick. After Feste's 'Thus the whirligig of time brings in
its revenges', he leaves the stage with his hoarsely threatening 'I'll
be revenged on the whole pack of you': an exit that, in no circumstances, should start a laugh. Alas, it can. 'He has been most
notoriously abused,' Olivia says sadly. The Duke's order is almost
casual: 'Pursue him, and entreat him to a peace.'

Malvolio must not re-appear: it was not Shakespeare's design,
though I remember that in one version, preserved by Donald Wolfit,
the man – presumably entreated to a peace – would kneel before
Olivia and in dumb-show receive his chain. That is quite unpersuasive.
By then the Illyrians will have swung back to the beginning of the

dream. On the darkening stage Feste sings his song of the wind and the rain that in its last lines returns us to the theatre: 'But that's all one, our play is done . . . .' We know, unquestionably, that at any moment it must begin again, the Duke with his musicians, Viola on an unknown shore.

NOTES

1 1943
2 Prologue for Birmingham Theatre Exhibition, 1949
3 'I had rather than forty shillings I had such a leg, and so sweet a breath to sing as the fool has.' (*Twelfth Night*, II, iii, 20–1). 'I had rather than forty shillings I had my book of Songs and Sonnets here.' (*The Merry Wives of Windsor*, I, i, 198–9).
4 'The Social Background' in *A Companion to Shakespeare Studies* (1934).

Hamlet, Prince of Denmark (1601–2)

I

A small-part officer, who has been called both Bernardo and Barnardo, begins with arguably the most exciting speech in the drama of the centuries. His two words 'Who's there?' which usher in nearly five hours of airs from heaven and blasts from hell, sound in the frigid darkness of the 'platform before the castle' of Elsinore. Francisco, sentinel on guard, his nerves taut, replies with the formal challenge. Nothing has happened; but 'for this relief, much thanks'. Presently others are there: Horatio, young Prince Hamlet's friend and fellow student from the University of Wittenberg, with a second officer, Marcellus, their footsteps ringing in the frost. The soldiers fear what has been, and will come again: the ghost of the dead King Hamlet. The scholar denies that it can appear. Voices are hushed, strained; only a glimmer of starlight, the spark of a lantern. (At the Globe on Bankside this would have been in the light of afternoon.) Then the Ghost is visible in full armour, his beard a sable silver'd; the majesty of buried Denmark. Even Horatio must acknowledge that this 'bodes some strange eruption to our state', to a Denmark ill at ease, with a new King come strangely to the throne, and Norway threatening.

It is a miraculous prologue, and it cannot be scamped. Often it used to be hurried through; even in our time we have known it, astonishingly, to be omitted. If director and actors find the sense of fear and wonder, we hardly notice that within less than two hundred lines we move from deep midnight to cock-crow and the dawn 'in russet mantle clad'. (Horatio sees this above a 'high eastward hill' absent from the map at Helsingör, but Shakespeare is never on oath.) When at length the lights rise, the stage is set for the Danish Court and for 'young Hamlet'.

Now what used to be, vaguely, a 'Court' assembly is treated as a royal Council. King Claudius presides; by him, his Queen. Hamlet sits apart. Often in the past the entry could be processional, with Hamlet, as Henry Irving did, walking behind the rest. 'The jewels, and crown, and sceptres dazzle,' wrote the critic Clement Scott of the Lyceum Theatre revival in 1874, 'and at the end of the train comes Hamlet. Mark him well . . .' Irving's Hamlet was to overwhelm all (as Hamlets did then, and do yet). 'Bernardo and Marcellus,' wrote Scott, 'the Ghost, the platform, the prologue or introduction . . . were, as usual, tolerated – nothing more.' Hamlet is still the observed of all observers; but we know now that practically everyone in the play is a personage, down to the almost 'thinking part' of Reynaldo, Polonius's servant, who must watch Laertes in Paris; and the Second Gravedigger, martyr to his chief's riddles, who at Stratford (1958) was a supercilious sacristan – a sound idea until the young man was despatched, implausibly, to that much-annotated off-stage figure Yaughan, for 'a stoup of liquor'.

II

This is another revenge play, but one in which revenge is fatally deferred. Throughout, like the soldier on the battlements, Hamlet is 'sick at heart'. His mother, Queen Gertrude, has been married again, to his usurping uncle, 'my father's brother; but no more like my father/Than I to Hercules'. The Ghost tells him of murder and adultery: 'If thou hast nature in thee, bear it not.' But Hamlet is agonisingly imaginative; though he can act quickly when he wishes, here his task terrifies him. He lives in perpetual mental fight; profoundly horrified by his mother's adultery, he lets his anger with womankind shatter the innocent Ophelia. He is 'punished with a sore distraction'; his treatment will drive her to true madness. Before then he has been elaborately feeling his way, arguing it out in the ratiocinative soliloquies, seeking confirmation for what is too surely confirmed. His purpose, the returning Ghost warns him, is 'almost blunted'. Then, suddenly, he strikes, and in doing so his own life is lost.

This – there is infinitely more – is the Hamlet, touched to the quick by death and disloyalty, we can think of in Matthew Arnold's phrase about Man being viewed as balancing and indeterminate, swayed by a thousand subtle influences, physiological and pathological. Few actors, directors, critics, will agree wholly with each other. Exegetists tie themselves in coils in searching for a single embracing phrase. Everyone will recognise some part of Hamlet, though maybe playgoers can never be truly satisfied with an actor who must play not one man but a confederation. Again and again we have waited instinctively for the Churchyard scene and the cry, 'This is I, Hamlet the Dane.' If we receive this without some immediate reservation, then the actor is near the truth.

The night is Hamlet's, yet all of those round him at once establish themselves: the King, suave and crafty diplomatist, a good mind fatally warped; his Queen, outwardly a lax sensualist, but, like him, with a conscience to be awakened; Polonius, the Lord Chamberlain, who wavers between shrewdness and an old man's blurring garrulity; Laertes, rash and loving, who does not delay revenge but will use any means to secure it; his sister Ophelia, helpless victim ('of ladies most deject and wretched');[1] the Ghost, who demands death for death ('Taint not thy mind, nor let thy soul contrive/Against thy mother aught'); and Horatio, wise and gentle friend, who spans the play from 'Friends to this ground' to 'Let me speak to the yet unknowing world/ How these things came about.'

III

Experienced playgoers may wonder now and then if they were not happier when *Hamlet* lay before them like a new book uncut, every passage an adventure, not a marginal note in sight. Too soon, maybe, there grows upon them the habit that the actor, William Charles Macready, noted in his journal:[2] 'The prescriptive criticism of this country, in looking for points instead of contemplating one entire character, abates my confidence in myself.' Perhaps there can be a danger sometimes in searching for points when we ought first to recognise the entire conception, a man, not a mosaic of emphasis. I recall a highly intellectual Hamlet who had combed the part to a comma; he remains only as a perambulating prompt-copy. Another performance, 'bold and forth on', by a traditional player who hurtled at any speech like a bolt from a crossbow while keeping in the precise geometrical centre of the stage, does dwell in the battered memory. We knew at least that this was a grand theatrical drama, not wholly a mental exercise. Its first audiences, waiting for the next move, would not have strayed out to the edges of the plot, or asked idly why Shakespeare was careless enough to use Claudio as a name for a gentleman in Claudius's household.

As a boy in the deep provinces, I entered this Castle Dangerous, C. E. Montague's 'monstrous Gothic castle of a poem, with its baffled half-lights and glooms', on a late February night of blistering cold. Tramcars jarred outside; every time a newsboy called the evening paper, we heard him in Elsinore. Mercifully, he had gone home by the second Ghost scene. The theatre, destroyed now, had an Ionic portico more impressive than anything upon the stage where curtains were bunched clumsily as pillars, the Court of Denmark lived against a background of frayed tapestry, Ophelia's grave was a tub of earth, and a patently empty cardboard goblet slipped from the Queen's hands as she died. But who troubled? Even now, after fifty years, I do not dare to question anything except – still baffled – to ask why Horatio wore the equivalent of a Roman toga. (Probably he was looking forward to 'I am more an antique Roman than a Dane'; even a 12-year-old thought this superfluous.) Hamlet then, like others of his period, was mature, a man over forty. If we take the Gravedigger's evidence (V, i) the Prince is 30, but lately he has been growing younger. Not that it is of much account. We do not ask an actor who excites us to produce his birth certificate.

Still, some things we are entitled to ask about, and to look for a reply. There are probably more in *Hamlet* than anywhere else. For all his neuroses (which psychiatrists now tiresomely define), Hamlet must be a man of breeding. It is absurd to overlook Ophelia's

> O, what a noble mind is here o'erthrown!
> The courtier's, soldier's, scholar's eye, tongue, sword;[3]
> Th'expectancy and rose of the fair state,
> The glass of fashion and the mould of form,
> Th' observ'd of all observers. (III, i, 150–4)

Had he lived, he would have proved 'most royal'. Denmark, in spite of a defiant production in the 1970s, is not a clutter of street corners. There must be a reasonable limit, and no Hamlet can discard the graces.

IV

Questions bristle. Thus, when, according to the Folio, Horatio says of the Ghost: 'So frown'd he once when, in an angry parle,/He smote the sledded pollax on the ice' (I, i, 62–3) are we to think of 'Polacks' or, less likely, of 'poleaxe'? In recent years more than one Horatio has shown by gesture how the King thrust down his weapon. How will Hamlet phrase 'Then saw you not his face' to Horatio and Marcellus – a statement or a question? How will he voice the quadruple appeal to the Ghost, 'I'll call thee Hamlet, King, father, royal Dane'? Can the Ghost (as Baliol Holloway said) convey the terror of that other world without seeming to read a spectral balance sheet? How will Hamlet speak: 'There are more things in heaven and

earth, Horatio, Than are dreamt of in your philosophy' (I, v, 166–7) –
something that, half a century ago, used to be invariably (and dis-
courteously) accented as a personal rebuke: '*your* philosophy'? John
Gielgud, more tactfully, took this from the particular to the general,
stressing the final word.[4]

In 'Yet, to me, what is this quintessence of dust?' will Hamlet
pause, searching for the word, before 'quintessence'? At the shout of
'Vengeance!' in the soliloquy, 'O, what a rogue and peasant slave
am I?',

> Bloody, bawdy villain!
> Remorseless, treacherous, lecherous, kindless villain!
> O vengeance! (II, ii, 575–7)

what will Hamlet do, merely draw his dagger and stay his hand (as if
still contemplating his own inaction) or, in an excess of frenzy, stab
furiously at the King's empty throne? Before the Play, does Claudius
see the revealing dumb-show, and what Hamlet calls its 'miching
mallecho', or is he talking to the Queen and looking idly away from
the players? In the Prayer Scene, while the King is, silently, on his
knees, does Hamlet – stealing up behind him – pick up the dropped
sword: 'Now might I do it pat, now 'a is praying', and check himself at 'Up, sword, and know thou a more horrid hent'?[5] In his
mother's closet – and will it contain a bed? there is no reason for one –
how does he illustrate

> Look here upon this picture and on this,
> The counterfeit presentment of two brothers.
> See what a grace was seated on this brow;
> Hyperion's curls; the front of Jove himself;
> An eye, like Mars, to threaten and command;
> A station like the herald Mercury
> New lighted on a heaven-kissing hill . . . (III, iv, 53–9)

Will he seize the locket the Queen wears and compare its picture of
Claudius with his own locket-miniature of his father? (This, assuredly,
was the original business.) Or will he – very rare now – indicate
portraits upon the tapestry? Or will he merely leave both pictures in
the mind's eye? How, in his soliloquy after watching the army of
Fortinbras, does he stress the line and a half, 'I do not know why
yet I live to say,/This thing's to do' – with melancholy resignation,
or, as Laurence Olivier spoke it at the Old Vic and Elsinore in
1937, with such desperate, pulsing force that James Agate said,
rightly, the words were 'trumpet-moaned'? In the Churchyard, what

is the pointing of the line to Laertes: 'I loved you ever; but it is no matter'?

Questions enough. We wait at once to see whether there are signs of a decadent Court, of 'heavy-headed revel', of the stifling quality of Elsinore ('Denmark's a prison'); whether the King is a plausibly smiling figure or, in the old manner, a villain fit for red fire; whether Polonius speaks the Precepts with a wise sententiousness, or unreservedly as a bore. Is Osric a comic popinjay or, as he has become lately, a sinister functionary round the Court? Does Ophelia bring with her the flowers of her madness or imagine them merely? Is Horatio a man of Hamlet's own age, or (National, London, 1975) a veteran tutor or perpetual student? And is the Gravedigger, who has long ceased to do a spade dance or to enliven the scene by shedding several layers of waistcoats, allowed for once to have his full text? That, perhaps, will do.

V

At the close, Fortinbras of Norway must enter the great hall to cry 'Where is this sight?' and to order four captains to bear Hamlet, like a soldier, to the stage. The ending is essential; and though Fortinbras need not be at least six feet tall and in gold armour – a critic's not too serious suggestion – he must always have the authority Bridges-Adams insisted upon at Stratford. Before his restoration in the Forbes-Robertson revival (Lyceum, 1897) he was practically unknown. So were the ambassadors from England.[6] It was partly because of the actor-managerial desire to end the play on 'flights of angels sing thee to thy rest' – as they did for Beerbohm Tree, occasionally out of tune – and partly because of the prescribed cutting for a shorter *Hamlet* which used[7] to reduce the play by nearly two-fifths. Horatio, in the first scene of the cut version, would pass straight from 'Some strange eruption to our state' to 'In the most high and palmy state of Rome', removing entirely the long speech about Denmark's standing with Norway. In the cut text we never heard of the ambassadors, Cornelius and Voltimand; we also had to do without that endearing little scene in which Polonius, rambling on about the need to watch Laertes in Paris, exclaims 'You have me, have you not?' and Reynaldo answers, 'My lord, I have.' (Reynaldo at the Old Vic, 1937, was a small masterpiece by the young Alec Guinness). Earlier, in the second Ghost scene, we never heard the lines beginning 'This heavy-headed revel' which are Hamlet talking nervously, with parentheses and sudden breaks ('These men, carrying, I say, the stamp of one defect') to fill in the time before the

Ghost must come. The Ghost's speech, too, was often heavily cut. So through the play: much of the Rosencrantz-and-Guildenstern scenes (Rosencrantz's full part is nearly twice the length of his companion's), the topical matter about the children's companies, the dumb-show and a good deal of 'The Mouse-trap', the last part of the Closet Scene from the return on 'One word more' to 'the neighbour room', a lot of the colloquy for the King and Laertes, beginning 'Now must your conscience my acquittance seal', and the first half of the passage for Hamlet and Horatio in the last scene but one. This, in the short version, would open at 'So Rosencrantz and Guildenstern go to 't' – a sad cut, for it removed the dramatic narrative of the voyage towards England and such lines as:

> Our indiscretion sometimes serves us well,
> When our deep plots do pall; and that should learn us
> There's a divinity that shapes our ends,
> Rough-hew them how we will.

HORATIO: That is most certain. (V, ii, 8–12)

Devisers of the short *Hamlet* would frequently cut pieces of the plot. It was assumed either that audiences would know already, or that in the flurry they would not ask awkward questions. A seasoned English provincial actor, who played over two hundred Shakespearian parts in his day, was shocked when he read the complete text of *Hamlet* which he had never seen, though he had spent his professional life as Bernardo and Rosencrantz and Second Gravedigger. All he said was: 'It does clear one or two things up.' It does.

Whether the text is cut or complete, our excitement endures, and even when we have lived so long with the play that we cannot help seeing and hearing double, plucking from almost every passage some reference to the historic past: Betterton's face turning 'as pale as his neckcloth' when he saw the Ghost; Macready, at 'I must be idle',[8] twirling his handkerchief as he moved to his place (the *pas de mouchoir* it was called, and it led to his feud with the American tragedian, Edwin Forrest); Charles Kean returning to the Churchyard after the others had left, to throw a rose upon Ophelia's coffin; Barry Sullivan's resolute reading, 'I know a hawk from a herne. Pshaw!'; and on through the years, to Tree's death (no Fortinbras), aided by a celestial choir; to the proud voice and bearing of John Barrymore; to Ernest Milton, most romantically moving Hamlet of his period, leaping all chasms; to John Gielgud, a man in revolt against an evil world, and using his voice as a virtuoso controls a Stradivarius; and to many, many other performances since. Most of them have had at least one thing new to say about the man of doubts and fears, a spirit in torment no less than his father: Granville-Barker's Hamlet of 'a rash and lonely mind', his native faith in life stunned, 'lapsing into impotent despair with crippled faith and enfranchised reason at odds within him'.

Actors may say with Gordon Craig: 'To play Hamlet is a very difficult job, and if we knew how difficult it was, we shouldn't go on at all.' They do go on; everywhere playgoers wait for them. A few years ago, after the noble Hungarian Hamlet of Miklós Gabór, I was talking to a Budapest scholar about the play's sheer theatrical drive. 'Yes,' he said instantly. 'Those first words. The platform before the castle. Night and darkness and frost, and the soldier speaking, his voice shaking a little: *"Ki az?"* ' Through the world the answer is constant: friends to this ground, and liegemen to the Dane.

NOTES

1 I have never known Ophelia's 'But I of ladies most deject and wretched/That sucked the honey of his music vows' to be spoken more touchingly than in the unflawed treble of a boy actor. This was in 1933 during an inconsiderable piece about Shakespeare in London and a *Hamlet* rehearsal at the Globe on Bankside.

2 8 January 1835.

3 We do perhaps overlook – and can we be blamed? – that 'the sense of derangement is heightened by the fact that the order of the genitive nouns does not correspond semantically with the order of the things possessed. But there is syntactic deviation too in the separation of each possessor from its possessed, so that both logic and the normal expectations of speech seem confounded, in the disaster.' (*Linguistics and Literature* by Raymond Chapman, 1973)

4 Richard Burton (New York, 1964) emphasised 'dreamt'.

5 John Gielgud (New Theatre, 1934) used to carry away the sword (later missed by the King) and, with it, stab Polonius through the arras in the Closet scene.

6 When *Hamlet* was done in early Victorian costume at Stratford in 1948, the players wondered among themselves what Queen Victoria and the Prince Consort would have done on receiving orders to kill Rosencrantz and Guildenstern.

7 I write hopefully in the past tense. Heavily cut texts are fewer now, though the 'entirety' *Hamlet* is not always possible.

8 Hamlet to Horatio: 'They are coming to the play; I must be idle./Get you a place' (III, ii, 88–9).

Troilus and Cressida
(1601–2)

> Like or find fault; do as your pleasures are;
> Now good or bad, 'tis but the chance of war.
>
> Prologue, 30–1

I

'Hector is dead: there is no more to say.' Shakespeare at the end of his bitterest work, is in lament for chivalry, for the great themes of love and honour debased to rankest deception and the appetite of 'cormorant war'. In youth he had been affected by the tale of 'strong-besiegèd Troy'.[1] In disillusioned middle years he was setting a legend awry. 'War and lechery confound all,' croaks Thersites. In *Troilus and Cressida* the legend is a victim to 'envious and calumniating time', though for all its distortion Shakespeare cannot help reminding us of a 'great morning' before the people of the epic had dwindled, romantic love declined to a Cressida, the splendour of arms to an Achilles. Where now is Argive Helen? She does say: 'This love will undo us all.'

A brambled play, we can tear ourselves on its briars. But the theatre returns to it regularly now that it suits the modern temper with its ambiguities, its shifting promises, its sense that nothing is but what is not. Probably acted privately in Shakespeare's time before sophisticated audiences, it had little stage history until the last forty years. William Archer, writing in the 1890s, never expected to see it in the theatre;[2] certainly it would never have suited playgoers, bred to heroics, for whom the ten years' war was as irresistibly romantic as the Arthurian legend. Though later there were transient revivals, including William Poel's in 1912, honoured now for the arrival of Edith Evans as Cressida, encounterer glib of tongue, a

Times critic had expressed the general feeling:[3] 'It is impossible to arrange this play for the stage . . . It is better left unacted and read in the study.'

II

In effect, Cambridge University salvaged the play. The Marlowe Society performed it not long after the First World War. Forty years on, at Stratford, Cambridge graduates who controlled the Royal Shakespeare Company were preserving the tradition. *Troilius and Cressida* had some inquiring revivals before then, one in modern dress (Westminster, 1938), two or three at Stratford, and one by Tyrone Guthrie (Old Vic, 1956) which caused more excitement than Archer could have dreamed. Presenting it as a struggle between Ruritania and a coalition of Central European powers about the year 1913, Guthrie showed the Trojans (undermined by frivolity) as resplendent musical-comedy dragoons, and the Greeks (undermined by faction) as jack-booted braggarts, Potsdam fashion. It was a pictorial commentary on the stupidity of blood-and iron militarism and the hollowness of love; but, deplorably, it lacked much feeling for the intricate and passionate verse. Among the harshness, the maggot-pocked, rotten-ripe prose of Thersites, and the windier arguments on the plains of windy Troy, Shakespeare was a poet strongly moved.

During 1960 *Troilus and Cressida* reached Stratford in what some critics called the 'cockpit' production by John Barton and Peter Hall; its stage was strewn thickly with sand, a comment on obliterating time that grates all to 'dusty nothing'. Time haunts the play. The thought is there during the first council in the Greek camp: 'After seven years' siege yet Troy walls stand.' Later, Hector salutes the ancient Nestor as 'good old chronicle,/That hast so long walk'd hand in hand with time.' Gazing up, with his hosts, at the towers of Troy, he exclaims: 'The end crowns all;/And that old common arbitrator, Time,/ Will one day end it.' Two passages are central. One is the warning of Ulysses to Achilles sullen by his tent:

> Time hath, my lord, a wallet at his back,
> Wherein he puts alms for oblivion,
> A great-siz'd monster of ingratitudes.
> These scraps are good deeds past, which are devour'd
> As fast as they are made, forgot as soon
> As done. (III, iii, 145–50)

And again:

> For Time is like a fashionable host,
> That slightly shakes his parting guest by th'hand;
> And with his arms outstretch'd, as he would fly,
> Grasps in the comer. The welcome ever smiles,
> And farewell goes out sighing. O, let not virtue seek
> Remuneration for the thing it was;
> For beauty, wit,
> High birth, vigour of bone, desert in service,
> Love, friendship, charity, are subjects all
> To envious and calumniating Time. (III, iii, 165–74)

Then Cressida's protestation to Troilus when her uncle has brought them together:

> If I be false, or swerve a hair from truth,
> When time is old and hath forgot itself,
> When waterdrops have worn the stones of Troy,
> And blind oblivion swallow'd cities up,
> And mighty states characterless are grated
> To dusty nothing – yet let memory
> From false to false, among false maids in love,
> Upbraid my falsehood. (III, ii, 180–7)

III

Yet Cressida is false. In spite of love speeches so passionately expressed, she gives herself to a Greek. Some directors (John Harrison at Birmingham Repertory in 1963 was one) will not accept her as the 'commodious drab' of Thersites, Ulysses' 'daughter of the game', a woman whose name is frailty. They hold that she is flawed not by professional infidelity but by weakness. Certainly – like so much else in the play – she is ambiguous. Responding instinctively to those round her, and honest with herself at any given moment, she is fatally unstable. The last we hear of her is in these lines, spoken to herself after the scene with Diomedes:

> Troilus, farewell! One eye yet looks on thee;
> But with my heart the other eye doth see.
> Ah, poor our sex! this fault in us I find,
> The error of our eye directs our mind.
> What error leads must err; O then conclude,
> Minds sway'd by eyes are full of turpitude.' (V, ii, 105–10)

The play itself, founded on the sand, is a fabric of ambiguities. Defying dogmatic assertion, people are not consistently what they seem to be. We are still discovering *Troilus and Cressida*, its complex structure, its folds of meaning, the intensity of its major verse:

TROILUS: We two that with so many thousand sighs
            Did buy each other, must poorly sell ourselves
            With the rude brevity and discharge of one.
            Injurious time now with a robber's haste
            Crams his rich thievery up, he knows not how.
            As many farewells as be stars in heaven,
            With distinct breath and consign'd kisses to them,
            He fumbles up into a loose adieu,
            And scants us with a single famish'd kiss,
            Distasted with the salt of broken tears. (IV, iii, 37–47)

and such tortured passages as this one where Shakespeare seems to be fighting his way to expression:

ULYSSES: Why stay we, then?
TROILUS: To make a recordation to my soul
            Of every syllable that here was spoke.
            But if I tell how these two did coact,
            Shall I not lie in publishing a truth?
            Sith there is yet a credence in my heart,
            An esperance so obstinately strong,
            That doth invert th'attest of eyes and ears;
            As if these organs had deceptious functions
            Created only to calumniate. (V, ii, 113–22)

We have to hear the play two or three times before it grows; every visit is an exploration. Troilus is by no means a simplified romantic. The cold wisdom of Ulysses, as in the homily on Degree – a matter that exercised Shakespeare all his life – can come to us like the ice-flowers fronded on a winter pane: it has been phrased acutely by such actors as Donald Wolfit, Robert Speaight, Eric Porter, and, at Stratford in 1976, Tony Church. Pandarus, the go-between, has a fussily professional goodwill and a last grim hint of the charnel; when Max Adrian played him in 1962 it was a death's head that spoke through the darkness of the Phrygian plain. Thersites, foul-mouthed camp-follower, is like an angry raven flapping over a knot of thorns in a marsh. The Greek and Trojan warriors have firm identities: Shakespeare has been remorseless to the cruel vanity of Achilles, and Ajax, beef-witted, would be a buffoon if it were not for the illuminating humanity of his final couplet:

DIOMEDES : The bruit is Hector's slain, and by Achilles.
AJAX :   If it be so, yet bragless let it be;
            Great Hector was as good a man as he. (V, ix, 4–6)

Aeneas, the Trojan, has a speech in the old chivalrous manner when he brings to the Greeks Hector's challenge to enliven a 'dull and long-continued truce':

> He hath a lady wiser, fairer, truer,
> Than ever Greek did couple in his arms;
> And will tomorrow with his trumpet call
> Mid-way between your tents and walls of Troy
> To rouse a Grecian that is true in love.
> If any come, Hector shall honour him;
> If none, he'll say in Troy, when he retires,
> The Grecian dames are sunburnt and not worth
> The splinter of a lance. Even so much. (I, iii, 275–83)

Troilus and Cressida has yet to create any substantial stage tradition.[4] We are unsure who will speak the Prologue, and how. I believe Paul Hardwick (Stratford, 1960) was right in his harsh assault, a Greek soldier behind his shield. Cassandra's first entrance, 'raving' (II, ii, 101), should be above the startled Trojan council, as it was in 1936 (Iden Payne's production) when, like a cry in the air, she passed across the upper stage. We wait to see how the night will close. Directors now generally stick to the Folio, with Pandarus; but in 1936 and 1948, at Stratford, we ended on the mourning for Hector, so foully surprised by Achilles and the sable-garbed Myrmidons. 'Hector is dead,' repeats Troilus dully. 'There is no more to say.' For a moment he storms at the Greek tents and at the distant murderer: 'Thou great-siz'd coward,/No space of earth shall sunder our two hates.' But darkness has fallen: 'Strike a free march to Troy. With comfort go;/Hope of revenge shall hide our inward woe.' We are accustomed to the macabre epilogue of Pandarus, addressing 'as many as be here of Pandar's hall' ('Brothers and sisters of the hold-door trade,/Some two months hence my will shall here be made'). Either ending is in the key of Thersites' line, the play's epigraph: 'Still wars and lechery! Nothing else holds fashion.'

NOTES

1 *The Rape of Lucrece.*
2 It is curious that W. S. Gilbert, in *The Grand Duke*, his final Savoy opera libretto (1895–6), chose *Troilus* as the coming production for the players in his imagined Grand Duchy.

3 After a revival at the Great Queen Street Theatre, 1 June 1907 (Lewis Casson as Troilus).

4 I doubt whether anyone will repeat the notion (Round House, London, 1977) of giving the men's parts to women and the women's parts to men. True, William Poel had some odd casting at the King's Hall, Covent Garden, in 1912: Thersites was played by Elspeth Keith, wife of Robertson Scott, who became editor of *The Countryman*.

All's Well That Ends Well (1602–3)

I

Dr Joseph G. Price, who has studied acutely 'a very human play', calls his book about it[1] *The Unfortunate Comedy*. That is just, though lately *All's Well That Ends Well* has found directors and audiences more receptive than in a far from happy past. Then, with a director 'wrapped in dismal thinkings',[2] it was often approached as a mildly unpleasant affair that had to be done once in a while to fill out the canon. Even now, after two or three unadorned revivals[3] that have rightly let audiences judge, drama criticism swings back, as if magnetised, to the loadstone of Tyrone Guthrie and the play in which, in effect, he collaborated with Shakespeare: he staged his *All's Well That Ends Well* at both Stratfords (Canada in 1953; England in 1959). The costumes were basically Edwardian at Court, more or less contemporary in camp. One frequently cut scene of eleven lines, the third of the third act, beginning 'The General of our horse thou art', Guthrie expanded into an irrelevant comic-military exercise. The Countess and Helena were not from the same world as the Irregular Humorists; Guthrie removed altogether the clown Lavache (or Lavatch). The Stratford-upon-Avon performance was expert in its mood; I can still hear the incantation of the rhymed couplets in Helena's scene with the King; and see Parolles like a dubious blowhard in tan shoes, and the palace thrones (and even their dais) joining in a dance. Most, I think now of the graciousness and compassion of Dame Edith Evans as the Countess. She was on one of her exploring ventures. Thus, at the awkward phrase, 'What's the matter,/That this distempered messenger of wet,/The many-colour'd Iris, rounds thine eye?' (I, iii, 141–3), one recalls her amused, almost startled, pause on 'wet', and then, holding up the words for us to inspect, the discovery of 'many-colour'd Iris'. Again she proved that, however fashionable it is to urge the colloquial speaking of Shakespeare, the verse need not be lost in a grey drizzle.

In general, it was an enjoyable night, a piece of romantic exhibitionism; but playgoers whose first *All's Well That Ends Well* it was might have been startled when they went to another revival, plainer, unchoreographed, curiously lonely. This is a lonely play: too many directors have had no real confidence in its text. I remember going in September 1953 to Michael Benthall's production at the Old Vic, straight from a holiday in the west of Pembrokeshire. That morning, from the summit of Carn Llidi, we had looked down on St David's Head lying below like a length of aged, stained velvet, rich where patched with sunlight, embroidered here and there with gold thread, and frayed and torn where the lining peeped through. It reminded me of *All's Well*, but there was little hint of it that night, at the Vic, where the central scenes were fantasticated and the King, who should have an autumnal poignancy, was minimised as a senile valetudinarian. Wearing a nightgown, and his crown over a nightcap, he sat on a litter; about him pressed a huddle of physicians, obvious quacks, who appeared to be ancestors of Molière's Dr Diafoirus and who would have enraged Helena, herself a physician's daughter. The King's lines were gabbled to nothing, with pauses for comic faintingfits and business with a sycophantic Court. This was maddening, especially as *All's Well* had appeared so rarely in any elaborate revival. Iden Payne's at Stratford (1935) had contained some sympathetic isolated performances that never fused into the complete comedy. I was sorry that Bridges-Adams, who had his own feeling for the play, could not have returned to it during his last Stratford decade. My other regret is that I missed Robert Atkins's production at the Vaudeville during the sustained air raids on London in October 1940: transiently it was the sole play in the West End – Atkins had chosen it because of the title – and Naomi Royde-Smith wrote movingly of Catherine Lacey's truthful Helena in her war journal, *Outside Information*.[4] The revival did not last, and no one could have expected it; again *All's Well That Ends Well* was unfortunate.

II

Today's playgoers would hardly regard it as a dark comedy. But other generations were doubtful of its heroine, the physician's daughter, Helena, even though such a high romantic as Coleridge had called her 'Shakespeare's loveliest creation'. On one level, Helena, who says 'My intents are fix'd, and will not leave me' can seem to be a resolute opportunist (a predecessor of Shaw's Ann Whitefield) with an unattractive method of getting her way. Yet, the more often I hear the play, the more such actresses as Lynn Farleigh and Penelope Wilton have persuaded me that, after all, this is not a problem to be treated with a creased seriousness. The tale of an intelligent young woman deeply in love with a weakly snobbish young man of a higher social station is something that might happen even now, if scarcely with the same theatrical devices. Bridges-Adams, at Stratford-upon-Avon, had his own method of rationalising what he held to be the indefensible in Helena:[5]

'I had a long argument with Barker about this play. He considers Helena one of Shakespeare's heroic women. Played so, she is an unendurable humbug by modern canons. Push the play an inch or so towards Cinderella, and that horrid trick she plays on Bertram is glossed over with the romance from which the story comes. Molly [Maureen Shaw] was the prettiest thing in the world with an elfin wisdom; you forgave her everything.'

Helena is a dependant, a gentlewoman in the house of the widowed Countess of Rousillon. Her father, Gerard de Narbon, was what William Painter, in his version of the *Decameron* story from which *All's Well* derives, calls 'a Phisition' whom the ailing Count maintained in his household. When Helena goes to Court and, with one of her father's remedies, cures the ailing King, she chooses as reward the hand of Count Bertram, her mistress's son. She loves him passionately; he is totally unreceptive. At the royal command he marries her; but before he escapes to the wars, fighting for the Duke of Florence against the Sienese, he warns her that he will recognise her as his wife only if she can get a ring from his finger. In the event she does so, through the dubious strategem known as the 'bed trick' when she takes the place, in the dark, of a Florentine girl with whose mother she lodges. At the end she and a dimly repentant Bertram come together: it is not for us to ask how they may fare beyond the play. These ring-time trickeries do not sound enthralling; still, few of the plays do if they are meagrely summarised. It is perfectly possible, given the right Helena, to take *All's Well That Ends Well* as outwardly romantic make-believe (a pity the word 'romantic' has been so rubbed) with a strange inner gravity. We can think then of Helena as a courageous and single-minded young woman in love, though Shakespeare does make it harder for her, and for us, than he need:

HELENA (to Widow):

> It is no more
> But that your daughter, ere she seems as won,
> Desires this ring; appoints him an encounter;
> In fine, delivers me to fill the time,
> Herself most chastely absent. After this,
> To marry her, I'll add three thousand crowns
> To what is pass'd already. (III, vii, 30–6)

It is, in fact, a comedy at which any playgoer must be a partisan: for or against the heroine. Most people on the stage, Bertram angrily excepted, are for her. Certainly the King is – that quiet, wistful figure, mournfully looking backward as when he remembers Bertram's father:

> Would I were with him! He would always say –
> Methinks I hear him now; his plausive words
> He scatter'd not in ears, but grafted them
> To grow there, and to bear – 'Let me not live' –
> This his good melancholy oft began,
> On the catastrophe and heel of pastime,
> When it was out – 'Let me not live' quoth he
> 'After my flame lacks oil, to be the snuff
> Of younger spirits, whose apprehensive senses
> All but new things disdain; whose judgments are
> Mere fathers of their garments; whose constancies
> Expire before their fashions.' This he wish'd.
> I, after him, do after him wish too,
> Since I nor wax nor honey can bring home,
> I quickly were dissolved from my hive,
> To give some labourers room.'(I, ii, 52–67)

Nothing in the play, if it is done without caprice, is more touching than the scene between the firm, persuaded girl and the shadowed King. Its couplets, glibly derided as jigging and periphrastic, can beat in the mind. They are not to be analysed, sternly debated. In the theatre this is just a formal pattern of sound, gently lingering:

> Ere twice the horses of the sun shall bring
> Their fiery torcher his diurnal ring,
> Ere twice in murk and occidental damp
> Moist Hesperus hath quench'd his sleepy lamp,
> Or four and twenty times the pilot's glass
> Hath told the thievish minutes how they pass,

What is infirm from your sound parts shall fly,
Health shall live free and sickness freely die. (II, i, 160–7)

and

More should I question thee, and more I must,
Though not to know could not be more to trust,
From whence thou cam'st, how tended on. But rest
Unquestion'd welcome and undoubted blest. (II, i, 204–7)

III

Helena, not always 'unquestion'd welcome', speaks boldly for youth;
but this is, first, a play for age. We respect the King, the Countess –
Shakespeare's most endeared *grande dame* – in her autumnal dignity,
and Lord Lafeu, the wise observer. Theirs is a world of experience,
courtesy, and grace. Against them is one of opportunism, irresponsi-
bility, and the kind of man, hollow at the core, represented by
Parolles; he is a parasitic braggart, a poltroon whose cowardice is
exposed, but who survives with the defiant: 'Simply the thing I am
shall make me live.' Jonathan Miller, in his Greenwich production
(1975) put him among the youth by making him the same age as
Bertram: 'The kind of young man', Miller said to Robert Speaight,[6]
'the Countess wished her son would not bring back to the house.'
Lafeu warned Bertram: 'There can be no kernel in this light nut;
the soul of this man is his clothes; trust him not in matter of heavy
consequence; I have kept of them tame, and know their natures.'
Bertram has been winning a small, and possibly growing, party to his
defence,[7] though again Shakespeare does not help with that single
and unfortunate final couplet: 'If she, my liege, can make me know
this clearly,/I'll love her dearly, ever, ever dearly.' (It goes better,
as so much does, in the theatre.) In Bertram's favour, social order,
'degree', among the Elizabethans, was rigidly defined. He would
have had sympathisers in the first audience – an audience, moreover, that would not have thought for a moment of the ethics of the
bed trick. Here playgoers seem to have come full circle.

Lavache, the play's clown, can be trying, though one day we
may find a comedian who can do justice to the variations of pitch
and accent in the repeated phrase, 'O Lord, sir!': it is the justification
for the scene between clown and Countess (II, i). Bridges-Adams,
at Stratford, tried to fit the man in by casting him as the gardener at
Rousillon. Noël Willman, directing another Stratford revival (1955),
turned him into a dwarf which meant that poor Edward Atienza

had to act all night on his knees. Other characters are there for the plot's sake (at Florence the silent and quickly lost Violenta is enigmatic), but we are glad to meet the determined Diana who has an immediate answer when Bertram refuses her the ring:

BERTRAM: It is an honour 'longing to our house,
          Bequeathed down from many ancestors;
          Which were the greatest obloquy i'th'world
          In me to lose.
DIANA: My honour's such a ring:
          My chastity's the jewel of our house,
          Bequeathed down from many ancestors;
          Which were the greatest obloquy i'th'world
          In me to lose. Thus your own proper wisdom
          Brings in the champion Honour on my part
          Against your vain assault.
BERTRAM: Here, take my ring. (IV, ii, 42–51)

One of Shakespeare's least predictable small parts is the 'gentle Astringer', a gentleman who is a keeper of hawks to the King. We find him in a street in Marseilles (V, i), and in Iden Payne's Stratford revival he was carrying, as identification, a falcon on his wrist.

Briefly, *All's Well That Ends Well* is like one of its own speeches, the Second French Lord's 'The web of our life is of a mingled yarn, good and ill together.' Listeners will select. If they have neither read nor seen the comedy, the actress of Helena may sway them. Certainly I must remember Lynn Farleigh (Aldwych, 1968) as she spoke the play's most quoted lines:

       My imagination
  Carries no favour in't but Bertram's.
  I am undone; there is no living, none,
  If Bertram be away. 'Twere all one
  That I should love a bright particular star
  And think to wed it, he is so above me.
  In his bright radiance and collateral light
  Must I be comforted, not in his sphere.
  Th'ambition in my love thus plagues itself:
  The hind that would be mated by the lion
  Must die for love. 'Twas pretty, though a plague,
  To see him every hour; to sit and draw
  His arched brows, his hawking eye, his curls,
  In our heart's table – heart too capable
  Of every line and trick of his sweet favour.

But now he's gone, and my idolatrous fancy
Must sanctify his relics. (I, i, 76–92)

That is romantic enough, no question. Robert Speaight[8] has expressed the other view of Helena: 'Just as her therapeutic powers are
able to cure the King's bodily sickness, so her implacable devotion
to Bertram will be able – or so we are asked to believe – to cure
his moral obliquity.' Playgoers will decide.

Two last points for the watcher. Helena is bound, in pilgrim's
dress, to Saint Jaques le Grand. She writes to the Countess (in a
sonnet-letter): 'Ambitious love hath so in me offended/That barefoot
plod I the cold ground upon' – explicit enough, but when did we last
see a Helena barefooted? Finally, the second and third scenes of the
fifth act contain about 380 lines; Helena speaks only twelve of them.

NOTES

1 1968
2 The King: *All's Well*, V. iii. 128
3 Such as John Barton's (Stratford, 1967; Aldwych, 1968) and Jonathan Miller's
   (Greenwich, 1975).
4 1941. Naomi Royde-Smith says also this (p. 125): 'The character of Diana seems
   to me to be the real blot on the play. No really nice girl would insist so emphatically
   on her virtue and behave as she did. Is it impertinent to suggest that a solution of
   the tangle might have been reached by letting Diana be a counterpart of Bianca in
   Othello and then showing a disillusioned Bertram turning to the passionate solace
   of Helena's integrity when he had been stripped of his money and thrown over by
   the Florentine gold-digger? Such an ending would be in key with Helena's beauty,
   a beauty destroyed by the trick she now plays.'
5 In a letter to the author, 1932. Maureen Shaw was Helena at Stratford-upon-Avon,
   1922.
6 *Shakespeare Quarterly* (Winter 1976).
7 Martin Holmes, in *Shakespeare's Public* (1960): 'A potentially pleasant young man
   in danger of being spoiled by the company he keeps . . . He must have been
   played as a sufficiently attractive person for audiences to feel pity for the way in
   which he is being misguided by Parolles.'
8 *Shakespeare Quarterly* (Winter 1976).

Measure for Measure (1604)

I

The theatre has always loved a Duke. Put that in quotation marks, with the grim little word 'Discuss' after it, and it would be useful in a paper on the ways of the British stage. *Measure For Measure* has the most bewildering Duke of all, an equivocal personage who leaves his post in Vienna and wanders round in a friar's habit to see how his understudy acts. A playgoer unused to him will be at the director's mercy. There seem to be endless methods of presenting a kind of Haroun al Raschid at large. Why has he chosen to leave so ostentatiously, and then to return as someone else? An answer too seldom offered, and usually scorned, is that the Duke is helping his dramatist to write a play; we ought for that to forgive his caprices, what Lucio calls his 'mad fantastical tricks' (Lucio himself is described as 'a fantastic').

This Duke, whom we rarely know as anything else, is actually named Vincentio: once more Shakespeare chose a name from stock. Angelo he had taken for the goldsmith in *The Comedy of Errors;* Claudio was in *Much Ado About Nothing;* and Juliet (how could he bring himself to the latest christening?) had done earlier and more important service. Escalus, too: a previous cast may have been running in Shakespeare's mind. It was among the riff-raff of Vienna that he suddenly let himself go, producing Lucio, Elbow, Froth, Pompey, Abhorson, and Mistress Overdone, as well as the mad procession in the gaol. Normally this is left only to a speech by Pompey, but Peter Brook at Stratford-upon-Avon in 1950 brought everyone on stage for us: Rash, Caper, Dizzy, Deep-vow, Copper-spur, Starve-lackey, Drop-heir, Forthlight, Shoe-tie, and – a near-cataleptic spasmodist – 'wild Half-can that stabbed Pots'.

The work in which all these people arrive, or are heard of, is now the theatre's favourite puzzle. Much influenced by another play, George Whetstone's *Promos and Cassandra*, set in Hungary and about 'the perfect magnanimity of a noble King in attacking Vice and favouring Virtue,' Shakespeare wrote a black comedy which critics have interpreted so variously that they do not seem to be talking of the same piece. It has appeared as a Christian allegory, a parable about sin and forgiveness in which the Duke is above temporal power; as an exposure of dictatorship; even, absurdly, as a near-farce quite unable to accommodate the figure of Isabella. The Duke is the enigma. Directors have had little trouble with the low life of a corrupt Vienna which is actually Shakespeare's London; but the Duke defeats them. An English actor who, between the wars, appeared as Angelo, the Duke, and Lucio, said once:[1] 'You can't explain the man. Keep him dignified, and let Shakespeare do the rest.' But does he? One production now will concentrate upon a sociological inquiry; another on the masquerading or, in effect, the practical joking – I have known this carried so far that the Renaissance prince might have strayed from Feydeau, with the gaol as Hotel Paradiso – and yet another will treat the Duke as a sinister, lying Machiavel whose great speeches are hypocrisy at its most ruthless. He has been a genial old meddler; a master of chicane; and, more strikingly, an embodiment of Power Divine, bearing the sword of heaven, and revealing himself (Tyrone Guthrie's view) when, at 'Look you sir, here is the hand and seal of the Duke', he shows the stigmata to the Provost.[2] Guthrie was resolved, we gather, that the Duke should be a figure of Almighty God: to Angelo a stern and crafty father, to Claudio a father stern but kind, to the Provost an elder brother, and to Isabella both a loving father and, at the end, the heavenly bridegroom to whom she is betrothed when the night begins.[3]

Angelo and Isabella, though taxing for their players, are apparently more direct. The first, a tempted neurotic, is a repressed puritan with a past: not crudely melodramatic, he must be able to suggest bonfires on the ice. Isabella, vulnerable novice of St Clare, is not yet of the cloister. Anxious to be the incarnation of goodness, and proud of it, she is fiercely tried. A sister's love or her brother's honour? The danger of damnation in yielding to Angelo? She will be tested again in the final minute of the play.

II

Measure for Measure opens with the Duke's command to Angelo:

In our remove be thou at full ourself;

> Mortality and mercy in Vienna
> Live in thy tongue and heart. (I, i, 44–6)

Here, according to the night's director, we shall know what kind of men these are. The Duke's last words as he leaves, allegedly for Poland:

> I'll privily away. I love the people,
> But do not like to stage me to their eyes;
> Though it do well, I do not relish well
> Their loud applause and Aves vehement;
> Nor do I think the man of safe discretion
> That does affect it. (I, i, 68–73)

are thought to refer to the dislike of King James (First of England, Sixth of Scotland) for the demonstrative English crowds.

During the ensuing street scene Claudio and Juliet enter under guard on their way to prison. Angelo has restored the old and forgotten penalties for fornication, and Claudio is in danger: though he and Juliet have declared themselves before witnesses to be man and wife, there has been no religious ceremony:

> We do the denunciation lack
> Of outward order; this we came not to,
> Only for propagation of a dow'r
> Remaining in the coffer of her friends,
> From whom we thought it meet to hide our love
> Till time had made them for us. But it chances
> The stealth of our most mutual entertainment,
> With character too gross, is writ on Juliet.
> LUCIO: With child, perhaps?
> CLAUDIO: Unhappily, even so. (I, ii, 141–9)

They pass to prison, and we to a monastery where the Duke is telling Friar Thomas, a trifle speciously, his reasons for the masquerade, why he has given his place to Angelo, 'a man of stricture and firm abstinence' who

> scarce confesses
> That his blood flows, or that his appetite
> Is more to bread than stone. Hence shall we see,
> If power change purpose, what our seemers be. (I, iii, 51–4)

Presently, in the nunnery of St Clare, Lucio urges Isabella, 'as a thing enskied and sainted', to plead for Claudio's life with Angelo 'whose blood is very snow-broth'.

So all is ready for the fanatical novice, who dreads the 'vice that I do most abhor', to meet the rigid judge; for him, promptly overcome, to order the choice between her chastity and her brother's life; and for the Duke-Friar, roaming about the prison, to manipulate events in the most tortuous way. He ruminates: 'O, what may man within him hide,/Though angel on the outward side . . . Craft against vice I must apply.' And he duly applies it.

III

If this is comedy, it is bleak. If we examine the Duke too closely, the play falls apart. Yet it has theatrical impulse and some fine and sombre verse; and several of its lesser characters are real: the honest Provost; the 'dissolute' Barnardine (a tiny part), prickly individualist, lord of his own republic in the straw of his cell and answerable to none; the touchily professional executioner, Abhorson, proud of the 'mystery' he is sure such a dubious assistant as Pompey must discredit; and Pompey himself, who takes life, in prison or out, with glib resource. Some of his associates are less conspicuous: the limp Master Froth, who would be a Lucio if he dared (which will be never), Mistress Overdone, who invites stereotyped exaggeration, and the constable Elbow, a trifling footnote to Dogberry.

More memorable, if actresses would let her be, is Mariana of the moated grange,[4] 'sister of Frederick, the great soldier who miscarried at sea', and once Angelo's betrothed. Escalus, who becomes deputy to the Deputy, is among Shakespeare's sage old men, Lafeu, Gonzalo, and the rest. Lucio, with a part (310 lines) longer than Angelo's, is a loose-tongued fellow, quick and ribald, a symbol of licentious Vienna who has the ultimate misfortune to be married to his whore, Kate Keepdown. Wordless, and without formal entrances, Kate can now slide flamboyantly into the cast, and she is far more alive than, say a Justice who has only three lines; Valentinus, Rowland, and Crassus, who do not appear; 'my gentle Varrius', who is on stage without a line to his name; or the absent Ragozine who loses his head for the plot's sake:

PROVOST: Here in the prison, father,
There died this morning of a cruel fever
One Ragozine, a most notorious pirate,
A man of Claudio's years; his beard and head
Just of his colour. What if we do omit

> This reprobate[5] till he were well inclin'd,
> And satisfy the deputy with the visage
> Of Ragozine, more like to Claudio.

DUKE: O, 'tis an accident that heaven provides!
> Dispatch it presently. (IV, iii, 66–73)

Those are merely functional lines. But much else is familiar: Isabella's 'O, it is excellent/To have a giant's strength! But it is tyrannous/To use it like a giant'; her

> Man, proud man,
> Dress'd in a little brief authority,
> Most ignorant of what he's most assur'd,
> His glassy essence, like an angry ape,
> Plays such fantastic tricks before high heaven
> As makes the angels weep . . . (II, ii, 117–22)

and the Duke-Friar's rhetoric:

> Be absolute for death; either death or life
> Shall thereby be the sweeter . . . (III, i, 5–6)

to the doomed Claudio. Alternating between hope and despair, the youth keeps his answer for Isabella later in the scene:

> Ay, but to die, and go we know not where;
> To lie in cold obstruction, and to rot;
> This sensible warm motion to become
> A kneaded clod; and the delighted spirit
> To bathe in fiery floods or to reside
> In thrilling region of thick-ribbèd ice . . . (III, i, 119–24)

To Shakespeare's audience, 'thrilling' in its Elizabethan sense of 'piercing' was a word of power: it is meaningless today.

What have been called the Duke's time-signals in the passing of the sultry Viennese night must be closely marked in the theatre:

> The vaporous night approaches. (IV, i, 56)

> As near the dawning, Provost, as it is. (IV, ii, 90)

> Look, th'unfolding star calls up the shepherd. (IV, ii, 192)

> Come away; it is almost clear dawn. (IV, ii, 198)

(The last phrase has a double implication.) During the last act, which has almost as many revelations in its Viennese judgement day as there will be five years on at the end of *Cymbeline*, the anxious moment is the pause before Isabella kneels to beg the Duke's pardon for Angelo. The longest pause in my experience (it lasted for thirty-five seconds) was in Brook's production at Stratford-upon-Avon, 1950. Brook had asked the actress, Barbara Jefford, to wait nightly until she felt the audience could stand it no longer. On some nights the timing could be two minutes – in the theatre very near eternity – 'silence', Brook said, 'in which all the inevitable elements of the evening came together – a silence in which the abstract notion of mercy became concrete for that moment to all those present.'

IV

Somebody, one day, will write a thesis on another pause. In the final minute the Duke who, long ago at the beginning of the play, had mocked 'the dribbling dart of love', has made his proposal to Isabella:

> Dear Isabel,
> I have a motion much imports your good;
> Whereto if you'll a willing ear incline,
> What's mine is yours, and what is yours is mine. (V, i, 532–5)

It seems obvious that in his last fifteen lines Shakespeare has been tidying the plot. The final couplets are simply a matter-of-fact completion; but no director now will miss his fun with the Duke.

When I first met *Measure for Measure* everyone remained calm. Shakespeare had to get his people off; we accepted the pairing as amiable, if clumsy. Isabella would bow to her fate with appropriate gratitude, and it did not sadden us after the Duke had been acted as a man who, in spite of his resolve to be 'a looker-on here in Vienna', had held his dignity through the convolutions and cruelties, the matter of life and death. But because of the current desire to wrest from any play more than its dramatist intended, the end has been firmly reconsidered. Isabella now must not tamely obey a man who has toyed with her emotions. In various revivals she has hesitated while the Duke looks nobly astonished. Some directors, too, have sought to transform him, not Guthrie-fashion as Power Divine, but in a manner sternly and politically class-conscious. Within a very few weeks in 1974 I saw him at Stratford-upon-Avon – the most perverse revival in memory – as a preposterous sinister sham; and at

Bucharest in a production, more restrained, that did insist on the will of an implacable autocrat. Each Isabella gave way as a virtual prisoner. In another English revival, Jonathan Miller's in modern dress at Greenwich (1975), she simply turned her back on a too complacently clever statesman and walked away, the proposal wordlessly rejected. At Edinburgh (1976) she slowly stripped off veil and habit and, a potential Duchess of Vienna, moved reluctantly towards the palace of her mischievous prince. We foresaw a weary marriage. The sourness of *Measure for Measure* cannot be mitigated by treating the Duke as a volatile refugee from light comedy. Maybe in the next revival Isabella will slap his face as, in Guthrie's early production at the Old Vic, she most heartily slapped Angelo's.[6]

NOTES

1 To the author.
2 At IV, ii, 181.
3 See Jane Williamson's valuable 'The Duke and Isabella on the Modern Stage' in *The Triple Bond*, edited by Joseph G. Price (Pennsylvania State University Press, 1975).
4 Curiously, she lives in two poems by the young Tennyson, especially the second, 'Mariana in the South'.
5 Barnardine.
6 'She fell upon Angelo as Mr Nupkins's cook fell upon Mr Job Trotter and "tore and buffeted his large flat face with an energy peculiar to excited females."' James Agate, *The Sunday Times*, 4 December 1933.

Othello, the Moor of Venice (1604)

I

In the third scene of the third act of *Othello*, the Moor says of
Desdemona: 'When I love thee not,/Chaos is come again.' Immediately his subordinate, Iago, speaks; and chaos enters with him.
If we have no sense of this, then the performance is faltering, for here
is the true beginning of the end. Iago, the demi-devil, who is the
Moor's ensign, or standard-bearer, has prepared his way; now he must
move relentlessly along it. If we seek to analyse, in the text, what has
happened and will happen in so short a space, the plot is quite
impossible; but the time problem, though it has been argued enough
outside the theatre, is of no account on the night: Shakespeare is so
expert an illusionist that we cannot question the structure of an
unsparing tragedy.

It is the tragedy of a man whom jealousy and disillusion destroy –
emotions roused by another man, of the most acute mind, whose
own jealousy has been malignant. In the 'Names of the Actors' at the
end of the Folio *Othello*, Iago is described simply as 'a villain': he
can be nothing else. He says to Roderigo in the first act: 'I have told
thee often, and I tell thee again, and again, I hate the Moor.' And when
Roderigo has gone out, he repeats to himself: 'I hate the Moor.' Why?
Because

> it is thought abroad that 'twixt my sheets,
> Has done my office. I know not if't be true;
> Yet I, for mere suspicion in that kind,
> Will do as if for surety. (I, iii, 380–4)

This is not the only reason, though he will return to it later. He hates
Othello because he has been passed over for the lieutenancy which

has gone to Cassio, an amiable inexperienced young officer and womaniser. He will then disgrace Cassio[1] and destroy Othello. He knows, none better, what jealousy can do – he even warns Othello of the 'green-ey'd monster'. Once he has begun his work, and he dulls not device by coldness and delay, nothing can stop it. Chaos has come again.

In its plainest terms, that is the narrative, Shakespeare's inspired transformation of a melodramatic tale by a sixteenth-century Italian. A constant, loving, noble nature is broken by devilry; by a man who tells himself, for the want of something better, that the thought of Othello with Emilia (of which we hear nothing more at any time) 'doth like a poisonous mineral gnaw my inwards'. But all derives from the very first scene when Iago is telling Roderigo, the 'foolish gentleman' (this and no more; never a sub-Aguecheek), why Cassio was chosen: 'Be judge yourself/Whether I in any just term am affin'd/To love the Moor.' He is a man of feverish invention, able to persuade himself of anything as he persuades others. When his imagination takes charge, it fans out extravagantly. Desdemona, a Senator's daughter, has been married in secret to Othello, the Moorish Negro general of the state of Venice; Roderigo is infatuated with her, and Iago urges him on:

> Call up her father.
> Rouse him, make after him, poison his delight,
> Proclaim him in the streets; incense her kinsmen,
> And, though he in a fertile climate dwell,
> Plague him with flies; though that his joy be joy,
> Yet throw such changes of vexation on't
> As it may lose some colour. (I, i, 68–74)

When Roderigo says: 'Here is her father's house. I'll call aloud,' Iago replies in three lines often sacrificed, though they are precisely in character:

> Do, with like timorous accent and dire yell
> As when, by night and negligence, the fire
> Is spied in populous cities. (I, i, 76–8)

A little later that night Othello's early speeches in the Venetian street tell us much about Iago's victim. He has great pride of race – 'I fetch my life and being/From men of royal siege.' He has done high service to the state (we shall hear this again at the end of the play). When Desdemona's father, Brabantio, brings men to attack him ('Down with him, thief'), his reply:

Keep up your bright swords, for the dew will rust them.
Good signior, you shall more command with years
Than with your weapons (I, ii, 59–61)

is the dignified voice of the Moor Desdemona knew when his stories to her father held her entranced. 'She lov'd me,' Othello says to the Senate;

She lov'd me for the dangers I had pass'd;
And I lov'd her that she did pity them. (I, iii, 167–8)

One word there takes us on to the cry at the night's end (to a man who has never known what the emotion means): 'The pity of it, Iago! O Iago, the pity of it, Iago!'

II

Othello used often to be acted (and frequently still is) as a handsome Berber; as Johnston Forbes-Robertson presented him early this century in white turban and flowing robe, and in an emasculated text, playgoers must have wondered why Brabantio was enraged. Othello's aspect is clearly indicated: 'thick lips', 'sooty bosom' – he is as much a Negro as Aaron of *Titus Andronicus*. Though several splendid Negro actors have played the part, they have not been able to voice it; even Paul Robeson became repetitively monotonous. It is much to have an Othello of temperament, one who is indeed roasted in sulphur and washed in steep-down gulfs of liquid fire; but we look, too, for the Othello music, the sheer grandeur of the verse; too many high-voltage players have offered power without glory. (This was the trouble with the redoubtable Czech, Frederick Valk, in 1942.[2])

On the other side, at Stratford (1961), Sir John Gielgud, looking like a Mauritanian eagle, presented an Othello whose nobility and command of the verse were unquestioned, but who lacked the man's temperament: he seldom got us to believe – as a critic said in another context – that he had been caught at the disastrous meeting-point of two cultural and spiritual traditions. It was a noble Venetian that cried in anguish 'Give me a living reason she's disloyal' and 'Would I were satisfied!' Sir Laurence Olivier (Old Vic – National, 1964) has been the only actor in our time to bring together the full Othello temperament and voice. In aspect – the text faithfully followed – he was the Moor. Out of intolerable agony he created a wild and surging music, particularly in 'Farewell, the tranquil mind' and the later:

> Like to the Pontic sea,
> Whose icy current and compulsive course
> Ne'er feels retiring ebb, but keeps due on
> To the Propontic and the Hellespont;
> Even so my bloody thoughts, with violent pace,
> Shall ne'er look back, ne'er ebb to humble love,
> Till that a capable and wide revenge
> Swallow them up. (III, iii, 457–64)

With Olivier the current grew and raged in desperate flood; suddenly a yearning remembrance on the two isolated words 'humble love'; then the flood again. The performance lived in its wind-tossed harmonies, its glimpse of the deities of primeval darkness, and the sobbing of 'O, Desdemona, Desdemona dead!' where the vowel 'o' carried a bitter burden.

III

Iago is really the easier part, taxing though it is, for the fellow must have an honest front – ironically, the epithet recurs – while revealing himself to us in his deadly soliloquies. How is he to be played? In a few of the performances this century he has been coldly, intellectually malign; a man of a vile gaiety; sinister and watchful, *faux bonhomme;* a barrack-room lawyer like a personified sneer; a coarse, chilling fox; a diabolist with a mask of carefully honest bluntness; boyish and pictorially vivid; and a stocky, black-bearded Judas with the face of a devil from a Renaissance picture. Actor and director must choose: the man is an affirmation of evil for its own sake, and he ends as he has begun:

OTHELLO: Will you, I pray, demand that demi-devil
          Why he hath thus ensnar'd my soul and body?
IAGO: Demand me nothing. What you know, you know.
          From this time forth I never will speak word.
                                                    (V, ii, 304–7)

In the play's last speech, with the bodies of Desdemona, Emilia, and Othello lying on the bed, Lodovico says:

> O, Spartan dog,
> More fell than anguish, hunger, or the sea!
> Look on the tragic loading of this bed.
> This is thy work – The object poisons sight;
> Let it be hid. (V, ii, 364–8)

The last words have sometimes continued the address to Iago. But Lodovico is ordering the curtains to be drawn across the bed and its 'tragic loading'.

Desdemona, trapped in a powerhouse, has more personality than many actresses allow. They take their cue from 'a maiden never bold', but she is neither a wilting lily nor, as a critic has expressed it, a junket run to whey. She is a courageous girl defying the sentiments and protocol of high-bred Venice, who declares herself – or should – with the lift of the head before the Senate at 'So much I *challenge* that I may profess/Due to the Moor, my lord.' Brabantio's anger will not be appeased: 'She has deceiv'd her father, and may thee.' And Othello's next lines are grimly, unconsciously ironic:

> My life upon her faith! Honest Iago,
> My Desdemona must I leave to thee. (I, iii, 294–5)

Othello is only partly a portrait of jealousy; it is also the fury of a noble, trusting nature on hearing that an adored wife is false ('No; my heart is turn'd to stone; I strike it, and it hurts my hand'). The part is compact of famous speeches and what used to be called 'points'. I name one of them: the end of the great outburst:

> O, now for ever
> Farewell the tranquil mind! farewell content!
> Farewell the pluméd troops, and the big wars
> That makes ambition virtue! O, farewell!
> Farewell the neighing steed and the shrill trump,
> The spirit-stirring drum, th'ear-piercing fife,
> The royal banner, and all quality,
> Pride, pomp, and circumstance, of glorious war!
> And O ye mortal engines whose rude throats
> Th'immortal Jove's dread clamours counterfeit,
> Farewell! Othello's occupation's gone.
>
> IAGO: Is't possible, my lord?
> OTHELLO: Villain, be sure thou prove my love a whore –
> Be sure of it; give me the ocular proof;
> Or, by the worth of man's eternal soul,
> Thou hadst been better have been born a dog
> Than answer my wak'd wrath. (III, iii, 351–67)

This, in a phrase coined by Tate Wilkinson, the provincial manager, at the end of the eighteenth century, was known as the 'collaring scene'.[3] Othello, at 'whore,' seizes Iago by the throat: business that has endured, we imagine, through the centuries. Donald Wolfit, when he played Othello in the 1940s and 1950s, would make a fierce sudden leap.

In the theatre Desdemona's waiting-woman, Emilia, Iago's wife, has become a more searching part than her mistress. Masefield, an admirer, says that her passionate instinct, without illusion, enables her to pierce Iago's web. The four words, 'O gull! O dolt!' when she turns upon Othello after Desdemona's death, are shattering.[4] Cassio, like Desdemona, needs a firmer hand than he generally gets. He also needs an actor who, in the first Cyprus scene, can deal with:

> Tempests themselves, high seas, and howling winds,
> The gutter'd rocks, and congregated sands,
> Traitors ensteep'd to enclog the guiltless keel,
> As having sense of beauty, do omit
> Their mortal natures, letting go safely by
> The divine Desdemona. (II, i, 68–73)

This is a scene that, because of the length of *Othello*, can be disappointingly trimmed, or, if not, lost in the tempests, high seas, and howling winds. At its beginning Shakespeare throws these lines to a Second Gentleman (there are, inevitably, three):

> For do but stand upon the banning shore,
> The chidden billow seems to pelt the clouds;
> The wind-shak'd surge, with high and monstrous mane,
> Seems to cast water on the burning Bear,
> And quench the guards of th'ever fixéd pole.
> I never did like molestation view
> On the enchaféd flood. (II, i, 11–17)

and Montano, Governor of Cyprus, urges them to the seaside: 'As well to see the vessel that's come in/As to throw out our eyes for brave Othello,/Even till we make the main and th'aerial blue/An indistinct regard.' Other probable straight cuts are the Musicians' scene (III, i) – a curious reminiscence of *Romeo and Juliet* – and the Clown (two brief entries) who, at the Old Vic in 1963, turned up in III, i as a one-man band. An *Othello* seldom gets through unscathed, though, uncut or cut, it is a headline drive towards the ultimate blow:

> Then must you speak
> Of one that lov'd not wisely, but too well;
> Of one not easily jealous, but, being wrought,
> Perplexed in the extreme; of one whose hand,

Like the base Indian, threw a pearl away
Richer than all his tribe. (V, ii, 346–51)

No tragedy is more nobly pitiful; and yet it was of this play that Thomas Rymer would write in 1693: 'Maybe a caution to all Maidens of quality how, without their Parents' consent, they run away with Blackamoors.'

NOTES

1 'He hath a daily beauty in his life/That makes me ugly' (V, i, 18–19).
2 New Theatre; for the Old Vic company. Later he appeared as Othello to Donald Wolfit's Iago.
3 Arthur Colby Sprague, *Shakespeare and the Actors* (1944), pp. 197–200.
4 Two exceptional Emilias of the period: Edith Evans (Old Vic, 1932) who, it was said, made one aware of her entire married life with Iago; and Elizabeth Spriggs at Stratford in 1971.

King Lear (1605)

> Men must endure
> Their going hence, even as their coming hither:
> Ripeness is all. (V, ii, 9–11)

I

Lear leads me instinctively both to Stonehenge and to three lines, in their contorted syntax, from Doughty's *The Dawn in Britain*:

> Hark bruit! and is the mighty mingled tread
> Of horse and foot-folk; which, in this dim night,
> Approach, with men that hold forth brands . . .

That was why it startled me at Stratford (1976) to discover Lear as a ruler of the late nineteenth, or early twentieth, century, disposing of the kingdom in a quiet little inner-court ceremony, and swearing by Apollo and by 'the sacred radiance of the sun,/The mysteries of Hecat and the night'. Gradually, time and place grew vaguer, less resolutely detailed; but the sight of that Lear in polished top-boots was alarming to anyone who must believe, as G. K. Hunter says in his New Penguin edition, that 'the play as a whole gives an impression of a monolithic and rough-hewn grandeur as if it were some Stonehenge of the mind'. The late Robert Speaight, actor-scholar, did not agree. It had nothing to do with Stonehenge, he said. 'It is a Jacobean tragedy in the sense that *The Duchess of Malfi* or *The Changeling* are Jacobean tragedies. It mirrors a period, and the thought of a period.'[1]

Doubtless; yet for me *King Lear* in the theatre must always rise from that dim world where Shakespeare set it; where, at the beginning of the night and at its end, we find an old King and his three daughters. At first, Lear, splenetic despot bent upon abdication, is giving away his land and rejecting Cordelia: I remember how, at 'With my two daughters' dowers digest this third', the German actor, Werner Krauss, cut the map in halves with an angry stroke. At the end all four, father and daughters, lie dead. 'Our present business/Is general woe.'

None would deny the greatness of *Lear*, tragedy of retribution, in its spiritual anguish and what Dr Gareth Lloyd Evans calls the 'terrible contrapuntal effect between delusion and reality' in the hovel scene.[2] The play is tremendous in the text while Lear, free of the large effects that troop with majesty, distils wisdom from madness. No man is so direly punished for the capricious choler of age, for arrogance and the lack of parental honesty. He has himself summoned the storm that he apostrophises, and that beats in his own mind: 'Thou, all-shaking thunder,/Strike flat the thick rotundity o'th' world.'

My trouble is that, like the director, Margaret Webster[3] (for that matter, Charles Lamb, and indeed Professor Bradley), I cannot rise easily to *Lear* in the theatre; what is hypnotic on the page has somehow to be minimised. Granville-Barker would not have this; I can say only that, in spite of cosmic utterances, an extraordinary profusion of imagery, and lines that search the heart, *Lear* does not reach me in the theatre as *Hamlet* does, or *Macbeth*, or *Othello*. It has taken a long time to realise – not that the King is unactable (I have nothing with the Lamb's tale about an old gentleman with a walking-stick) – simply that the tragedy does not carry as it ought. In our time there have been variably fine performances: those of John Gielgud (four revivals), Randle Ayrton, William Devlin, Laurence Olivier, Michael Redgrave, Donald Wolfit, Charles Laughton, Paul Scofield, Eric Porter, Robert Eddison, Donald Sinden. The stage has sent out its strongest actors to hold the bridge, yet I am left now remembering, in isolation, such incidentals as the tenderness of Ayrton when he spoke 'We two alone will sing like birds i'th'cage'; the wild coherence that Gielgud (in 1950) gave to the colloquy with blinded Gloucester, and, earlier, his twist of the lip at the third repetition of the name in 'Lear, Lear, Lear! Beat at this gate that let thy folly in'; Olivier kneeling at 'Let me not be mad'; Wolfit in the hovel ('The little dogs and all . . . see they bark at me'); Redgrave in his massive quietness; Scofield's 'Blow winds!' the first vowel extended; Eddison's extreme pathos at 'She's gone for ever'; Sinden acting with his eyes. A grand mosaic; but it does not take account of hours when the tragedy, in performance, has seemed to be at a remove, a cry from the dawn in Britain that is borne away upon the gale.

We realise that Lear's first action is incredibly stupid, as the Fool keeps on telling him. But the play has to begin, and it is a theatrically direct scene, however we may disbelieve in Cordelia. She is true to her nature, no doubt, but she appears to be behaving like a fairy-tale heroine who gets herself into immediate difficulty so that the tale can begin – with the difference that there is no happy ending here for anyone. Dame Peggy Ashcroft (Stratford, 1950) got me to understand the girl as few actresses have done: it is easy for the part to go the way of Desdemona, probably because the two elder sisters are so dominating that the 'unpriz'd precious maid' can seem to be pallid.

II

The first scene over, much of the rest is what Webster's Bosola *(The Duchess of Malfi)* calls 'a hideous storm of terror'. Goneril and Regan are fiends, though there is a disposition in these days to excuse Goneril in the early scenes. We cannot do it; and I cannot imagine that Shakespeare intended it. Cordelia leaves the pair with these lines ('washed eyes' can mean either 'washed with tears' or a new clear-sightedness):

> The jewels of our father, with wash'd eyes
> Cordelia leaves you. I know you what you are;
> And, like a sister, am most loath to call
> Your faults as they are named. Love well our father.
> To your professèd bosoms I commit him;
> But yet, alas, stood I within his grace,
> I would prefer him to a better place.
> So, farewell to you both. (I, i, 267–75)

It is Goneril who says to Regan at the end of this scene: 'We must do something, and i'th'heat.' She continues as she has begun. 'Old fools', she says to her steward Oswald, 'are babes again, and must be us'd/ With checks as flatteries, when they are seen abus'd.' What she says may not warrant Lear's all-embracing curse – inevitably he goes to extremes – but she acts as well as speaks, and Lear is thrust rapidly towards the madness some players have suggested in him from the first. The word is used as he prepares to leave for Gloucester's castle where Regan is staying: 'O, let me not be mad, not mad, sweet heaven!/Keep me in temper; I would not be mad!' What he has feared comes after the encounter with both daughters:[4]

> No, you unnatural hags,
> I will have such revenges on you both
> That all the world shall – I will do such things –
> What they are yet I know not; but they shall be
> The terrors of the earth. You think I'll weep.
> No, I'll not weep.
> I have full cause of weeping; but this heart
> Shall break into a hundred thousand flaws
> Or ere I'll weep. O fool, I shall go mad! (II, iv, 277–85)

In the Folio, after 'full cause of weeping', there is the direction: 'Storm and tempest'; and when Cornwall, Regan's husband, speaks after Lear has left the stage, it is with the ominous 'Let us withdraw; 'twill be a storm.' It is the fiercest known to the theatre. A Gentleman, one of Shakespeare's innominate reporters, tells Kent how Lear 'strives in his little world of man to outscorn/The to-and-fro conflicting wind and rain'. Almost at once we are on the heath where the tumult in Lear's brain is identified with the elemental fury; after the first words, an actor will not attempt to match the cataracts and hurricanes. During the storm and its aftermath Shakespeare's two lines of narrative – for there is a substantial sub-plot – come together; the tragedy drives on inexorably to the meeting of the two fathers on whom retribution has so fearfully descended: the blinded Earl of Gloucester, and Lear in his madness, 'crown'd with rank fumiter and furrow weeds'. This calls for major acting: if it is only roughly played, the passage, so charged in the text, will slip away from us. Lear's last scenes are some of the most actable: when he is reunited with Cordelia:

> You do me wrong to take me out o'th'grave.
> Thou art a soul in bliss; but I am bound
> Upon a wheel of fire, that mine own tears
> Do scald like molten lead. (IV, vii, 45–8)

when, after the losing battle, he and Cordelia are made prisoner:

> Come, let's away to prison.
> We two alone will sing like birds i'th'cage;
> When thou dost ask me blessing, I'll kneel down
> And ask of thee forgiveness; so we'll live,
> And pray, and sing, and tell old tales, and laugh
> At gilded butterflies, and hear poor rogues
> Talk of court news; and we'll talk with them too –
> Who loses and who wins; who's in, who's out –

And take upon's the mystery of things
As if we were God's spies; and we'll wear out
In a wall'd prison packs and sects of great ones
That ebb and flow by th'moon.   (V, iii, 8–19)

and finally, when the old man enters bearing Cordelia in his arms, the scene of the triple 'Howl!' and the quintuple 'Never':

No, no, no life!
Why should a dog, a horse, a rat have life,
And thou no breath at all? Thou'lt come no more,
Never, never, never, never, never.   (V, iii, 305–8)
Death is lord of all, and men can do no more than die.

III

The most debated production in our period was Brook's at Stratford (1962), a Beckettian *Lear*, without pity or sympathy, from which any awkward lines were cut. Scofield's Lear, ruling a pagan realm in a rusting Iron Age, was a man of still abounding strength; he could resemble for a moment an ancient sea-captain commanding the bridge of his vessel, defying the cosmic fates, as he drove unmanned to death. For years we have watched our principal actors and directors battling with the play. Donald Wolfit, during the war, was greatly praised, though I recall him better as a Kent of clear and uncoined constancy, with Ayrton at Stratford in 1936. His own Lear could be genuinely theatrical; I would have admired it more if, from long experience, I had not known every inflection. For many years John Gielgud has felt towards the heart of the play, once (Old Vic, 1940) under the direction of Granville-Barker in person on that storm-ridden journey of the mind and spirit. He was poorly served in a West End revival (Palace, 1955). The original idea, according to a programme note, was 'to find a setting and costumes which would be free of historical or decorative associations, so that the timeless, universal, and mythical quality of the story may be clear. We have tried to present the place and the characters in a very simple and basic manner, for the play to come to life through the words and the acting.' In practice, as I wrote later,[5] the 'simple and basic manner' ensured that at nearly every stage of the tragedy we were baffled by some fresh excrescence. No revival was so calculated to withdraw the mind from the timeless, universal, and mythical quality of Shakespeare's text: it took Gielgud until the last half-hour to outplay the décor by a Japanese-American artist. Sad; but his earlier Lears are safe in record.

The tragedy contains one of the most horrible scenes in the
Folio: the blinding of Gloucester by Cornwall and Regan (whose
cruelty here is implacable: 'The other, too'; 'Go, thrust him out at
gates/And let him smell his way to Dover'). It must be years since I
have been able to watch the entire scene. Many who are like me
remember Lilian Baylis's decision, at the Old Vic, always to have the
Blinding played immediately after the interval so that those who wished
could come in later. (The whole play, Brook believes, is about sight
and blindness.) There is, less fiercely (but only fleetingly), a semi-
romantic resolution of the sub-plot in which, on the third call of the
trumpet, Edgar appears, his face hidden, to fight with his bastard
brother. When Edmund has fallen, Edgar reveals himself:

EDGAR: Let's exchange charity.
                I am no less in blood than thou art, Edmund;
                If more, the more th'hast wronged me.
                My name is Edgar, and thy father's son.
                The gods are just, and of our pleasant vices
                Make instruments to plague us:
                The dark and vicious place where thee he got
                Cost him his eyes.
EDMUND: Th'hast spoken right, 'tis true;
                The wheel is come full circle; I am here. (V, iii, 166–74)

Edmund is a sardonic egotist who knows his dark power ('Yet
Edmund was beloved'). Edgar, as some return for the grotesquerie of
his Poor Tom scenes,[6] has the Dover cliff speech, imagined for the
benefit of his blinded father:

The crows and choughs that wing the midway air
Show scarce so gross as beetles. Half-way down
Hangs one that gathers samphire – dreadful trade!
Methinks he seems no bigger than his head.
The fishermen that walk upon the beach
Appear like mice; and yon tall anchoring bark
Diminish'd to her cock; her cock, a buoy
Almost too small for sight. (IV, vi. 13–20)

Gloucester, who could order his house no better than Lear, is the
sensual man delivered to fate. Kent, in disguise or out, is the oaken-
true follower of his King. Lear's other follower, the Fool, voice
of his conscience, had to fit uneasily into the post-dated 1976
production at Stratford, though Michael Williams was, gallantly, a
kind of superannuated Whimsical Walker. The Fool has been played

as a very old man, as an arch jester, as a youth like a frightened bird (Alan Badel at Stratford, 1950), as a stray from some Tibetan monastery, and, as Alec Guinness acted him so touchingly to Olivier (New Theatre, 1946), wry, quiet, and true, with a dog's devotion. In the hovel he slides out of the play:

LEAR: So, so, we'll go to supper i'th'morning.
FOOL: And I'll go to bed at noon. (III, vi, 84–5)

Some have thought that Lear refers to him at the last 'And my poor fool is hang'd.'[7] It is more likely to be Cordelia.
The final words of the tragedy:

> The weight of this sad time we must obey;
> Speak what we feel, not what we ought to say.
> The oldest hath borne most; we that are young
> Shall never see so much nor live so long

will go now, and reasonably, to Edgar; they are assigned to him in the Folio. Many productions used to prefer Albany, who is the elder statesman left in command; but the tone is Edgar's.

IV

Just as *Richard III* was in the grasp of Cibber, so *King Lear* for a long time was controlled by the Nahum Tate version of 1681. The end of this (which I quote to show what a pirate could really do when he tried) finishes everything off with the briskest good cheer:

EDGAR: Your Leave, my Liege, for an unwelcome Message.
              Edmund (but that's a Trifle) is expir'd;
              What more will touch you, your imperious Daughters,
              Goneril and haughty Regan, both are dead,
              Each by the other poison'd at a Banquet;
              This, Dying, they confest.
CORDELIA: O fatal Period of ill-govern'd Life!
LEAR: Ingratefull as they were, my Heart feels yet
              A Pang of Nature for their wretched Fall; –
              But, Edgar, I defer thy Joys too long:
              Thou serv'd'st distrest Cordelia; take her Crown'd;
              Th'imperial Grace fresh blooming on her Brow;
              Nay, Gloster, thou hast here a Father's Right,
              Thy helping Hand t'heap Blessings on their Heads.

KENT: Old Kent throws in his hearty Wishes too.

To which we can say merely; O fatal period (but that's a trifle now!)

NOTES

1 *Shakespeare: The Man and His Achievement* (1977), p. 279.
2 *Shakespeare IV: 1601–1605* (1972), p. 83.
3 *Shakespeare Today* (1957).
4 When Charles Laughton played Lear at Stratford in 1959, in some ways his most touching point was the pause (in the scene with the daughters) before the last word of his line to Goneril: 'And thou art twice her love.'
5 *Shakespeare on the English Stage 1900–1964* (1964), p. 221.
6 The dialect he uses with Oswald always sounds Mummerset in the theatre: 'An chud ha'bin zwagger'd out of my life, 'twould not ha' bin zo long as 'tis by a vortnight . . . Chill be plain with you.' It reminds one of the Elizabethan ballad, 'Plain Truth and Blind Ignorance', with such lines as 'Chill tell thee what, good vellowe' and 'And this che zay my zelf have zeene'.
7 In 1952, at the Old Vic, the Fool was left weaving a noose at the close of the hovel scene.

Macbeth (1606)

I

This, the shortest of the tragedies – what we have may be a cut version – is a study in damnation, an exploration of evil, that is a terror to act. A superstitious profession has made a terror of it, in two senses: its record on the stage is blackened by disasters that may or may not have been fortuitous. Once, during the Princes Theatre production in 1926, the atmosphere of evil grew so inescapably that Sybil Thorndike and Lewis Casson, who were playing Lady Macbeth and Banquo, shut themselves in their dressing-room to read aloud the 91st Psalm.

Macbeth is the agonising part. Valour's minion, and, by virtue of his dramatist, poet of the haunted imagination, he has to use the full tragic stride on his path between the three castles of Inverness, Forres, and Dunsinane. For much of the way he is on a narrow bridge across the depths of hell. The verse falls in flakes of fire until it smoulders in those last embers:

> And be these juggling fiends no more believ'd
> That palter with us in a double sense,
> That keep the word of promise to our ear,
> And break it to our hope! (V, viii, 19-22)

Many players in our time have made us aware of some part of the journey. Few, at the end, have persuaded us that the cornered wolf of the last bravado is the man, straight from battle, who cried to the Weird Sisters: 'Stay, you imperfect speakers, tell me more.' John Masefield held that the early scenes of temptation and resolve should be played 'not like a moody traitor, but like Lucifer, star of the morning', and the later scenes 'not like a hangman who has taken to drink, but an angel who has fallen'. Ideally, yes; but the Macbeths are in a world where blood must have blood, and where it is seldom day. Through the shadows move the two victims of ambition – the wife who drives on her husband; the husband who, as she weakens, strains desperately forward:

> For mine own good
> All causes shall give way. I am in blood
> Stepp'd in so far that, should I wade no more,
> Returning were as tedious as go o'er.   (III, iv, 135–8)

This echoes Richard the Third's

> But I am in
> So far in blood that sin will pluck on sin.
> Tear-falling pity dwells not in this eye. (IV, ii, 65-7)

I think it was Ivor Brown who said that Macbeth can unite two Richards, the Second as well as the Third.

The play begins in storm, in thunder, lightning, and in rain; but the storm in Macbeth's mind is slow in breaking. The idea of Duncan's death must grow as his wife, obsessed by her own ambition for him, urges him to screw his courage to the sticking-place. The Weird Sisters have spoken to her unspoken thoughts, yet (she says to herself as she reads his letter from 'the day of success'):

> Yet do I fear thy nature;
> It is too full o'th'milk of human kindness
> To catch the nearest way. Thou wouldst be great;
> Art not without ambition, but without
> The illness should attend it. What thou wouldst highly,
> That wouldst thou holily; wouldst not play false,
> And yet wouldst wrongly win. (I, v, 13–19)

Though we are aware on good authority that sound and fury alone signify nothing, people can still be disappointed if Macbeth fails at once to be a *basso profundo*. This has often been the cause of disaster: a Macbeth unable to sustain a premature frenzy. Moreover, our conception of Lady Macbeth has changed since the heavy artillery of Sarah Siddons. The part, surprisingly brief (255 lines), should not be over-gunned or – in another popular reading – turned to a seductive harpy. Wholly possessed and possessive, a warmly loving wife and a woman of cold resolution, she will not rest until her husband is on the throne. Dorothy Tutin (Guildford, 1976) said all in a single movement[1] when, on Macbeth's entry in the Letter scene, she knelt to him at

> Great Glamis! Worthy Cawdor!
> Greater than both, by the all-hail hereafter! (I, iv, 51-2)

In these days we see Lady Macbeth as a young woman (she was designed for a boy player); but, brought up on a Shakespearian tradition carried over from the nineteenth century, I thought of this for too long as a tragedy of middle age. The notion was strengthened as a rule by what we now call 'shaggy-dog' dressing, and by the casting of the Macbeths as a general, uncomfortably hirsute, and a massive wife with a voice of bell-metal. Robert Speaight, praising a Jacobean-style production, said that he had 'grown rather tired of the subtle reasoning and sophisticated imagery sitting on heads that might have worn the antlers of Hengist and Horsa'.[2] At another extreme, experiments with modern dress have led to such foolishness as Macbeth's emphasis in the 1928 revival (Court Theatre) on 'this *blasted* heath'.

II

A director has immediately to consider the Weird Sisters, the equivocating fiends who, to King James and the Jacobeans, were not just legendary figures. We have seen them in all guises from wild scaly shapes and conscientious crones to the nightmare emanations of the Fuseli picture or, simply, to prowling fortune-tellers. They have crouched in a circle, or stood in echelon, or, literally, hovered through the fog and filthy air (Stratford-upon-Avon, 1955). Favoured casting now is either two women and a man, or two old women and one young and lividly beautiful. The less fantasticated the better, and the fewest cackling laughs: 'Satan's kingdom does not laugh,' said Masefield sagely. Agents of evil, they do no more, with their triple greeting, triple prophecy, than encourage Macbeth's secret ambition:

> that suggestion,
> Whose horrid image doth unfix my hair
> And make my seated heart knock at my ribs
> Against the use of nature. (I, iii, 134-7)

Thenceforward the play, on an uncluttered stage, can move with the speed the Jacobeans expected and the theatre lost when realistic scenery had to be shifted and there could be three twenty-minute intervals and a sequence of isolated episodes. There were twenty-one of these in the Princes Theatre revival of 1926, with the Ricketts setting; and the provinces were accustomed to wait while a fresh bit of gauze was added or another curtain arranged. Beerbohm Tree, at His Majesty's Theatre early in the century, would have thought this kind of thing elementary. Even before he entered, his stage directions called for lightning and a thunder-crash, raging winds, toppling rocks, the fall of a blasted oak, and distant trumpets. Lightning then revealed Macbeth poised upon a crag.

Elaboration is never needed less than in *Macbeth* where the verse is, triumphantly, the scene painter, though a director (Royal Court, 1966) who confined the tragedy within three canvas walls, and in an unaltered glare of light, did make me ask wistfully for aid from the switchboard. We must hope for imaginative, disciplined simplicity; but what the next man will do is never remotely predictable; I marvel yet at a revival (1967) in which the stage of the Royal Shakespeare Theatre was matted in a tumble of rust-coloured sheepskin.

III

Like the Macbeths, the people round them have got younger through the years. In the theatre, Banquo, that 'root and father of many kings', has sometimes been treated unguardedly as a plain soldier. He is not. At once he recognises shrewdly what Macbeth means by 'If you cleave to my consent when 'tis,/It shall make honour for you.' He has, says Macbeth, 'a wisdom that doth guide his valour/To act in safety.' Believing that time is on his side, he knows too much for his own good; and he has his own bad dreams ('Merciful powers/Restrain in me the cursèd thoughts that nature gives way to in repose)'. It is a test for an actor who at least can look wary and indicate his deep distrust of Macbeth. 'In the great hand of God I stand' (II, iii, 129) has added meaning if his position is clear: not an accomplice, but a man who has heard the prophecies. Macduff is the avenger. One day, when he learns of his wife and children's murder, we may find an actor isolating the phrase 'At one fell swoop'. It is the cry of a man whose castle has been taken and his 'wife and babes savagely slaughter'd', but the words, which must have come in fire from Shakespeare's pen, have flickered to the ashes of a cliché. Earlier in the same speech, we shall notice whether Macduff applies 'He has no children' to Malcolm, who has just spoken, or, more reasonably, to Macbeth. Malcolm, during this English scene at Edward the

Confessor's Court, has some grating passages of self-accusation in an effort to probe Macduff's loyalty; apparently clogging at first, their value increases the more we hear them.

Other characters are unambiguous. Though the Porter at Inverness is often dabbed in unwisely as comic relief, the text shows that he is no longer drunk. The knocking at the gate is superbly dramatic; what the Porter has to say about equivocation and hell-fire should not be overlaid by the customary staggering and hiccoughing. We may observe also that, while on the night of murder Lady Macbeth heard only the owl scream and the crickets cry, Lennox, who comes to Inverness with Macduff, talks of gales and portents. ''Twas a rough night,' responds Macbeth, his thoughts elsewhere. 'My young remembrance', says Lennox, 'cannot parallel a fellow to it.' And on the cue, Macduff re-enters with 'O, horror, horror, horror!', four words which used to be shouted at the pitch of an actor's voice but more·often now are gasped on a hoarse exhalation of the breath.

How old is the murdered Duncan? In the theological context some-times emphasised today, with Duncan, in effect, both king and high priest, and Macbeth adding sacrilege to regicide, he may be much older than the rest.[3] He need not resemble Macaulay's ancient Tarquin, who was 'white as Mount Soracte,/When winter nights are long', and whose 'beard flowed down o'er mail and belt', – an exact description of the average Duncan from an inter-war revival. Komisarjevsky, in the so-called 'aluminium' *Macbeth* (Strat-ford, 1933), would have none of this: his Duncan, played by Eric Maxon, was a soldierly figure in his early forties. On the other hand, I remember that fine actor, Nicholas Hannen, in the Gielgud revival (Piccadilly, 1942), bestowing on the king what James Agate called 'the Maeterlinckian quality of sweetness in old age'.[4]

We meet Duncan in the second scene when the Wounded Sergeant brings a report on the last battle of the civil war. Here he can be a virile general applauding the news of victory, or a gentle old man whose lip twists wryly at 'So well thy words become thee as thy wounds.' Meanwhile, the Weird Sisters wait for Macbeth upon the heath. 'Her husband's to Aleppo gone, master o'th'Tiger' must always remind me of a letter from T. E. Lawrence, who was reviewing an edition of Hakluyt, to Francis Yeats-Brown in 1927:[5] 'My first dis-covery was a letter which said: "My last I sent you from Aleppo by the purser of the *Tiger*." It was like finding a human footprint in the desert. W.S. had passed.' Upon the entrance of Banquo and Macbeth ('His 'so foul and fair a day' echoes the 'Fair is foul, and foul is fair' of the first scene), the Third Witch's 'All hail, Macbeth, that shalt be king hereafter!' releases the tragedy. It has yet to grow, but we should see it in Macbeth's eyes, hear it in his aside, 'Why do I yield to that suggestion?', and, possibly, observe it in his response to Duncan's 'We will establish our estate upon/Our eldest, Malcolm.' In Michael Redgrave's revival (Aldwych, 1947) Macbeth was the last to draw his sword in the ceremonial salute to the Prince of Cumberland.

Next, what the stage knows as the Letter scene: Lady Macbeth, in the castle of Inverness, reading her husband's letter from the 'day of success' (a phrase that can have two meanings). The ensuing soliloquy, with its invocation to the dark spirits, is the whole of Lady Macbeth in her boldest hour, and there is no need to add to it by such business as the descent of a long staircase. Presently, at Macbeth's arrival, there is the laden exchange:

MACBETH: My dearest love,
                      Duncan comes here tonight.
LADY MACBETH: And when goes hence?
MACBETH: Tomorrow – as he purposes.
LADY MACBETH: O, never
                  Shall sun that morrow see! (I, v, 55-8)

He is still uncertain; for his wife he is already crowned. Within a few minutes' stage time she is at Duncan's feet while he greets her as 'our honour'd hostess!' and 'Fair and noble hostess,/We are your guest tonight.' The rest follows with extraordinary speed. In Macbeth's fraught 'If it were done when 'tis done', we expect the actor to pause, searching, before 'Horsed/Upon the sightless couriers of the air', just as Hamlet will search for 'this quintessence of dust'. After midnight, and with all yet to do, imagination conjures the dagger from the air, and it is a Macbeth's task to make it palpable to us, 'the handle toward my hand'. Throughout the play we shall not forget the word 'hand':

As they had seen me with these hangman's hands . . . (II, ii, 27)

What hands are here? Ha! they pluck out mine eyes.
Will all great Neptune's ocean wash this blood
Clean from my hand? No; this my hand will rather
The multitudinous seas incarnadine,
Making the green one red. (II, ii, 59-63)

Thence to be wrench'd with an unlineal hand . . . (III, i, 62)

        Come, seeling[6] night,
Scarf up the tender eye of pitiful day,
And with thy bloody and invisible hand

> Cancel and tear to pieces that great bond
> Which keeps me pale. (III, ii, 46-50)

> Look, how she rubs her hands. (V, i, 26)

> What, will these hands ne'er be clean? (V, i, 41)

> All the perfumes of Arabia will not sweeten this little hand.
> (V, i, 49–50)

And, at the last:

> this, dead butcher, and his fiend-like queen,
> Who, as 'tis thought, by self and violent hands
> Took off her life. (V, viii, 69–71)

The other words that constantly recur are 'murder', the dominating 'blood', and, with a peculiar chill, 'sleep'. Apart from the Witch's 'Sleep shall neither night nor day/Hang upon his pent-house lid', the first use is Lady Macbeth's 'When Duncan is asleep . . .' We hear it again and again: Macbeth's 'wicked dreams abuse/The curtain'd sleep', and the great outburst 'Methought I heard a voice cry Sleep no more;/Macbeth doth murder sleep . . .'

> Still it cried 'Sleep no more' to all the house;
> 'Glamis hath murder'd sleep; and therefore Cawdor
> Shall sleep no more – Macbeth shall sleep no more.' (II, ii, 41–3)

The reiterated phrase is the key to what follows. Duncan, after life's fitful fever, may sleep well; not so Macbeth and his queen. The play is never more frightening than when, together but apart, they sit lonely in the darkness before morning, and Lady Macbeth says wearily and tonelessly : 'You lack the season of all natures, sleep.' Those, with terrible irony, are her last words before the Sleepwalking. Then, in her thick-coming fancies, plagued by an unsleeping conscience, she lives again through the night of the murder until she vanishes from us for ever. We hear no more but an offstage cry of women:

SEYTON :   The Queen, my lord, is dead.
MACBETH :   She should have died hereafter. (V, v, 16–17)

IV

Though *Macbeth* should be given uncut, the brief, atmospheric scene for the Old Man, Ross, and Macduff is sometimes, and unluckily, sacrificed. Little else goes except those tempting Hecate couplets which are probably unShakespearian, and the part of the English Doctor in the 'King's Evil' passage (IV, iii), a compliment to James the First,[7] often mocked as superfluous. Professor G. K. Hunter says that the report of Edward the Confessor's virtues is meant 'to establish the potency of virtuous kingship in our minds before the play plunges in to demonstrate the fate of vicious kingship (and queenship).'

In these days, at the pit of Acheron, the cauldron-apparitions (crowned head, bloody child, crowned child) are likely to be puppets voiced by the Weird Sisters, a device damaging to a scene that demands the most powerful atmospherics. Elsewhere, the two Murderers who are dispatched to wait for Banquo and Fleance (and who probably reappear at Macduff's castle in Fife) need not be simple thugs: they are two of life's failures, 'weary with disaster, tugged with fortune'. The Third Murderer, never disclosed, is doubtless Macbeth's faithful Seyton who is to him what Catesby is to Richard III. Some writers have been tempted boldly (but it can be only boldness) to suggest Macbeth himself.

The two entrances, at that inhospitable banquet, of Banquo's ghost, shaking its 'gory locks', are matters for a director's juggling; some have shirked by employing an empty stool and a quivering green light, but this is a cowardly way out. Other revivals have left it to the imagination, though Shakespeare is explicit: 'Enter the Ghost of Banquo and sits in Macbeth's place,'[8] and, after another fifty lines, 'Enter Ghost.' At the return, Macbeth should drop in terror the goblet he has just raised in bravado to toast 'our dear friend Banquo, whom we miss. Would he were here!'

In the fifth scene of the last act, when Macbeth is a wolf beleaguered, we wait for the pointing of the first line and a half which can be

Hang out our banners on the outward walls;
The cry is still 'They come.'

or

Hang out our banners! On the outward walls
The cry is still 'They come.'[9]

or

Hang out our banners on the outward walls!
The cry is still. They come.

It is almost over except for the fight between Macduff and Macbeth when the tyrant is killed off stage and we have the daunting direction: 'Re-enter Macduff, with Macbeth's head.' John Masefield insisted on the head: 'Actors complain that it makes people laugh; of course it does; the laughter is hysterical, it comes from deep feeling, from relief that justice has been done. On the stage, in poetry, justice is done.'[10] Still, it is safer, where practicable, either for Macduff or an attendant to carry on a long pole with the head safely out of sight, or, upon an open stage, to point helpfully off. We do not dwell upon it, for Macduff, as he turns towards Malcolm, is speaking:

> The time is free.
> I see thee compass'd with thy kingdom's pearl
> That speak my salutation in their minds;
> Whose voices I desire aloud with mine –
> Hail, King of Scotland! (V, viii, 55-9)

It is then that we remember again the voice of the Third Witch in the mists of the lonely heath: 'All hail, Macbeth, that shalt be King hereafter!'

NOTES

1 Noted by Professor Arthur Colby Sprague, November 1976. The young Madge Kendal did this more than a century before, but Dorothy Tutin, not waiting for the 'Greater than both', knelt immediately on her husband's entrance.
2 *Shakespeare on the Stage* (1973), p. 242.
3 How do we read 'His silver skin lac'd with his golden blood' (II, iii, 111)?
4 *The Sunday Times*, 10 July 1942.
5 *Francis Yeats-Brown* by Evelyn Wrench (1948).
6 Blinding.
7 New Penguin edition, 1967. 'By the date of the play,' says Professor Hunter, 'James had begun, after some hesitation, to touch for the King's evil.'
8 At the moment Macbeth is saying to his wife, 'Sweet remembrancer.'
9 A famous early nineteenth-century reading.
10 *A Macbeth Production* (1945), pp. 22-3.

Antony and Cleopatra
(1606–7)

I

Hamlet opens unmatchably; but *Antony and Cleopatra* is very close to it. In *Hamlet* we have the armoured frost of a northern night, awed watchers, pacing ghost. *Antony* is in the torrid splendour of Alexandrian revel. Before the lovers enter, a shadowy soldier, Philo, has thirteen lines of fire. Antony must fulfil them:

> Those his goodly eyes
> That o'er the files and musters of the war
> Have glow'd like plated Mars, now bend, now turn
> The office and devotion of their view
> Upon a tawny front. (I, i, 2–6)

We shall remember the ensuing lines, 'His captain's heart,/Which in the scuffles of great fights hath burst/The buckles on his breast . . .'. A lifetime afterwards, with Antony close to his end, he cries to Eros: 'Heart, once be stronger than thy continent,/Crack thy frail case.' On the first Alexandrian night he has yet to know defeat. Philo is still addressing the shadow called Demetrius when, on the gong-note of 'Behold and see!', Antony, 'the triple pillar of the world transformed/Into a strumpet's fool', enters with Cleopatra, the whole court behind them. Oblivious, the lovers speak antiphonally in four world-spanning phrases, stayed by the single word 'Rome'. The future is at the doors; there are messengers from Rome. 'Grates me,[1] the sum,' rasps Antony in a phrase powerfully compressed. A moment, and again he is crying, not in the voice of the triumvir but of the lover: 'Let Rome in Tiber melt, and the wide arch/Of the rang'd empire fall! Here is my space.'

All his days that opening fanfare haunted Sir Barry Jackson. The Birmingham Repertory Theatre's *Antony and Cleopatra* in 1961 was the last production before he died. Ill during rehearsal, he fixed his mind on the play and told his director, Bernard Hepton, to open upon a half-lit stage and suddenly to bring the lights up when the flourishes for Antony and Cleopatra[2] were heard. The lovers must enter in a blaze. Thenceforward, through victory, defeat, despair, and approaching death, the blaze of language persists. Shakespeare is at his most prodigal: realms and islands are 'as plates dropped from his pocket'.

His opening is sovereign. Throughout, he must speak undistracted by scenic pomp that, in a dead fashion, would overwhelm the stage with lotus columns, marble halls, and quantities of sand. Glen Byam Shaw (Stratford, 1953) placed *Antony and Cleopatra* against a wide-arched sky. A hint of a sail for the revel aboard Pompey's galley; thrones for Cleopatra; the wings of the Roman eagle. It was enough; but the simplicity would have been alien to older actor-managers who thought only in display. The incorrigible Herbert Beerbohm Tree (His Majesty's, 1906) used all kinds of extravagance. Moreover, he began ridiculously with the fourth scene of the first act, Caesar's house in Rome, followed by the entrance of the lovers in Alexandria ('If this be love indeed'), and, upon their exit, Enobarbus with Philo's first speech: 'Nay, but this dotage of our general's/O'erflows the measure.' Such a production as this overflowed like the floodwaters of Nile, and not beneficently.

Upon the stage *Antony and Cleopatra* cannot hesitate; it must sweep by in a rapid panorama and in Shakespeare's ordering of the scenes – near Misenum, Pompey's galley, a plain in Syria, Cleopatra's palace. Some are very brief indeed (III, viii has six lines, and III, ix four), and the wisest production lives on a bare stage that the verse transforms. Glen Byam Shaw knew this; and so did László Vámos in a Budapest revival (1974) where, except for the emblems of Egypt and Rome that faced each other across the stage, there was nothing in sight to stem the rushing progress. As Enobarbus and Menas were running out after the revel on the galley, Ventidius was already marching on from his victory over darting Parthia. This was Granville-Barker. 'We are to keep Shakespeare's stage well in mind,' he wrote[3], 'if we are to realise the dramatic value to the spectator of the quick shift from singing and dancing and the confusion of tipsy embracings to the strict military march that brings Ventidius "as in triumph" upon the stage. There is no pause at all.' *Antony and Cleopatra* is made of these contrasts.

II

'A man may, if he were of a fearful heart, stagger in this attempt,' says Touchstone on another occasion. A director of *Antony and*

Cleopatra might echo that. He must assemble his cast: an Antony near the close of day, with a voice for the sunset, a Cleopatra who can take all hearers in her strong toil of grace, an Enobarbus who can assume the purple without self-consciousness, and an Octavius Caesar to stand marmoreally for Rome. Given these bounties, he must cope with dozens of scenes, the pomps of the ranged Empire, the revelling, the legions' tread and 'the noise of a sea-fight', music in the air when 'the god Hercules' leaves his Antony, and all those complexities about Cleopatra's monument. They begin at a moment, one that scholars consider anxiously, when the dying general is hauled up to Cleopatra. We have feared now and then that he might crash, leaving us to exclaim in the words of John Philip Kemble's 'Grand Chorus':

> No monument, till now, could boast a pair
> So fam'd, yet, ah! so luckless in their doom.

This is a moment every fresh revival must solve for itself.

There have been calamities with the play. Theodore Komisarjevsky, who had succeeded with his Stratford *Lear,* failed tragically in 1936 (New Theatre) – not only because his Cleopatra, a clever Russian comedienne, was nearer to Neva than to Nile and unable to project the verse intelligibly,[4] but also because he scuffled round with the text. Thus he deferred Philo's overture and opened trivially with Iras, Charmian, and the Soothsayer; the same Soothsayer would wander in to grab such lines as 'Swallows have built in Cleopatra's sails their nests' and even the magical ' 'Tis the god Hercules, whom Antony lov'd, now leaves him.' Cuts – such as 'Call to me all my sad captains' – were inexplicable. Enobarbus was a velvety gallant blessed by the voice of Leon Quartermaine, but quite wrong; and the costumes were disastrous. Both Granville-Barker and Bridges-Adams had faith in Veronese: 'the only way of saving "Cut my lace, Charmian," from absurdity, and *one* way out of Wardour Street'.[5] Komisarjevsky merely used anything he considered decorative. 'Incredible though it sounds,' wrote James Agate, 'Cleopatra attends the sea-fight in a costume consisting of a Roman helmet, a golden breastplate, and a slashed skirt of forget-me-not blue satin, the whole irresistibly reminiscent of Miss Renee Houston in some naval-cum-military skit.'[6]

Since that night there have been genuine revivals, especially Glen Byam Shaw's with Michael Redgrave and Peggy Ashcroft, and Trevor Nunn's with Janet Suzman and Richard Johnson (Stratford, 1973). I revert to the Komisarjevsky failure simply because one certain way of reducing any major tragedy is to let the eye rule the ear and verbal splendour dwindle before visual caprice.

III

As with Romeo and Juliet, most of us have preconceived ideas of the lovers. Created by a boy actor of (we can only suppose) genius, Cleopatra would go three hundred years later, as of right, to a stately contralto. One actress, Dorothy Green, had superbly the grand manner that bridged the periods. Today we think in terms of more volatile players – Vivien Leigh; Peggy Ashcroft, so royally sustaining the long adagio of her end; and Janet Suzman. Everybody waits for the Barge speech, but three early lines for Antony show what we must look for: the queen

> Whom everything becomes – to chide, to laugh,
> To weep; whose every passion fully strives
> To make itself in thee fair and admir'd. (I, i, 49–51)

In her myriad moods, contradictions, passions, she must be at the core of the Alexandrian scenes. She is never alone with Antony – the part was framed for a boy player and much is done by report and inference – but as the moods vary, and as Shakespeare finds the music for them, we know why Cleopatra must obsess Mark Antony; why, when his world has fallen, and she has beguiled him to the very heart of loss, he can still look towards reunion in Elysium:

> Where souls do couch on flowers, we'll hand in hand,
> And with our sprightly port make the ghosts gaze.
> Dido and her Aeneas shall want troops,
> And all the haunt be ours. (IV, xiv, 51–4)

Cleopatra, in her last sublimation, robed, crowned, and marble-constant ('Now the fleeting moon no planet is of mine') utters Antony's name with her last breath. Octavius, cold conqueror of the Roman world, reunites them in his last speech:

> She shall be buried by her Antony;
> No grave upon the earth shall clip in it
> A pair so famous. (V, ii, 355–7)

Antony, ravaged triumvir at the close of day, the man who had superfluous kings for messengers, must glow first like plated Mars, present majesty in ruin, and at his end, in Cleopatra's monument, remember his former fortunes:

> Wherein I liv'd the greatest prince o' the' world,
> The noblest; and do not now basely die;

Not cowardly put off my helmet to
My countryman – a Roman by a Roman
Valiantly vanquish'd. (IV, xv, 54–8)

As his spirit goes, Cleopatra mourns for him as no man had been
mourned before:

The crown o'th' earth doth melt. My lord!
O, wither'd is the garland of the war,
The soldier's pole is fall'n! Young boys and girls
Are level now with men. The odds is gone,
And there is nothing left remarkable
Beneath the visiting moon. (IV, xv, 63–8)

In the last act, before Cleopatra, with her maids Charmian and Iras,
makes 'death proud to take us', she can still revert to her old self in
her conscious acting with Octavius, and in the petty deception that
her treasurer discloses. These things pass. All the while she remembers
Antony:

For his bounty
There was no winter in 't; an autumn 'twas
That grew the more by reaping. His delights
Were dolphin-like; they show'd his back above
The element they liv'd in. In his livery
Walk'd crowns and crownets; realms and islands were
As plates dropp'd from his pocket. (V, ii, 86–92)

At length: 'I am again for Cydnus/To meet Mark Antony.' There
follows the passage – in the theatre an anxiety – with the countryman
who brings the poisonous asps from the banks of Nile. By then an
audience is so wrought that laughter breaks easily, and the peasant
with his iteration of 'worm' – eight times in eight speeches – will save
it only by holding the intensity and refusing any indulgences of a
character-comedian. The part asks for the eerie whisper of George
Hayes, one of the few inspirations of the Komisarjevsky revival.
When the man has gone, Cleopatra is ready: 'I am fire and air;
my other elements/I give to baser life.' As she fades into death ('Dost
thou not see my baby at my breast/That sucks the nurse asleep?')
Charmian rises in farewell:

Now boast thee, death, in thy possession lies
A lass unparallel'd. Downy windows, close;
And golden Phoebus never be beheld

> Of eyes again so royal! Your crown's awry;
> I'll mend it and then play— (V, ii, 313–17)

At once she does so; Iras has already died of a broken heart. And Caesar, entering, salutes the Queen: 'She looks like sleep,/As she would catch another Antony/In her strong toil of grace.'

IV

I have concentrated on the fifth act because what's past is prologue to these great events. As the play lingers in the Alexandrian palace, Cleopatra releases every emotion: mark only the anger, cajolery, and vanity in the Messenger scene. Antony leaves her, returns, and is lost; and Octavius, forbiddingly cold in wrath as in policy, remains the marble pillar that will be Imperial Rome. Famous passages come upon us unawares. It can astonish when Enobarbus, who is matter-of-fact now – the day of the isolated purple patch is over – says quietly: 'I will tell you,' and begins the Barge speech that Shakespeare transmuted from the prose of North's Plutarch:

> For her own person,
> It beggar'd all description. (II, ii, 201–2)

With no warning, as Antony's fortunes fail, there is a brief wonder in the still, glimmering midnight of Alexandria. Soldiers of the guard, waiting for tomorrow's battle which will 'determine one way', hear ghostly music:

2ND SOLDIER: Hark!
3RD SOLDIER: Music i'th'air.
4TH SOLDIER: Under the earth.
5TH SOLDIER: It signs well, does it not?
4TH SOLDIER: No.
3RD SOLDIER: Peace, I say!
2ND SOLDIER: 'Tis the god Hercules, whom Antony lov'd,
        Now leaves him. (IV, iii, 13–17)

Enobarbus, who leaves his Antony as the god Hercules does, is the blunt man who, like other blunt men, can flower into unaccustomed eloquence. He forsakes his loyalty in a tragic end ('A master-leaver and a fugitive') when Antony's quick forgiveness has overpowered him. Randle Ayrton acted him so staunchly at Stratford in 1931 that other performances have seemed to be unfinished. Several small parts come and go, and a few (like Lepidus, the weakling of the triumvirate), have character.

Three, beyond others, exist for me. One is Eros, whose crowning loyalty is in his suicide ('Thus do I escape the sorrow/Of Antony's death'). Another is Euphronius, Antony's schoolmaster. Sent as envoy to Caesar, he announces himself unforgettably in lines that, as often as not, are cut:

> Such as I am, I come from Antony.
> I was of late as petty to his ends
> As is the morn-dew on the myrtle-leaf
> To his grand sea. (III, xii, 7–10)

Certain post-war revivals have run the smaller people together in what the writer, Arthur Machen, who was an Old Bensonian, once called 'conglomerate or pudding-stone parts': Philo Canidius, Scarus Dercetas, Alexas Diomedes, Euphronius Lamprius. The last (St James's, 1951; Old Vic, 1957) is a false partnership because Lamprius is the Soothsayer who has nothing whatever in common with Euphronius of the 'morn-dew on the myrtle leaf'.

Finally, Cleopatra's second waiting-woman, Iras, ever-present, loving, usually silent. When she speaks in the last scene she puts the tragedy of Antony and Cleopatra into fourteen words:

> Finish, good lady; the bright day is done,
> And we are for the dark. (V, ii, 192–3)

NOTES

1 It irritates.
2 Elizabeth Spriggs was Cleopatra; Tony Steedman, Antony.
3 *Prefaces to Shakespeare: Second Series* (1930), pp. 121–2.
4 Charles Morgan said in *The Times* next morning (15 October 1936) that he heard 'O, wither'd is the garland of the war' as 'O weederdee degarlano devar.'
5 Bridges-Adams in a letter to the author.
6 *Sunday Times*, 17 October 1936.

Timon of Athens
(1607–8)

I

Probably this is the loneliest of the plays; in the theatre almost the
least popular: 'only an incident with comments on it', said William
Charles Macready, rejecting it for production at Drury Lane in 1840.
Performed more often than any of the *Henry VI* trilogy, or *Titus
Andronicus*, it is greeted as a rule only by collectors, though I have
met it in both Hungarian and French translations. In Budapest it
was staged irrelevantly under a circus tent; but in Paris, using the
decayed beauty of the Théâtre des Bouffes-du-Nord, Peter Brook
contrived an inventive variety of mood for a play often slow and
muscle-bound. In another poet's phrase, it was 'signed with
conflagration'.

On the page *Timon of Athens* offers some incandescent verse but
little drama. What there is, presumably suggested to Shakespeare
by paragraphs in North's Plutarch, could have been designed by
Jaques after a frigid winter in Arden. 'I am Misanthropos, and hate
mankind,' says Timon in a Wood near Athens that must be on the
other, and darker, side of the city from *A Midsummer Night's Dream*.
Efforts to modernise a production have commonly been misguided;
I do recall one of the Senators (in a revival from Stratford, Ontario,
brought to Chichester) undergoing massage and pedicure in a Turkish
bath. Some years before this, Sir Barry Jackson, most selfless of theatre
philanthropists, chose modern dress at the Birmingham Repertory,
hinting with a quick gleam of mischief that much in the play
reminded him of contemporary Birmingham; he had known, and
harshly, the frustrations of patronage. The afternoon lingers because
the then director of the National Theatre of Greece insisted mildly
that few hosts in contemporary Athens flung lukewarm water and
empty dishes at their guests.

The tragedy has had more than its share of frivolous criticism. Thus an American petroleum geologist, who claimed that Queen Elizabeth was Shakespeare, proposed *Timon of Athens* as her first play: after the Leicester marriage, it appears, she knew that 'her cure for grief was hard work'. More seriously, Shakespeare's *Timon of Athens* must have been bred of disappointment and disillusion. It is confidently asserted that what we have, written under stress, unfinished, and unrevised, was a manuscript thrust into the First Folio to fill a gap. Maybe; we have to take it as it moves ferociously into the theatre.

The key to its narrative is a line for Timon's faithful steward, Flavius: 'Bounty, that makes gods, does still mar men.' During the five acts which some call tragic, and others ironical and critical, we observe the fate of a noble Athenian flawed by his unselectively generous nature. On the stage a single-minded parable, it is overpeered by a cumulus cloud of language through which, again and again, the lightning strikes. Timon conducts himself with a princely air. When he says 'To Lacedaemon did my land extend', the words seem to reveal the country, fold upon fold, into a misty Hellenic distance. Then, for he is a man of extremes, the misanthrope absorbs the patron. He turns his back on Athens as Coriolanus upon Rome. His heart is stone: we realise that, as with Othello, if he strikes it now it will hurt his hand.

II

The cast numbers twenty-five or so, with extras. Timon aside, only the Athenian general, Alcibiades, Apemantus, 'a churlish philosopher', and Timon's unimpeachable Flavius have any personality on the page. Alcibiades deserves more credit (and, in the theatre, authority) than he often gets. The character may be incomplete. One speech to the Senate, begging for the life of a man condemned, is argued cogently, though its versification sounds like a draft:

I SENATOR: You cannot make gross sins look clear:
            To revenge is no valour, but to bear.
ALCIBIADES: My lords, then, under favour, pardon me
            If I speak like a captain:
            Why do fond men expose themselves to battle
            And not endure all threats? Sleep upon't,
            And let the foes quietly cut their throats
            Without repugnancy? If there be
            Such valour in the bearing, what make we

> Abroad? Why, then, women are more valiant,
> That stay at home, if bearing carry it;
> And the ass more captain than the lion; the fellow
> Loaden with irons wiser than the judge,
> If wisdom be in suffering. O my lords,
> As you are great, be pitifully good.
> Who cannot condemn rashness in cold blood?
> To kill, I grant, is sin's extremest gust;
> But, in defence, by mercy, 'tis most just.
> To be in anger is impiety;
> But who is man that is not angry?
> Weigh but the crime with this. (III, v, 48–58)

The man dies. Alcibiades lives; but who, may we ask, are Sempronius, Ventidius, and Caphis; Lucius, Servilius, Hortensius, and Hostilius? And what of that uncertain and rapidly dropped Fool? In performance we can get something from an affected aspen of a man, the 'glass-fac'd flatterer', Lord Lucullus. The only women, those greedy whores, Phrynia and Timandra – a careless echo-name – are trivial in text and theatre: dragged in for womankind to be mowed down in a few misanthropic bursts. Ivor Brown believed that Shakespeare had been 'reduced to anguish by some overwhelming personal experience in which a faithless woman had played a devastating part', but there is no evidence of this.

In the theatre we are wholly at a director's mercy. Tyrone Guthrie held that the Thersites-play satirised materialism, exposed the deceitfulness of riches. Others see it as, primarily, a condemnation of ingratitude, a sin Shakespeare through life abhorred. Timon tosses lukewarm water at the parasitic guests; his second-half speeches are boiling lava, the fury of a deceived benefactor. Both he and Alcibiades face Athenian ingratitude. Where Timon yields ('I am Misanthropos'), the general returns indomitably to conquer the Senate.

Still, it is one man's tragedy. Its beginning is easier: Timon in what he misinterprets as the blaze of noon – actually thunder and storm-light. Nothing troubles him in these hours when Fortune, as in attendant poet's allegory, beckons from her high and pleasant hill. We are warned at once what the 'glib and slippery creatures may do', yet Timon remains rapt in a kind of self-destructive philanthropic euphoria. Apemantus, a tiresome professional cynic, is about the place, 'discontentedly like himself' – or like Timon's conscience – to mutter that 'men shut their doors against a setting sun'. Never mind. There must be a lavish banquet, a masque of Cupid and the Amazons (not inevitably in a theatre script), and the flatterers' off-stage gifts of four milk-white horses trapp'd in silver, and two brace of greyhounds, before Flavius, as loyal to his master as Kent to Lear, discloses the truth:

FLAVIUS: Now's a time
           The greatness of your having lacks a half
           To pay your present debts.
TIMON: Let all my land be sold.
FLAVIUS: 'Tis all engag'd, some forfeited and gone;
           And what remains will hardly stop the mouth
           Of present dues . . .
TIMON: To Lacedaemon did my land extend.
FLAVIUS: O, my good lord, the world is but a word;
           Were it all yours to give it in a breath,
           How quickly were it gone!
TIMON: You tell me true. (II, ii, 144–55)

We know what must follow – the turning of the sycophants upon their patron, an exercise that can be tedious when only occasional lines glint:

     He ne'er drinks
But Timon's silver treads upon his lip (III, ii, 69–70)

and

  'Tis deepest winter in Lord Timon's purse;
  That is, one may reach deep enough and yet
  Find little. (III, iv, 15–17)

One sentence for Flavius keeps the mind:

  I have retir'd me to a wasteful cock
  And set mine eyes at flow. (II, ii, 163–4)

Long considered to be a crux, editors toyed with such an alternative as 'wakeful couch'. It is accepted now that the speech refers to a flowing barrel of wine of which the tap has not been turned off. Interleaved with these scenes is the political conflict in which Alcibiades is exiled from Athens; his time will come. In the scene where Timon banquets his false friends on what they imagine to be 'royal cheer', actor and director have at length a chance. Presently a new Timon, the second half of the double character, begins under the Athenian wall the commination service, the cry of hate, that might be engraved upon asbestos. Or we can say that the play here is like a spring that, having been drawn to fullest length, starts to recoil fiercely along its course.

It is unwise to exaggerate the parasites at the banquet. To present them, as Guthrie did at the Old Vic (1952), as a covey of harried grotesques, is ruinous: we do not look for pantomime comedy, a dish-cover on that man's head, this man's girdle about his ankles. The more serious it is, the more violent the impact of Timon's wrath. In a soliloquy of forty lines he scorches Athens. Then:

> Timon will to the woods, where he shall find
> Th' unkindest beast more kinder than mankind.
> The gods confound – hear me, you good gods all –
> The Athenians both within and out that wall!
> And grant, as Timon grows, his hate may grow
> To the whole race of mankind, high and low!
> Amen. (IV, i, 35–41)

III

The remainder of the play is in the Athenian woods. As listeners and spectators we can only hope. Guthrie decided to establish Timon not in a cave but in a form of burrow, a trap in the stage from which he rose from time to time like a distraught golfer sorely bunkered. I have yet to find a production that, at one notable passage, answers the cue of Edmund Kean's performance in 1816, as Leigh Hunt described it:

'The finest scene in the whole performance was the one with Alcibiades. We never remember the force of contrast to have been more truly pathetic. Timon, digging in the woods with his spade, hears the approach of military music . . . Kean started, listened, and leaned in a fixed and angry manner on his spade with frowning eyes, and lips full of the truest feeling, compressed but not too much so; he seemed not to be deceived, even by the charm of a thing inanimate; the audience were silent; the march threw forth its gallant note nearer and nearer; the Athenian standards appear, then the soldiers come treading on the scene with that air of confident progress which is produced by the accompaniment of music; and at last, while the squalid misanthrope still maintains his posture and keeps his back to the strangers, in steps the young and splendid Alcibiades in the flush of victorious expectation. It is the encounter of hope with despair'.[1]

The last scenes are like a variation on a mood of *Lear*: now and then 'a terrible beauty is born'. True, the vituperation can be more bearable to read; on the stage monotony can supervene, even though lit by phrases that endure when the cursing is still:

> embalms and spices
> To th'April day again (IV, iii, 40-1)

> Will these moist trees,
> That have outliv'd the eagle, page thy heels
> And skip when thou point'st out? (IV, iii, 222-4)

(Here the speaker is Apemantus.)

> Lie where the light foam of the sea may beat
> Thy gravestone daily (IV, iii, 376-7)

> Behold, the earth hath roots;
> Within this mile break forth a hundred springs;
> The oaks bear mast, the briars scarlet hips (IV, iii, 415-17)

> The sea's a thief, whose liquid surge resolves
> The moon into salt tears. (IV, iii, 437-8)

Timon's opening speech in the woods contains the phrase:

> It is the pasture lards the rother's sides,
> The want that makes him lean. (IV, ii, 12-13)

'Rother' is an ox; one of the open spaces in Stratford-upon-Avon is the Rother Market. It was odd that in 1966, at the Royal Shakespeare of all theatres, the word was changed in the acting text to 'wether'. Possibly the director was unsatisfied with a famous emendation of the Folio line ('It is the Pastour, Lards the Brothers sides'): if so, he chose the wrong place to express it.

Ironically, Timon discovers gold in the cave where he lives and will die. Nothing can placate him. The treasure he gives to a procession of visitors, bandits, and Senators, painter and poet, Alcibiades and the women. Alcibiades returns to subdue Athens. News arrives that Timon is dead. In his final speech we have heard him say, as Paul Scofield did superbly in his rifted voice[2]:

> Timon hath made his everlasting mansion
> Upon the beachèd verge of the salt flood,

Who once a day with his embossed froth
The turbulent surge shall cover. (V, i, 213–16)

In Shakespeare's mind, as Robert Speaight once observed to me, the
sea was likelier to have been the Channel than the tideless
Mediterranean.

For such lines as those we must value the tragedy. Now and then,
upon our stage, such a man as Scofield can join the halves of the
character and keep 'the light foam of the sea' or 'the turbulent
surge' actively in our remembrance. Timon can never respond to an
oleographic artist who wants only a visual pomp. If we cry 'O, hollow,
hollow, hollow!' the night is finished: Timon must crumble in marble,
not flake in plaster. Moreover, round him the play cannot be allowed
to creep; to drag the feet is fatal. That said, I think that some of the
angrier reviewers on the least fruitful occasion might ponder the final
speech of Alcibiades:

> Dead
> Is noble Timon, of whose memory
> Hereafter more. Bring me into your city,
> And I will use the olive, with my sword (V, iv, 79–82)

NOTES

1 *The Examiner* (4 November 1816) reprinted in *Leigh Hunt's Dramatic Criticism 1808–
  1831*, ed. L. H. and C. W. Houtchens (1949), pp. 134–9; also in *Theatre Bedside
  Book* (1974).
2 Stratford, 1966.

Coriolanus (1607–8)

I

Early in this Roman play (which, on the whole, Granville-Barker thinks should be pronounced 'Corry-o-lanus'), the unreconcilable First Citizen, one of the 'mutable, rank-scented many' with staves and clubs, and some cause for rage, says of Caius Marcius and 'what he hath done famously':

> Though soft-conscienc'd men can be content to say
> it was for his country, he did it to please his mother . . . (I, i, 34–7)

In these words, so often passed over during the clamour of an opening crowd scene, the later tragedy is compressed. Always the phrase must be linked with Caius Marcius Coriolanus's 'But for your son . . . most dangerously you have with him prevail'd' when the Supplication is over. Here is the man Volumnia bred ('To a cruel war I sent him, from which he return'd, his brows bound with oak'). Here is the father of a child content to 'mammock' the gilded butterfly. Here is the scourge of the common people. He is brave and he is honest: 'What his heart forges, that his tongue must vent.' Menenius says of him:

> He has been bred i'th' wars
> Since 'a could draw a sword, and is ill-school'd
> In bolted language . . . (III, i, 320–1)

('Bolted' is 'refined'.) He is also, fatally, his mother's son. In the theatre this man, at the heart of all, might be intolerable without the bounty of the late-Shakespearian phrase; in *Coriolanus* it can be harsh, though it can also glide suddenly into such lines as the salute to Valeria:

The moon of Rome, chaste as the icicle
That's curdied by the frost from purest snow,
And hangs on Dian's temple – dear Valeria! (V, iii, 64–7)

Often, and unaccountably, the salute is cut; playgoers should listen for it early in what modern editions call the third scene of the fifth act.

Even if he can speak the verse, an actor must have a harder time with Coriolanus than with most of the other heroes or anti-heroes. ('Not worth a damn,' said the disappointed Henry Irving, who was cast so wrongly.) The obdurate autocrat, the egoist, the noisy, petulant child, protagonist of what Masefield calls 'the clash of the aristocratic temper with the world', does not fix our sympathy until late in the play. While we detest his enemies, those steam-jets of bitterness, the opportunist tribunes of the people, we see that what is happening is largely his own fault. To win us in the theatre he should have the power of a burning-glass; ideally he could be charged with arson. When we find such an actor as this our prejudices do flake away. Though we may not often be fortunate, and though without a supreme Coriolanus the tragedy can be in complex trouble, there is still a great deal to observe. When Menenius is pleading to the tribunes, one of them grinds out indignantly: 'This is clean kam.' The phrase means 'cock-eyed' or 'crooked', and I would use it for any suggestion that the play is unexciting; better to look hopefully to another few words, 'a shower and thunder . . . I never saw the like'. Of all the tragedies, it must not be too fluently presented and spoken: the stream – rather too small a word – should never appear to slip easily over the river-bed.

II

A director has at once to consider his crowd, even more important than in *Julius Caesar*. Half a dozen actors with dubious beards are not enough, and the noise has to be genuine. O. B. Clarence, the Bensonian actor, recalled[1] how when Arthur Machen, a writer then, joined the company, he would stand on the edges of the crowd, muttering mildly: 'Down with him! Distinctly traitor! Yes, an impossible fellow!'

We can miss at first what the crowd is shouting about. After all, it is by no means easy. Leaders of modern demonstrations are seldom heard to cry, at the pitch of their voices: 'The leanness that afflicts us, the object of our misery, is as an inventory to particularise their abundance; our sufferance is a gain to them.' Moreover, the opening

does demand a forcible Menenius Agrippa; we have to listen to the
old man's apologue of the Belly and its Members, taken from
Plutarch, and it is not really a compulsive fable. Then Caius
Marcius enters with the injudicious greeting:

> What's the matter, you dissentious rogues
> That, rubbing the poor itch of your opinion,
> Make yourselves scabs? (I, i, 162–4)

'We have ever your good word', exclaims the First Citizen; and in
that exchange, too, the play is summarised. It is customary now, as
in the days of John Philip Kemble, noblest Roman, for the crowd
to flinch back at the sight of Marcius. Warrior of the oaken garland,
twenty-seven times wounded, he is also the most disdainful of men;
the critic, A. V. Cookman, called it a 'pig-headed splendour'.[2]

This is a tragedy that has invited simplification, the modern search
for relevance. Hence directors' pleasure in translating it into a limbo
of trades unions, demagogic officials, and scenes that might be re-
ported in a morning newspaper. It can be a worrying approach.
Emphasis on politics is generally tedious in the theatre; we have
never enjoyed them as the French (*Coriolanus* has been explosive
material in Paris) and the Germans do. Even so, the play has been
labelled through the centuries: see Nahum Tate's dire Restoration
treatment, *The Ingratitude of a Commonwealth*. *Coriolanus* is the tragedy
of one man, a hot-tempered egoist, but we have had any number of
curiosities. Thus Tyrone Guthrie, at the opening of the new
Nottingham Playhouse (December 1963), chose costumes of the
French First Empire for a revival that – among other things –
examined what a programme-note called 'the love-hate between
Coriolanus and Aufidius; the hysterical and homosexual element
which seems so usual and powerful an ingredient in the composition
of intensely vigorous men of action'.

The problem in the theatre is to play fair: not to be whirled
off by theories; to exaggerate neither the aspect of the mob, all hair
and sackcloth, nor the tribunes of the Left whose speeches are jags
from a rusty blade; and to keep some humanity in the Roman
matriarch, Volumnia Victrix (Swinburne's name for her) – one
early nineteenth-century actress 'stepped about with her head thrown
half a yard back as if she had a contempt for her own chin'.
Volumnia has a high dignity that cannot be minimised, and it is not
simply that of a Lady Bracknell carrying her thunderbolts in a hand-
bag. She does stand for eternal Rome, albeit a conquering and des-
tructive Rome. Virgilia, wife of Coriolanus, is not much more than
'my gracious silence' (though we do not like Volumnia when she

mocks a 'faint puling'). Valeria is much more of a personage. Her amusing gossip has to be expended in one of the few private scenes in this very public play: 'You would be another Penelope,' she tells Virgilia, 'yet they say, all the yarn she spun in Ulysses' absence did but fill Ithaca full of moths.' Good; but silent though she is thereafter, the 'noble sister of Publicola' cannot be dismissed as an incidental wit.

For that matter, the far more important Menenius Agrippa, self-described as 'a humorous patrician . . . one that loves a cup of hot wine with not a drop of allaying Tiber in it', is not just a synthetic 'character', mouthing, rubious, and rheumatic. He is as much a professional of the right as the people's tribunes are of the left. Hardly maybe the 'noble fellow' that one of the guards calls him as he leaves the inflexible presence in the Volscian camp, he is loving and courageous, he has a silver scorn, and he should not be undervalued in performance.

III

Indeed, the sharpest production of *Coriolanus* will come straight from the text, with no efforts to explain more than Shakespeare does himself. The first half is the danger: a director has to present plausibly the sway of battle in and round Corioli and the passage when Marcius is shut within the city gates and apparently repels an entire army. Again and again, what the Jacobeans accepted easily on the platform stage of the Globe has been a chaotic affair of noise and smoke. '*Enter the Army of the Volsces.*' '*Alarum. The Romans are beat back to their trenches.*' '*Marcius is shut in.*' '*Enter Marcius bleeding, assaulted by the enemy.*' It does work out; and Marcius is honoured. Playgoers had better take the battle as it comes. There should be at least some effort at realism. When Iden Payne was in difficulty while grappling with these scenes at Stratford in 1939, he had a habit of crying 'Stylise!' – advice that Alec Clunes, the Coriolanus, found unhelpful. 'What could I do,' he said,[3] 'while left without a soldier to support me while I hurled defiance at the Volsces?'

A small final scene snatches at the imagination. As victor of Corioli, Marcius refuses princely gifts but begs the freedom of a poor Volsce, now a Roman prisoner, who had befriended him. 'O well begged!' the general, Cominius, replies:

> Were he the butcher of my son, he should
> Be free as is the wind. Deliver him, Titus.

TITUS LARTIUS: Marcius, his name?

There is a pause. Slowly Coriolanus answers:

> By Jupiter, forgot!
> I am weary; yea, my memory is tir'd.
> Have we no wine here? (I, ix, 88–92)

The Volscian's fate we cannot know. The play's rising tide hides the scene and swells again towards a distant shore.

The thirty lines or so, immediately following, for the Volscian Tullus Aufidius ('Enter bloody') and a few soldiers can be unwisely thrown away; I once saw it pushed away upstage in a melodramatic dull greenish glow. Yet it is a scene to mark, for Aufidius is vowing the fiercest vengeance on Marcius ('Five times I have fought with thee': at Antium he makes it 'twelve several times', but no matter), and he goes on:

> Nor sleep nor sanctuary,
> Being naked, sick, nor fane nor Capitol,
> The prayers of priests nor times of sacrifice,
> Embarquements all of fury, shall lift up
> Their rotten privilege and custom 'gainst
> My hate to Marcius. Where I find him, were it
> At home, upon my brother's guard, even there,
> Against the hospitable canon, would I
> Wash my fierce hand in 's heart. (I, x, 19–27)

It was upon this speech, and on that later at Antium, after Coriolanus has disclosed himself,[4] that Guthrie based his love-hate theory. 'Let me,' cries Aufidius;

> Let me twine
> Mine arms about that body, where against
> My grained ash an hundred times hath broke,
> And scarr'd the moon with splinters. Here I clip
> The anvil of my sword, and do contest
> As hotly and as nobly with thy love
> As ever in ambitious strength I did
> Contest against thy valour. Know thou first,
> I lov'd the maid I married; never man
> Sigh'd truer breath; but that I see thee here,
> Thou noble thing, more dances my rapt heart
> Than when I first my wedded mistress saw
> Bestride my threshold (IV, v, 106–18)

In any event, it is a grand theatrical outburst. Aufidius, with a part less than one-third the length of Coriolanus, cannot be weakly cast: I have not forgotten the young Albert Finney (Birmingham Repertory, 1956) as he waited, a lithe, dangerous cat, poised ready to spring, with a prismatic sky, fire in the clouds, behind him.

IV

Earlier, when Coriolanus stands for Consul and is driven from Rome by mob law, we have to watch for such lines as Volumnia's couplet, so typical of the play's craggy diction:

> Death, that dark spirit, in 's nervy arm doth lie,
> Which, being advanced, declines, and then men die. (II, i, 151–2)

and the tributary speech of Cominius with its strangely compelling rhythm (even though Ben Jonson disliked the last line):

> He prov'd best man i'th' field, and for his meed
> Was brow-bound with the oak. His pupil age
> Man-ent'red thus, he waxed like a sea,
> And in the brunt of seventeen battles since
> He lurch'd all swords of the garland. (II, ii, 95–9)

We look for 'points', as the old actors termed them, at the end of the scene in which Coriolanus, urged to humility when he reaches the Forum, leaves with the flint-flashed snap, 'The word is *mildly*' (Olivier turning on his heel; Old Vic, 1938); the invective of

> You common cry of curs, whose breath I hate
> As reek o'th' rotten fens (III, iii, 122–3)

and the massive exit on

> Thus I turn my back;
> There is a world elsewhere. (III, iii, 136–7)

Presently, at the city gate, we catch the repetition of a word, a common occurrence when a dramatist is writing fast, and Shakespeare must have been doing so:

> Like to a lonely dragon, that his *fen*
> Makes fear'd and talk'd of more than seen. (IV, i, 30–1)

Hard upon this, and after the little street scene where Volumnia (lamenting 'in anger, – Juno-like', a clear direction to any player) comes back with Virgilia and Menenius, we reach what is now a familiar break in performance. Most probably, the play will restart at the appearance of Coriolanus 'in mean apparel, disguised and muffled', before the lighted doorway of Aufidius's house in Antium. Collectors hope, without confidence, for the dialogue that should precede this, something that Granville-Barker called 'a marginal passage of cheerful trading in the ignoble' on a highway between Rome and Antium. There a Roman fifth-columnist, Nicanor, meets the Volsce, Adrian, and they prepare for much interchange of news (not all of it accurate) and supper at the end.

Coriolanus, at Antium, has one of his rare breaks into soliloquy. Though he seldom talks to himself, everybody is ready to discuss him at some length. Normally we lose the talk of the Volscian servants after the generals have met: another unfortunate cut, but this is the fifth longest of the plays.

Once Coriolanus is reconciled to Aufidius, which will not be for long, for the Volsce is a subtle politician with the future in his eyes, we move rapidly to the advance on Rome and to the chaos in the city. On the way there is Aufidius's magnificent speech[5] to a lieutenant in which he says of Coriolanus:

> I think he'll be to Rome
> As is the osprey to the fish, who takes it
> By sovereignty of nature. (IV, vii, 33–5)

V

Earlier I spoke meagrely of the action as a 'stream'. But, as it nears the Supplication, *Coriolanus* rolls forward with the compulsion and majesty of a slow-pouring wave – a comber that finds its crest during the Volumnia scene and shatters upon the marbled shore during the last brag among the Volscians.

When Cominius has brought tidings that

> he does sit in gold, his eye
> Red as 'twould burn Rome, and his injury
> The gaoler to his pity. (V, i, 63–5)

and even Menenius has failed to woo his 'son' to forgiveness, all is set for the Supplication, the three black-robed women (in 'mourning habits'), and Aufidius and the Volsces standing by, watchful and speechless, while Coriolanus meets his last challenge. Volumnia's plea is a driven passion that, until 'Down, ladies: let us shame him with our knees', no gesture should disturb. Twice she utters the great monosyllable, 'Rome', the name that, as if beaten out in bronze, sounds in the play about sixty times. At the words,

> I am hush'd until our city be afire,
> And then I'll speak a little . . . (V, iii, 181–2)

there is, while Coriolanus holds her by the hand, as long and tense a silence as the players can dare. Then:

> O, mother, mother!
> What have you done? (V, iii, 182–3)

and the slow tolling of

> You have won a happy victory to Rome;
> But for your son – believe it, O believe it! –
> Most dangerously you have with him prevail'd,
> If not most mortal to him. (V, iii, 186–9)

North's version of Plutarch, upon which, with several variations, Shakespeare framed the tragedy, put it like this: 'O mother . . . you have wonne a happy victorie for your countrie, but mortall and unhappy for your sonne: for I see myself vanquished by you alone.'

When Coriolanus turns to Aufidius, with the last almost beseeching repetition of the name,

> Were you in my stead, would you have heard
> A mother less, or granted less, Aufidius? (V, iii, 192–3)

we listen for the tone of the reply, coldly impersonal: 'I was mov'd withal.' The sun has set; Coriolanus must go, a rejected renegade, to Corioli and to the enfolding darkness through which rings the splendour of his last brag, prompted by the contemptuous 'boy of tears!' from Aufidius:

> 'Boy'! False hound!
> If you have writ your annals true, 'tis there,
> That, like an eagle in a dove-cote, I
> Flutter'd your Volscians in Corioli.
> Alone I did it. 'Boy'! (V, vi, 113–17)

A moment more, and after his last *fortissimo* he falls among the swords or, as we have sometimes known (Olivier, Stratford, 1959) leaps headlong to his death. Next, the chilling direction: '*Aufidius stands on his body.*' We do not forget this when the Volscian general says, all too glibly (after a Second Lord's perilously colloquial 'Let's make the best of it'):

> My rage is gone,
> And I am struck with sorrow . . . (V, vi, 147–8)

> . . . Though in this city he
> Hath widow'd and unchilded many a one,
> Which to this hour bewail the injury,
> Yet he shall have a noble memory. (V, vi, 151–4)

In this play, of all others, that is for the audience to decide. Herbert Farjeon was right, I think, when he said[6] that *Coriolanus*, carved from the imperishable rock of human nature, could as well be called *Strife* or *Loyalties*.

NOTES

1 *No Complaints* (1943).
2 *The Times*, 8 July 1959.
3 To the present author.
4 Coriolanus's 'Of all the men i'th'world/I would have 'voided thee' echoes Macbeth (V, viii, 4): 'Of all men else I have avoided thee.'
5 Towards the end of this speech we notice a reminiscence of *Romeo and Juliet*, though only in a proverbial saying: Benvolio's 'One fire drives out another's burning' echoed in Aufidius's 'One fire drives out one fire; one nail, one nail.'
6 *The Shakespearean Scene* (1949)

Pericles, Prince of Tyre
(1607–8)

Because, in my parents' Shakespeare, a snobbish editor had hidden
Pericles away at the end, beyond the glossary, it was one of the plays
I read first. The fact that it had been relegated as a non-Folio
outcast[1] meant nothing to me. Indeed, to a reader straight from the
long trail of the Arabian Nights, it seemed to be a reasonable, if
intermittently baffling, narrative; and grandly, at the age of 9, I
assumed that one day I would meet it in a theatre – whatever a
theatre was – and there all would be made clear. Whereupon twenty-
two years elapsed, more than in the text. During the interval I
learned that *Pericles* was seldom acted because of the incest-riddle of
Antioch in its first act and the brothel scene in its fourth. Today
both seem unimportant: *Pericles*, familiar now upon the stage, remains
a good rambling tale that reaches a deep and quiet beauty at the
reunion of Marina and her father, a scene still not fully valued.
Popularly for many years it was dismissed as a brothel-play;[2] and an
expertly performed revival at Her Majesty's in 1974 emphasised this
with superfluous enthusiasm by using the establishment at Mytilene
as a permanent set.

Presumably the first and fourth acts were why Ben Jonson, in some
of his most peevish verses, threw out *Pericles* as 'a mouldy tale'. It has
delighted disintegrators: those who, faced anywhere with a suggestion
of joint authorship, give the best passages to Shakespeare and the
worst to some half-wit Hand B. Here the problems are nearly insoluble; but Professor Philip Edwards has suggested,[3] most persuasively, that the text we have (deriving from an edition in 1609) is
the work of two 'pirate' reporters. One, the feebler, rewrote the first
two acts 'in humdrum verse'; the second gave 'an incomplete
rendering of the original language'. Though Professor Edwards does

not believe that the whole of the original play as acted was Shakespeare's, he does think that the design indicates conception by a single mind; and he adds: 'The comparison with *The Winter's Tale* and *The Tempest* leaves me in no doubt whatsoever that that mind was Shakespeare's.' Alas, the authentic text is not recoverable.

II

As we have it – and other opinion proposes Shakespeare's revision of a piece by a brisk hack, George Wilkins – *Pericles, Prince of Tyre* is a Levantine tour, set dispersedly in many countries and unafraid of the romantic marvel. A 'field of stars' hangs in the violet night above Antioch. We are taken to Tyre, to Tharsus, to Pentapolis, to the stormy Mediterranean, to Mytilene, and to Ephesus. Pericles, shipwrecked, 'enters, wet'. He wins a king's daughter. Later, on shipboard, he calls imperiously upon 'thou god of this great vast':

>   Rebuke these surges,
> Which wash both heaven and hell; and thou that hast
> Upon the winds command, bind them in brass,
> Having call'd them from the deep! O, still
> Thy deaf'ning dreadful thunders; gently quench
> Thy nimble sulphurous flashes! (III, i, 1–6)

A princess rises, alive, from a sea-borne casket driven to land in a pelting storm. Towards the end, as the sky above Mytilene streams with celestial light, we hear Diana, queen and huntress, 'goddess argentine', calling on Pericles to 'do upon mine altar sacrifice'.

The first and second acts, beginning with the black riddle of Antioch, straggle wildly, though certain lines can glint like mica in a pebble:

>   The blind mole casts
> Copp'd hills towards heaven, to tell the earth is throng'd
> By man's oppression, and the poor worm doth die for 't.
>   (I, i, 100–2)

> Why should this change of thoughts,
> The sad companion, dull-ey'd melancholy,
> Be my so us'd a guest as not an hour
> In the day's glorious walk, or peaceful night,
> The tomb where grief should sleep, can breed me quiet?
>   (I, ii, 1–5)

Yet cease your ire, you angry stars of heaven!
Wind, rain, and thunder, remember earthly man
Is but a substance that must yield to you. (II, i, 1–5)

Apparently so haphazard in the text, the piece can keep its hearers
locked. It is absorbing make-believe, a narrative that insists upon
being heard out. Some of the early writing is patently absurd:

All poverty was scorn'd, and pride so great
The name of help grew odious to repeat (I, iv, 30–31)

and yet this did not sound at all ridiculous when Cecil Ramage, as
Cleon, governor of famine-ridden Tharsus, spoke it to his wife Dionyza
(Cathleen Nesbitt) on a turfy bank in Regent's Park during the hot
summer of 1939. There are other crudities in the same scene; but
the night proved that imaginative acting can make one believe in
anything; it can offer the sense and the spirit. From that production,
too, I recall the command of Wilfred Walter's Antiochus when he
showed to Pericles in the first scene the lost princes, 'drawn by
report, advent'rous by desire', who

Tell thee, with speechless tongues and semblance pale,
That, without covering, save yon field of stars,
Here they stand martyrs, slain in Cupid's wars. (I, i, 36–8)

Poor verse; but the speaking is what matters, and at least the dramatist
is pressing on with his story – in these cynical days, I suppose, the
worst of invitations to the play.

A play or a novel, riddled with faults, may still insist on being
heard for the fable's sake. *Pericles* might almost have been written as a
serial. The Prince of Tyre has escaped from Antioch. Thaliard
pursues him with (curiously) a pistol. What will happen in tomorrow's palpitating instalment? Forward to the eve of the jousting,
the end of the shipboard scene, the capture of Marina, the vision of
Diana ('Awake and tell thy dream'). It is a set of romantic effects,
episodes to be continued in our next: we are not startled when
Thaisa, after being thrown, coffined, to the 'humming water' – a phrase
that has stuck with me since I read *Pericles* on that winter night by the
southern Cornish sea – is restored within possibly three minutes by a
noble miracle-worker, Cerimon of Ephesus:

The fire and cloths,
The rough and woeful music that we have,
Cause it to sound, beseech you.
The vial once more . . . (III, ii, 92–5)

III

We have for this play the affection we give to a fractious child. Marina we love for her own sake. She has 'as chiding a nativity/ As fire, air, water, earth, and heaven, can make'. As a 14-year-old girl she has to know the griefs of Mytilene before reunion with her parents in Diana's temple. The brothel passages of the fourth act may be disfiguring in the text; played without fuss they have in the theatre a quality strangely touching. Marina shines, an unsmutch'd lily, among the rank weeds. She strews the play with flowers, 'the yellows, blues, the purple violets, and marigolds'. No one will question the artifice of the recognition scenes. What stay with us are the words of Pericles when he looks on his recovered daughter, still unknown to him:

> Thou dost look
> Like Patience gazing on kings' graves, and smiling
> Extremity out of act (V, i, 136–8)

and, later:

> Put me to present pain,
> Lest this great sea of joys rushing upon me
> O'erbear the shores of my mortality,
> And drown me with their sweetness. O, come hither,
> Thou that beget'st him that did thee beget;
> Thou that wast born at sea, buried at Tharsus,
> And found at sea again! (V, i, 190–6)

Marina, too, when the scene begins:

> I am a maid
> My lord, that ne'er before invited eyes,
> But have been gaz'd on like a comet. She speaks,
> My lord, that, may be, hath endur'd a grief
> Might equal yours, if both were justly weigh'd.
> Though wayward fortune did malign my state,
> My derivation was from ancestors
> Who stood equivalent with mighty kings;
> But time hath rooted out my parentage,
> And to the world and awkward casualties
> Bound me in servitude. (V, i, 83–93)

In performance it will be only ten minutes before Thaisa,[4] Marina's mother and Diana's priestess, is crying 'O, my lord, are you not Pericles?' and, to Marina, 'Blest and mine own!'

Pericles was written by an actor for actors; in the swift traffic of the stage we are less conscious than we should be of smudged authorship (Wilkins or Hand B). Samuel Phelps, at Sadler's Wells in 1854, was the first manager to bring back most of the Shakespearian text, fairly free from clumsy adaptation, though he did jettison the Gower chorus, inserted explanatory passages, and made the Bawd into 'an old woman of the town'. He spent £3,000, a good sum at the time, on a production that is remembered now for the advancing and ebbing of the waves on the shore at Pentapolis, and for a sliding panorama behind the vessel of Pericles on the journey towards Ephesus. William Charles Macready, who had retired by then, might have heard wryly of Phelps's success. Writing in his journal twenty years earlier (26 April 1834) he had noted: 'An author called with a version of *Pericles*, which I very courteously persuaded him I could not assist by my influence.' I have often thought of the craggily stern tragedian restraining his impatience with a conscious effort. We can guess what he would have said, had he known of it, of John Coleman's Stratford production in 1900.

Coleman was the kind of amiable, leathery old actor who said once to a super at the rehearsal of another play: 'My dear sir, when you ascend the raking piece and leave the stage, be good enough to emit a greasy laugh of truculent defiance.' He became obsessed by *Pericles*, its brine and cloudy billow, its coffin thrown overboard, its romantic plumage; everything except the first scene and the fourth act which he could easily transform in lamentable *Sign of the Cross* verbiage. 'Fortified', he said, 'by the many eminent authorities who subscribe to his opinion as to Shakespeare's actual share in the authorship of this play, the writer has not hesitated to expunge the first act, to eradicate the banality of the second, to omit the irrelevant Gower chorus, and altogether to eliminate the obscenity of the fourth act.' Vaguely, Frank Benson, who was occupied with a London season at the Lyceum, let Coleman have his head at the Stratford Festival, and the result of the expunging, eradication, omission, and elimination, with the old man appearing himself as Pericles, created general dismay. W. H. Hutton, in *Literature* (April 1900), spoke of 'tragic bungling', quoted some of Coleman's additions ('the foaming juice of the purple grape' and 'Thou art a stranger in these parts'), and lamented that Marina, 'whose every word was beautiful, is a miracle now of tedium and contempt'.

Inevitably, such a production as this damaged the chances of *Pericles* for many years. Robert Atkins did it twice, at the Old Vic (1921), in the simplest of black draperies and white columns, and at

the Open Air Theatre in the sultry midsummer of 1939 when Robert
Eddison, with his lyric voice and bearing, sailed round the Levant.
Sir Barry Jackson restored it to Stratford in 1947; Nugent Monck,
cutting the first act, reduced the playing time to 100 minutes. Eight
years later, at the Birmingham Repertory, Richard Pasco gave his own
glow to Pericles, and Bernard Hepton half spoke, half chanted, the
chorus couplets for ancient Gower (John Gower, the poet, who
had adapted the old tale in his *Confessio Amantis*). John Harrison, not
long before, had staged *Pericles* uncut, for two Sunday night performances at a remote London theatre where Paul Scofield could
extend his Stratford performance to full length, and one actress,
Daphne Slater, doubled mother and daughter, as tempting though
ultimately as difficult as doubling Hermione and Perdita in *The
Winter's Tale*. Mary Morris, fantastically dressed, was Gower, a part
that has always bothered directors. At Stratford in 1958 he became
a coloured sailor, a calypso man whose song encouraged the rowers
of the Prince's vessel but practically blotted out his exposition, and in
1969 he was a Welsh-accented bard. Although the last production
did theorise about neo-Platonic allegories – what would this have
meant to Hand B? – it was fortunate in Ian Richardson, one of the
country's major verse-speakers, who in the reunion looked as if he had
come from a mosaic in the cathedral of Torcello. Marina and
Thaisa were doubled; so again, in observing the ingenuity, emotion
faded:

MARINA: My heart
Leaps to be gone into my mother's bosom
                              (Kneels to Thaisa)
PERICLES: Look who kneels here! Flesh of thy flesh, Thaisa;
Thy burden at the sea, and call'd Marina,
For she was yielded there.
THAISA: Blest and mine own! (V, iii, 45–9)

IV

However the play is staged, a director should leave this fifth act alone:
recognition, vision, reunion, all enclosed in Thaisa's

     O, my lord,
Are you not Pericles? Like him you spake.
Like him you are. Did you not name a tempest,
A birth and death? (V, iii, 32-5)

So far, in the theatre, *Pericles* has very little traditional business. We cannot say what Gower will do with his couplets, archaic octo-syllabics, which are a mixture of the bare – 'Till fortune, tired with doing bad,/Threw him ashore, to give him glad' (II, Chorus, 37–8) – and the evocative:

> The cat, with eyne of burning coal,
> Now couches 'fore the mouse's hole;
> And crickets sing at the oven's mouth,
> Aye the blither for their drouth. (III, Chorus, 5–8)

The procession of the jousting knights before Simonides is sometimes curtailed; so, also, is the scene between Helicanus and the Lords of Tyre. Normally, we have the last three acts in full. In Act Three the clamour of the storm fades to the tranquility of the scene in which Cerimon – and it would be pleasant to think of this as Shakespeare's tribute to his son-in-law, Dr Hall – revives the coffined Thaisa. The ensuing melodrama of Dionyza (a first sketch for Cymbeline's Queen), Leonine, and the pirates, and the rough stuff of the brothel (directors must observe that there are no extraneous whores), simply prepare the way for the last act: tremulous recognition, discovery, joy upon joy, to which all that has passed has been a prelude.

Marina is one with Imogen, Perdita, and Miranda, and she must be our memory:

> My dearest wife was like this maid, and such a one
> My daughter might have been: my queen's square brows;
> Her stature to an inch; as wand-like straight;
> As silver voic'd; her eyes as jewel-like,
> And cas'd as richly; in pace another Juno;
> Who starves the ears she feeds, and makes them hungry
> The more she gives them speech. (V, i, 106–12)

NOTES

1 It did reach the second edition of the Third Folio in 1664.
2 Mary Lamb, in her version for *Lamb's Tales*, was agreeably tactful: 'The pirate who had made Marina his prize carried her to Mytilene and sold her for a slave, where, though in that humble condition, Marina soon became known through the whole city for her beauty and her virtues.'
3 New Penguin edition (1976).
4 Pronounced 'Ty – eesa'.

Cymbeline (1609)

I

For many of us, this late romance, which might equally have been called *Imogen, Princess of Britain,* is like the song ordered by Cloten as an aubade, a 'wonderful sweet air, with admirable rich words to it'. Yet, though Imogen (with that ecstatic cry, 'O, for a horse with wings!') has reason to be called the nonpareil of Shakespeare's women, the play, one of the final romances, is acted relatively seldom. It is the sort of fairy-tale, a tall story getting progressively taller, that in its indulgent confusion has no relevance to the twentieth century. Directors are coy about it; they will not be 'committed' to something that, like all the last plays, demands unequivocal belief, to be accepted for what it is, as a neo-romantic reader will take, say, Tolkien's *The Lord of the Rings.* No one can theorise about the apposition of skins and furs, Renaissance modes, and the Rome of Caesar Augustus. *Cymbeline* shuffles them together, and there is nothing else to be said.

The scene is, more or less, Lear's pagan Britain (which will not prevent its transference to nineteenth-century Turkey). The plot, briefly, is Snow White in collision with a few words from the Decameron. Its last act and the cumulative disclosures that so delighted Quiller-Couch – there are twenty-four dénouements in five hundred lines – must always be technically astonishing, even if in the theatre, as layer upon layer is peeled off, newcomers may lose their place. They have to receive each fresh explanation ('Guiderius had upon his neck a mole, a sanguine star') without asking too anxiously why. Fairy-tales are like that; and *Cymbeline* in essence is nothing more. Shaw's effort to improve it by rewriting the last act, with topical allusions to 1936,[1] is just capricious:

IMOGEN: Subtle Italian villain!
                 I would that chest had smothered you.
IACHIMO: Dear lady,
                 It very nearly did.

Today, *Cymbeline*, which would have flowered indoors, under the candelabra of the Blackfriars Theatre, as well as upon the open stage of the Globe, yields only to a director who keeps his head, and Shakespeare's, without faltering. I have known the play to be staged Brechtianly (and, it follows, disastrously), tongue-in-cheek; to be cut to rags; and to be overwhelmed with scenery. Though one director, using a number of isolated 'features' set beneath great oaks cast from Stratford trees, did try to meet the plot on its own terms, his belief in detail was perilously unselective. Ben Iden Payne did it at Stratford (1937) as a Jacobean court masque in a permanent architectural setting, Inigo Jones fashion; it was visually right, but, a few players aside – Joyce Bland, Wolfit, Baliol Holloway – Payne lacked the cast to fortify his ideas.

II

Twenty years before the play begins, the two sons of Cymbeline were stolen in infancy; we find later that Belarius, a banished lord, is bringing them up in a Welsh cave as his own children. By a previous marriage, the King's second wife has a dire son, Cloten, whom she wants to marry to her stepdaughter Imogen (could it have been ·Innogen? – we think of that spectral figure in *Much Ado*). But the girl is already married, without her father's consent, to a worthy gentleman, Posthumus Leonatus. The Queen contrives his banishment; he travels to Rome; and we go on from there. Shakespeare swoops into what Hamlet would call 'a dream of fiction': the play is intended for rapid performance, and it is fruitless to analyse it in the study, to ask whether A would have done this and B would have said that.

In the theatre, after twenty minutes or so, we meet Iachimo, 'slight thing' of Renaissance Italy, a dark spirit of the romantic imagination given to 'high-coloured harlequin phrases' (Granville-Barker). A villain for the leading man, he is, after Imogen, the play's most considerable figure, wildly out of tune with Cymbeline's Britain but an artist in deliberate Renaissance mischief. From the first we must be conscious of his swift, silky intelligence, his irony, and his purring pleasure. Far less evil than Iago, he has far more personality and pictorial glow than Don John. By the time he has arrived in Britain actor and director should have reconciled us to practically anything. Iachimo has wagered with Posthumus about Imogen's chastity. When she repulses him, he quickly placates her. 'You make amends,' she says, and agrees politely to keep for one night in her bed chamber the trunk about which Iachimo is so circumstantially glib:

> Some dozen Romans of us, and your lord –
> The best feather of our wing – have mingled sums
> To buy a present for the Emperor;
> Which I, the factor for the rest, have done
> In France. 'Tis plate of rare device, and jewels
> Of rich and exquisite form, their values great;
> And I am something curious, being strange,
> To have them in safe stowage. (I, vi, 184–91)

Not remarkably, just after midnight, while Imogen is asleep after reading for three hours ('Fold down the leaf where I have left,' she says naughtily to her woman Helen), Iachimo emerges from the trunk. The ensuing speech is marvellously composed, though any Iachimo must have to calm the laughter when the lid of his trunk first rises. (These devices, at the wrong time, can be irresistible²). Most actors have conquered – Wolfit for one, Eric Porter, Ian Richardson. The speech is gold for anybody with a communicated sense of language right to the moment when, the clock striking and three hours having passed in forty lines, Iachimo re-enters the trunk, exclaiming: 'One, two, three: time, time!' Before then he has observed exactly the appearance of the room – carefully left undescribed in detail until the later scene with Posthumus – and he has removed Imogen's bracelet:

> Come off, come off;
> As slippery as the Gordian knot was hard!
> 'Tis mine; and this will witness outwardly,
> As strongly as the conscience does within,
> To th' madding of her lord. (II, i, 33-7)

Posthumus, so cruelly treated, who must yield Imogen's ring on the evidence of the bracelet, is just an uncomplicated hero. He has in the last act one shining phrase when Imogen embraces him: 'Hang there like fruit, my soul,/Till the tree die!' Cloten, whose name is frequently mispronounced – the clue is the line about 'Cloten's clotpoll' – is a coarse-grained oaf with a moment of verbal valour during the embassy from Augustus Caesar. Usually, he may remind us of a line from another dramatist: 'Dost thou understand that, changeling, dangling

thy hands like bobbins before thee?'[3] Cymbeline himself has a last-act
challenge where he has to keep up with so many recognitions and
comment on a narrative going almost too fast for him; Leon
Quartermaine, in this brocaded voice, did this at Stratford (1949)
with a subtly mounting joy. Elsewhere, the King has a touch of Capulet
('Nay, let her languish/A drop of blood a day and, being aged,/Die
of this folly'). His unnamed Queen is simply the evil stepmother of all
the stories, with one speech, at the demand of the Roman tribute,
that is oddly out of character:

> Remember, sir, my liege,
> The kings your ancestors, together with
> The natural bravery of your isle, which stands
> As Neptune's park, ribb'd and pal'd in
> With rocks unscalable and roaring waters,
> With sands that will not bear your enemies' boats
> But suck them up to th'top-mast. A kind of conquest
> Caesar made here; but made not here his brag
> Of 'came and saw and overcame'. With shame –
> The first that ever touch'd him – he was carried
> From off our coast, twice beaten; and his shipping –
> Poor ignorant baubles! – on our terrible seas,
> Like egg-shells mov'd upon their surges, crack'd
> As easily 'gainst our rocks; for joy whereof
> The fam'd Cassibelan, who was once at point –
> O, giglot fortune! – to master Caesar's sword,
> Made Lud's town with rejoicing fires bright
> And Britons strut with courage. (III, i, 16-33)

Belarius, the old lord of the Welsh cave, is another Kent – an actor
in Shakespeare's company must have specialised in oaken staunchness
– and the two young Princes in his charge speak (presumably because
the original players could not sing) the loveliest crystalline elegy in
the Drama, the dirge for Fidele, Imogen disguised and apparently
dead:

> Fear no more the heat o' th' sun
> Nor the furious winter's rages . . .   (IV, ii, 259-60)

With responsive voices, Arviragus and Guiderius cannot fail, but in
the dirge they must beware of seeming to celebrate a famous passage
rather than mourning for a death.

Imogen, deceived and true, is one of the enchanted royal children
of the last period; we can think of her, in a couplet from *The Phoenix*

and the Turtle, as 'Beauty, truth, and rarity,/Grace in all simplicity'. Her most trying scene is the discovery of the headless corpse of Cloten that she mistakes for Posthumus. In the theatre this passage can hover on the absurd, and its writing is strangely variable. After 'so small a drop of pity as a wren's eye', we have:

> A headless man? The garments of Posthumus?
> I know the shape of's leg; this is his hand,
> His foot Mercurial, his Martial thigh,
> The brawns of Hercules; but his Jovial face –
> Murder in heaven! How! 'Tis gone. (IV, ii, 309–13)

Otherwise the part is unflawed; and such actresses as Joyce Bland, Barbara Jefford, Peggy Ashcroft, Vanessa Redgrave, and Susan Fleetwood have shown us that it is so. Designers should be wary of Imogen's aspect when disguised; Dame Peggy, in 1957, had to overcome the modes of Little Lord Fauntleroy.

III

Simplicity must be the word for *Cymbeline* in the theatre, though one might not use it in the study for the opening and typically compressed exchange between two Gentlemen:

FIRST GENTLEMAN : You do not meet a man but frowns; our bloods
No more obey the heavens than our courtiers
Still seem as does the King's.
SECOND GENTLEMAN :   But what's the matter? (I, i, 1–3)

What indeed? This is exposition in the old manner, but to a difficult tune. It works in performance if the parts are safely cast and not merely handed on (as Solanio and Salerio used to be) to anybody who is about. The First Gentleman knows everything. The Second knows nothing. His questions:

And why so?

What's his name and birth?

But, pray you, tell me . . . ?

How long is this ago?

prompt the First Gentleman to the most gratified explanation. (We meet a similarly helpful personage in *The Winter's Tale*.) When Shakespeare thinks we have had enough, he ends the dialogue with the First Gentleman's 'Howsoe'er 'tis strange,/Or that the negligence may well be laugh'd at,/Yet is it true, sir.' To which the Second replies: 'I do well believe you.' During the first half-hour the players have to accustom our ears to odd, hauntingly scored melodies (and occasional dissonances) as well as to a plot that includes the last of Shakespeare's rings. With the agreeably informal 'Look here, love', Imogen gives to the banished Posthumus a diamond that was her mother's; he replies with a bracelet – as a 'manacle of love; I'll place it/Upon this fairest prisoner.'

Even a novice will spy worries ahead. They begin in a house in Rome during a prose scene – often presented as a banquet – at which, beside the vaguely indicated host, the guests are the Italian, Iachimo (remember, the Renaissance inside the house, Caesar Augustus without), and an unnamed Frenchman, Dutchman, and Spaniard. The last two are silent. This is the scene of the wager on Imogen's chastity; Posthumus's ring against the Italian's ducats. Do not ask why Iachimo behaves like this; for the play's sake he must. Thereafter, in the tangling of the plot, which has an often parodied way of fixing on the name of Milford Haven, a director's main puzzles are with Cloten's body, the treatment of the fight between British and Romans, and the apparitions of the Leonati, with Jupiter's descent on an eagle as an additional bonus.

In the text Shakespeare disposes of the battle in a series of stage directions. The first is, embracingly:

'Enter Lucius, Iachimo, and the Roman Army at one door, and the Britain Army at another, Leonatus Posthumus following like a poor soldier. They march over and go out. Alarums. Then enter again, in skirmish, Iachimo and Posthumus. He vanquisheth and disarmeth Iachimo, and then leaves him'. (V, ii)

Later, there will be a long speech by Posthumus to a 'Britain Lord' in which he describes the 'ancient soldier' and the 'two striplings' – these are Belarius, with Arviragus and Guiderius – who hold a sunken lane, 'ditch'd and wall'd with turf', against the entire Roman army. We cannot wonder when the Lord murmurs: 'This was strange chance:/A narrow lane, an old man, and two boys.' Today the battle is often stylised (Stratford, 1957 and 1962); not much else can be done with it, though the duel in which Posthumus 'vanquisheth and disarmeth' Iachimo must not be blurred. W. Graham Robertson, writing in 1923,[4] looked back on an effect in the Irving production at the Lyceum, a quarter of a century before, which we would never find now. The princes, he said, were 'angelic figures who turned the tide of battle in the last scene by the force of their supernatural beauty, as they stood for a moment on a sunlit crag before plunging into the fight'. And again: 'Irving's battle was small and fought in a narrow, shadowy gorge, with cliffs rising into sunshine, so as to get the (momentary) supernatural effect of the two white boys in golden light high above the dark valley.'

There remain the Apparitions and the ultimate Recognition. The Apparitions, who appear to Posthumus in prison, are his parents and his brothers, the Leonati. After they have encircled him while he lies asleep, they join in a supplication to Jupiter who promptly 'descends in thunder and lightning, sitting upon an eagle. He throws a thunderbolt. The Ghosts fall on their knees.' After a certain gruffness, Jupiter is responsive:

> Rise, and fade!
> He shall be lord of Lady Imogen,
> And happier much by his affliction made.
> This tablet lay upon his breast, wherein
> Our pleasure his full fortune doth confine;
> And so, away; no farther with your din
> Express impatience, lest you stir up mine.
> Mount, eagle, to my palace crystalline. (V, iv, 106–13)

It is all pleasantly theatrical, but few critics have defended it except Professor Wilson Knight, who takes it to be an important symbolic theophany, or divine appearance; and, of all people, Bernard Shaw, who thought it eminently possible as a masque, with suitable music and enough splendour of declamation; here Masefield agreed. What Shaw called 'careless woodnotes wild', Granville-Barker dismissed as 'jingling twaddle'. We cannot judge from the text; inevitably, a theatrical rendering is the answer. When I last heard these 'petty spirits of region low' (the voice is Jupiter's) they could be amiable company; moreover, in a fairy-tale, it is right that a magical voice ('he shall be lord of Lady Imogen') should show the path to a happy ending.

The Apparitions are followed by the uncompromising naturalism of the Gaoler ('O, the charity of a penny cord!') who acts as death's advocate more persuasively than the Duke does in *Measure for Measure*. So to the last scene in 'Lud's town' and the 'huddle of mechanical recognitions' (M. R. Ridley[5]) which is actually a technical triumph, one recognition growing from the next, and, in the midst, such a phrase as Belarius's:

The benediction of these covering heavens
Fall on their heads like dew! for they are worthy
To inlay heaven with stars. (V, v, 350–2)

That, for many of us – and I end where I began – is the true voice
of *Cymbeline*.

NOTES

1 *Cymbeline Refinished:* A Variation on Shakespeare's Ending (staged at the Embassy, London, 1937).
2 At Stratford in 1961 (Peter Wood's production of *Hamlet*), Ian Bannen jumped into a trunk left by the Players and began the 'Rogue and peasant slave' soliloquy. At its peak, when he cried 'O vengeance!' the lid fell down upon him, and he propped it up again, exclaiming: 'Why, what an ass am I!'
3 Lady Wishfort speaking in Congreve's *The Way of the World*.
4 *Letters from Graham Robertson*, (edited by Kerrison Preston, 1953), pp. 111, 113.
5 New Temple edition.

The Winter's Tale (1611)

I

The anonymous chronicle of *Edward III,* in the Shakespeare Apocrypha, has a speech that I have often thought tempting to a theorist:

> The stern Polonian and the warlike Dane,
> The King of Bohemia, and of Sicily,
> Are all become confederates with us. (III, i, 34–6)

Later, we feel, they would all become confederates with Shakespeare. Certainly the Kings of Bohemia and of Sicily arrive in the oddly misshapen, yet as oddly unified, Janus-play that pairs a Sicilia of the darker passions with Shakespeare's idea of *la vie de Bohème* so manifestly of pastoral Warwickshire. No title is more misquoted than this. Over and over, a play that demands its definite article appears as *A Winter's Tale:* even Professor Dover Wilson yielded to this when he was editing his Folio facsimiles in the 1920s.

Its construction is awkward. First, that emotional fury in a palace that we can picture as heavily Byzantine (though a modern stage setting is unlikely to help), the knotted speeches of Leontes, and the alarums of tragic trial and error. Next, the direction, 'Exit, pursued by a bear', on the sea-coast of Bohemia; then Time's stilted couplets to span sixteen years, after a rather shorter interval in today's theatre. So to the lyric garland of the sheep-shearing, interrupted by King Polixenes (who, said the actor Baliol Holloway, can be as angry as the next monarch); and, at length, Sicilia again in the quiet airs of forgiveness. Surprisingly, the astrologer-diarist Simon Forman, who saw *The Winter's Tale* at the Globe in 1611, made no mention of the great Statue scene which must have excited audiences on Bankside, and in the fashionable candle-lit Blackfriars Theatre across the river. Forman thought more of Autolycus; he took care – typically, we daresay – to write: 'Beware of trusting feigned beggars or fawning fellows.'

All begins in near-melodrama. Plagued by the yellow fever of jealousy, Leontes, apparently megalomaniac King of Sicilia – or so he must seem to an audience as unprepared as the courtiers – puts his chaste Queen, Hermione, on trial for adultery with Polixenes of Bohemia. We gather that he has been a good ruler with no suggestion of tyranny; his people do not fear to speak to him. Now, without warning, the gale blows; there is no evidence and the slightest of theatrical preparation. He is a man in whom jealousy can flame without cause; in Britain today he would be a Celt. Observing the framework and the tenuous exposition, we have to remember that Shakespeare was dramatising, altering, and enriching a popular novel, Robert Greene's prose romance of *Pandosto* (1588), reprinted in 1607 as *Dorastus and Fawnia*. This opens with the words:

'Among all the passions wherewith human minds are perplexed, there is none that so galleth with restless despite as the infectious sore of jealousy . . . Whoso is pained with this restless torment doubteth all, distrusteth himself, is always frozen with fear and fired with suspicion, having that wherein consisteth all his joy to be the breeder of his misery.'

The Queen in *Pandosto* dies at the news of her son's death; years later, after the recognition of his daughter, the King kills himself in remorse. But Shakespeare, at the time of *The Winter's Tale,* was in his final period of charity and reconciliation. Nothing must mar the end of what is twice called an 'old tale': the reunion of Leontes and Hermione; the young Florizel and Perdita as further symbols of serenity; and, in an expected symmetrical resolution, the loyal Paulina (the 'i' here is long) paired at the last moment with Camillo.

II

Almost as many learned pages have been wasted in finding reasons for the jealousy of Leontes as in seeking to rationalise Iago's malice. The truth is that each is a good beginning for a play. An English director, John Harrison, chose as epigraph for his revival at Nottingham (1955) the words, 'Once upon a time there was a jealous king.' Like all the later plays, it is a once-upon-a-time invention, not to be too closely scanned, or its anachronisms – the Delphic Oracle coeval with 'Whitsun pastorals' – too freely and derisively listed. Granville-Barker, in 1912, insisted that it should be spoken rapidly; the first thing was to get it alive; all must be continuous, intimate, vital. 'To hear these swift words delivered at speed in Henry Ainley's wonderful voice', wrote W. A. Darlington of the Savoy production, 'was to be shown the very ecstasy of jealousy.'[1]

Newcomers may not get from a Leontes more than a general idea of the early speeches. That is enough. They will have no time in the theatre to explore such a statement as this, and I doubt whether a Jacobean audience, for all its instant responses, would have done more than catch the drift:

>   Can thy dam? – may't be?
> Affection! thy intention stabs the centre.
> Thou dost make possible things not so held,
> Communicat'st with dreams – how can this be? –
> With what's unreal thou coactive art,
> And fellow'st nothing. Then 'tis very credent
> Thou may'st co-join with something; and thou dost –
> And that beyond commission; and I find it,
> And that to the infection of my brains
> And hard'ning of my brows. (I, ii, 137–46)

We understand why Polixenes says: 'What means Sicilia?' and why Hermione answers: 'He something seems unsettled.' Hermione is not a simple speaker at first. We hear her saying:

> What! have I twice said well? When was't before?
> I prithee tell me: cram's with praise, and make's
> As fat as tame things. One good deed dying tongueless
> Slaughters a thousand waiting upon that.
> Our praises are our wages; you may ride 's
> With one soft kiss a thousand furlongs ere
> With spur we heat an acre. (I, ii, 89–96)

On the stage the compressed, urgent utterance, and particularly the King's – as if 'the earth in fast thick pants were breathing' – can be raspingly dramatic: provided always that the speaking is sovereign and the director unobtrusive. It took me some time to appreciate a performance at Stratford-upon-Avon in 1976, simply because Sicilia had been translated from the Deep South to the glooms of Scandinavia. 'The iceman cometh,' said one sardonic spectator, not without cause. It reminded me of the actor-antiquarian Charles Kean's decision in 1856 to change Bohemia to Bithynia. That disposed completely of a mythical coast. Moreover, he could present 'the costume of the inhabitants of Asia Minor at a period so intimately associated with Greece'. It was said, not unkindly, of Charles Kean, that if an actor coughed on the Princess's stage you could be sure that this exactly reproduced the cough in some medieval manuscript.

Few revivals of the fusion of tragedy and romantic comedy have been entirely sure. Leontes can be baffling, though John Gielgud (asking us to accept a man jealous from his opening syllables) could persuade us in the Peter Brook production of 1951. This is the overwhelming delusion of an honest man who becomes, as Paulina tells him, a traitor to himself; but it is far from easy for an audience and a frightening exercise for a player to make sense and music of what, on the page, swirls like a sea beach in storm, or the fountain of *Kubla Khan*

> Amid whose swift half-intermitted burst
> Huge fragments vaulted like rebounding hail
> Or chaffy grain beneath the thresher's flail.

Many years after Granville-Barker, one could still find a minor Leontes chiselling away as though each word must be carved from granite.

The man who divines what is wrong, who recognises the King's frenzy as near-madness, is his cupbearer, Camillo. Wisely, when ordered to poison Polixenes, he warns the victim and escapes with him to Bohemia. Leontes, he knows, 'in rebellion with himself, will have/All that are his so too (I, ii, 355–6). It will be safer 'to avoid what's grown than question how 'tis born'. Merely a functionary of the plot, Camillo can do far more in performance than the text promises.

III

Early, the play is dark with sorrow. 'A sad tale's best for winter', says the child Mamillius (whom Ellen Terry, with go-cart modelled on a Greek vase, acted for Charles Kean; fifty years later she played Hermione). The Sicilian winter has little indeed to lighten its imperious melodrama. We cannot have time to ponder while Leontes is in the naphtha-flare of his passion. Such lines as these emerge:

There may be in the cup
A spider steep'd, and one may drink, depart,
And yet partake no venom, for his knowledge
Is not infected; but if one present
Th'abhorred ingredient to his eye, make known
How he hath drunk, he cracks his gorge, his sides,
With violent hefts. I have drunk, and seen the spider. (II, i, 39–45)

Hermione, an Emperor of Russia's daughter who unwittingly has caught a Tartar for a husband, is carried off to prison where she gives birth to the child who will be Perdita. Thence she is brought to trial in the open air. This, treated often as a night scene alive with torches and braziers, can be grandly theatrical. I think of the Hermione of Vivienne Bennett (Old Vic, 1936) when her dignity and snow-crystal speech transcended the humiliation of her appearance, guarded closely and in chains. Hermiones now are seldom chained or, for that matter, allowed to sit at the end of their defence ('I do refer me to the Oracle; Apollo be my judge!'). It is an eloquent defence; we hear something similar during Katharine's trial in *Henry VIII*. Besides the frenzy of Leontes it is like a flashing stream:

If pow'rs divine
Behold our human actions, as they do,
I doubt not then but innocence shall make
False accusation blush, and tyranny
Tremble at patience. You, my lord, best know –
Who least will seem to do so – my past life
Hath been as continent, as chaste, as true
As I am now unhappy (III, ii, 26–33)

Leontes has sought confirmation from the Delphic Oracle; but when Hermione's innocence is declared (I once saw the scroll brought in among what seemed to be the flames of a chafing-dish), he will have none of it. Now, as in the best of melodramas, everything happens pell-mell. Off stage the winter's-tale child, Mamillius, has died; and, in performance, the words 'is dead' are almost certainly a cue for thunder and for the King's:

Apollo's angry, and the heavens themselves
Do strike at my injustice. (III, ii, 143–4)

Fainting, Hermione is carried off. Presently, her gentlewoman, Paulina, announces her presumed death; and Leontes, his sorrow as extreme as his anger, is led off to prolonged despair. Though

Paulina says to the distraught King, 'I'll speak of her no more, nor of your children,' the fifth act suggests that she goes on doing so for sixteen years. What she thinks she speaks – the words of Leontes, 'the great comfort I have had of thee' – can be, in two senses, pathetic. It is a longer part than Hermione, 294 lines against 183, and one that can stand by the Emilia of *Othello*. (An Emilia in *The Winter's Tale* is a minor gentlewoman).

By now the tragedy has almost burned itself out. Hermione, reserved for an ultimate *coup de théâtre*, will have only another eight lines at the far end of the play. Meanwhile the scene must shift to Bohemia and the tempest in which Paulina's husband, Antigonus, sent by the King, leaves the baby princess, Perdita, upon the barren shore. In Greene's novel 'the mariners descried the coast of Bohemia, shooting off their ordnance for joy'. Shakespeare took the name without the ordnance. It is, in any event, as much of a Never-Never land as the Illyria of *Twelfth Night*. Antigonus, depositing the child upon it ('Blossom, speed thee well') is himself lost in the blizzard: 'Exit, pursued by a bear' – a tricky business for a modern director. We assume that the Globe people borrowed from the Southwark bear-pit which was near the theatre, though I suppose this was too late for Sackerson, a Bankside favourite, who was 'meat and drink' to Slender of *The Merry Wives*.[2] Inevitably, Charles Kean would be reassuring; he would find chapter and verse for anything: 'The existence of bears in the East is exemplified in the second chapter of the Second Book of Kings.'

Immediately, the old Shepherd arrives to discover the child; and soon his son, the slow-speaking, furry-vowelled Clown (or peasant), will describe the end of Antigonus. My heart is with the critic Herbert Farjeon in his review of the Old Vic production of 1925: 'Antigonus . . . seems to have been a man of great presence of mind. The bear got him, and the Clown describes how, even as the brute was busy on his shoulder-bone, "he cried to me for help, and said his name was Antigonus, a nobleman." In the teeth of a savage bear I, too, would cry for help, but I should be too much put about to think of adding: "My name is Herbert Farjeon, a dramatic critic. . . . " '

IV

On to the stiff, Gower-like couplets of Time, beckoning us across sixteen years. In Peter Brook's production (1951) the ancient advanced down stage through a dazzling whirl of snow as if one of those endearing glass toys had been shaken. But it will be high summer in

Bohemia, though the mood is spring-like, Perdita is dressed as 'Flora peering in April's front', and Autolycus, a 'snapper-up of unconsidered trifles' – like the bear he is entirely Shakespeare's invention – sings of daffodils beginning to peer: one standard edition glosses this gravely as ' "peep above ground" but possibly meaning "appear" '. We have the rustic feast and the wooing of the cottage-bred shepherdess Perdita – bravely her mother's daughter – by the disguised Florizel, son of Polixenes and heir to Bohemia; and a sudden gust of narrative whisks all the important people back to a Sicilia gently autumnal. In the sunlight of Bohemia we may have forgotten those torch-lit rages. The sheep shearing is the world of Autolycus's robberies and rogueries which should be quick and deft, not dwelt upon in anxious detail; and of the flower-speeches of Perdita:

> O, Proserpina,
> For the flowers now that, frighted, thou let'st fall
> From Dis's wagon! – daffodils,
> That come before the swallow dares, and take
> The winds of March with beauty; violets, dim
> But sweeter than the lids of Juno's eyes
> Or Cytherea's breath . . . (IV, iv, 116–22)

Spoken very simply, this must enchant, in spite of the 16-year-old shepherdess's wealth of classical allusion. The spirit of the scene, if not of its allusions, is from Shakespeare's own land. The sheep shearing belongs to Cotswold or the Vale of the Red Horse; the young shepherd is a broadly bucolic youth, dulcified in good humour, from the wattle-cotes of Arden; and Autolycus, conceivably, from a Stratford fair (certainly not, as one production seemed to believe, from a discotheque); Granville-Barker liked to think that it was at Stratford that Shakespeare happened on a man who 'compass'd a motion[3] of the Prodigal Son, and married a tinker's wife, within a mile where my land and living lies'.

Directors must be cautious in the fourth act where a comedian can transform Autolycus into an expansive variety act. He may be a vagrant rich in ballads, songs, and snatches; but he is also a fellow, sharp of mind and eye, who in his time has served Prince Florizel and worn costly velvet, and who can affect a plausibly patronising hauteur in the meeting with Shepherd and Clown. In the theatre the Shearing ought not to broaden into a Mummerset revel like something from a bad production of Phillpotts: 'Be happy, if you like,' a director said to his cast, 'but for heaven's sake don't be as happy as all that.' Little can be so false as synthetic fooling and fabricated accents; still, it will be wrong if Perdita, from her cottage, uses any strained gentility or puts her flower-garland into a florist's window display. An 'old tale' does not live on its naturalism; but, to the end, the girl's voice should hint at her rustic youth.

The fifth act, moving very slowly – and we do not want it faster – reunites everyone. It completes the cycle with resurrection after life and death; it includes the memory of Hermione – a line once spoken by Sir John Gielgud with agonised longing: 'Stars, stars,/And all eyes else dead coals!' (V, i, 67–8) – and it ends with the theatrical *coup* of the Statue scene, prodigiously stage-managed by Paulina. Hermione, marble upon her pedestal, can be a noble sight for an audience, agony for an actress until the phrase 'You perceive she stirs', and a final challenge to Leontes as it was to William Charles Macready at Covent Garden in 1837. The Hermione, Helen Faucit, wrote many years later:

'His passionate joy at finding Hermione really alive seemed beyond control. Now he was prostrate at her feet, then enfolding her in his arms. The hair which came unbound, and fell on my shoulders, was reverently kissed and caressed. It was the finest burst of passionate speechless emotion I ever saw.'

Now and then, like another mother and daughter, Thaisa and Marina in *Pericles*, Hermione and Perdita have been doubled. Though we realise it can be done, and affectingly – as by Mary Anderson in London (1887), and by Judi Dench at Stratford-upon-Avon (1969) – it has to be a dangerous expedient. Perdita has two speeches. No mechanics must distract us from the last direct emotion.

When the theatre wasted its time with elaborate place changes, one passage used to be cut. Today we can hardly do without it: the second scene of the fifth act when Shakespeare, either from laziness or (I prefer to believe) sheer pleasure in technical craft, reports in a form of Messenger speech the reunion of Leontes and Polixenes, and all that went with it. To begin, Autolycus questions a First Gentleman; then they turn to a second, called Rogero, and at length to a star witness, Paulina's Steward, talkative and smug in his hour of exquisite importance. I have wondered sometimes how Paulina had kept Hermione's presence secret; but this is a matter we are not supposed to discuss. Anyway, the Steward is not talking of Hermione whose hour has not yet come. There are other matters:

	. . . Did you see the meeting of the two kings?
2ND GENTLEMAN:	No
STEWARD:	Then have you lost a sight which was to be seen, cannot be spoken of. (V, ii, 39–41)

He goes on to speak of it in relishing and relished detail: 'I never heard of such another encounter, which lames report to follow it, and undoes description to do it.' Whereupon he undoes description. Granville-Barker knew the impact the scene must have in performance; even so, it has often been ignored. Twice here the phrase recurs, 'Like an old tale'; and that, in brief, is the play. The four words give a clear hint (if only he will keep his fantastication and mood-lighting within bounds) to any new and sensitive director.

NOTES

1 *Six Thousand and One Nights* (1960).
2 *The Merry Wives of Windsor*, I, i, 295.
3 Contrived a puppet show.

The Tempest (1611)

Like its off-stage Queen of Tunis, *The Tempest* dwells ten leagues beyond man's life. We may ask, as in another context, who has measured the ground; but it is incontestable that the fantasy, Shakespeare's final adventure of the spirit, is frighteningly elusive in performance; it is easy to lose direction and to find a shore that is not Prospero's – a play that becomes, indeed, a dream about an old scientist who tortured Caliban with rheumatism and frightened him with 'spangled spooks'. This irreverence is from James Bridie's Lady Pitts in *Daphne Laureola*. Since hearing it I have instinctively divided revivals of *The Tempest* into plain and spangled. The spangled can get in Shakespeare's way, nudging him along unwisely. The plain trust him; how far the director himself may be trusted we are likely to guess from the opening scene. Thus, do we hear the words as the ship is splitting during a wreck (all will be magically restored at the last) where, as Masefield said, the master would infallibly have lost his certificate? I have known the scene attempted in many ways: a majestic galleon in the trough of the waves, a stylised balletic storm, all nymphs o'the sea and brandished scarves, and – from the first *Tempest* I saw – a mast-head lantern swinging in a dizzy arc against a grey curtain. No more. I was reminded of this in Peter Brook's production at Stratford and Drury Lane thirty-four years later, though Brook added flailing ropes, burning fire-balls, and clambering sailors as well as a moment few directors had vouchsafed, a spell-stopped, ominous quiet before the final split. In none of these productions were the words entirely audible: a loss, because Alonso (in his one speech), Gonzalo, Sebastian, and Antonio are all – in Max Beerbohm's phrase elsewhere – making remarks highly characteristic of themselves; and the Boatswain, in his score of lines, is a fellow we would not willingly lose. Moreover, we have the directions, 'Enter Mariners, wet' and 'A confused noise within', and Gonzalo leaves us with the admirable wish:

Now would I give a thousand furlongs of sea for an acre of barren ground – long heath, brown furze, any thing. The wills above be done, but I would fain die a dry death. (I, i, 62–6)

As we know, he does not have any kind of death. No one does, for this is a magician's storm that puts the courtiers in Prospero's power until the ultimate forgiveness inseparable from Shakespeare's last plays.

II

First performed at Whitehall on Hallowmas Night, 1611, *The Tempest* was very largely inspired by a newsletter about the wrecking on Bermuda – the 'still-vexed Bermoothes' – of the *Sea Venture* bound for Virginia. Its sounds and sweet airs were fit, too, for the English Princess Elizabeth; with her bridegroom, the Elector Palatine of the Rhine, she heard and watched a revival in the Banqueting House early in 1613.

What is there beyond ingeniously devised masquing and epithalmic spectacle? A popular idea is that Prospero, bidding farewell to his art and breaking his staff, speaks for Shakespeare retired to Stratford. Peter Brook, in *The Empty Space* (1968) goes much further:

'When we realise it takes place on an island and not an island, during a day and not during a day, with a tempest that set off a series of events that are still within a tempest even when the storm is done, that the charming pastoral naturally encompasses rape, murder, conspiracy, and violence; when we begin to unearth the themes that Shakespeare has so carefully buried, we see that it is his complete final statement, and that it deals with the whole condition of man.'

Few playgoers would go so far on hearing *The Tempest* first. They find a narrative of a studious Italian Duke who, during twelve years' exile from his kingdom upon an isle in the far-off seas, has become a master of arts of the earth and air, with spirits at his command. By bringing to the isle all those who had worked against him – and one old counsellor, who had been his friend – he manages within a day to get his dukedom back; to see his daughter betrothed to the son of the King of Naples; magnanimously to heal all wounds; and to return to his Milanese duties where 'every third thought shall be my grave' – his subjects may find a curiously detached ruler. Before he goes he frees the spirits who have attended him, and he leaves behind the 'savage and deformed slave' Caliban – an anagram of cannibal – who is as much a thing of the earth as Ariel of the air and skies. After its loitering exposition the play is full of theatrical effects, a banquet brought in by strange Shapes, Ariel in the form of a harpy, the removal of the banquet by 'a quaint device', spirits in the shape of dogs and hounds, and a lovely internal masque of goddesses – all reinforced by verse of Shakespeare's gravest beauty and some exquisite songs.

It is clear that the Prince Palatine and his Princess ('th'eclipse and glory of her kind') were seeing an entertainment far rarer than the customary Court shows. But we can consider it too deeply: I would pause before regarding *The Tempest* as a statement of the whole condition of man, or as Shakespeare's last theatrical message. It is, as Ivor Brown would maintain, as much of a diversely imaginative invention as *The Winter's Tale* and *Cymbeline*, and we need not blur its pleasures by an earnest search for the improbable.

III

Thomas Campbell, as far back as 1835, suggested that Prospero could be Shakespeare: a tempting ascription that fits less neatly than it seems. *Henry VIII* had yet to come; later still, Shakespeare collaborated in *The Two Noble Kinsmen;* and, in any event, would he have applauded himself so indiscreetly:

> Graves at my command
> Have wak'd their sleepers, op'd and let 'em forth
> By my so potent art. (V, i, 48–50)

Shakespeare was 47 when *The Tempest* was performed. Certainly Prospero might not be more than 35 or 40. His daughter Miranda is 15. In the theatre he was once an ancient, a major prophet who would be the girl's great-grandfather; today he is usually beardless, and we think of him in the El Greco image of John Gielgud at Stratford in 1956 and the Old Vic (National Theatre) in 1974. Besides being the oldest inhabitant of the globe, Prospero has been in his time a ponderous schoolmaster,[1] a man of an aloof noble dignity, and once (at Stratford-upon-Avon) a complicated personage with book in one hand and in the other a wobbling staff poised over the cauldron – he looked uncommonly like an anxious chef.

Many have charged him with tedium, and it is true that the part, static at first and unrelenting in exposition, demands vocal virtuosity. It has had such players as Ion Swinley, whose voice, free from any theatrical vibrato, would remind me of Flecker's 'great bell swinging in a dome'; Gielgud, who has acted it more often than anyone; Robert Eddison, Ian Richardson, and Paul Scofield (John Harrison's Prospero at Leeds in 1975 and later in London). Charles Laughton's casting for the Old Vic in 1934 was curious. A potentially terrifying Caliban, he preferred to see Prospero as a decayed Father Christmas with a dubious past. Another collector's piece was Alastair Sim's Old Vic performance in 1962: a genial whimsical housemaster, neither proud of his magic – which indeed perpetually astonished him – nor lord of the Shakespearian harmonies; his voice was the familiar aerated purr with a sudden spring-heeled leap at the end of a phrase.[2]

Prospero may sound most schoolmasterly when he is narrating to Miranda. Here he insists on concentration: 'Obey, and be attentive'; 'Dost thou attend me?'; 'Thou attend'st not'; 'Dost thou hear?' By the time she does fall off she knows all that had happened in 'the dark backward and abysm of time': the perfidy of Antonio, the usurping Duke – who could go straight into *As You Like It* – the evil-doing of Alonso, King of Naples, and the 'sea-sorrow' in 'the rotten carcass of a butt':

MIRANDA: How came we ashore?
PROSPERO: By Providence divine.
                Some food we had and some fresh water that
                A noble Neapolitan, Gonzalo,
                Out of his charity, who being then appointed
                Master of this design, did give us, with
                Rich garments, linens, stuffs, and necessaries,
                Which since have steaded much; so, of his gentleness,
                Knowing I lov'd my books, he furnish'd me
                From mine own library with volumes that
                I prized above my dukedom.
MIRANDA: Would I might
                But ever see that man! (I, ii, 158–69)

Miranda asleep, there comes to Prospero the spirit Ariel he had once released from the cloven pine where the witch Sycorax had imprisoned him. Ariel is Prospero's servant as Puck is Oberon's, but he is a spirit infinitely more delicate, a part that in our time has been expressed uncannily by the silver flash of Elsa Lanchester (1934), by Leslie French many times in the Open Air Theatre of the 1930s, and by Alan Badel (Stratford, 1951) like a Donatello figure given radiant life. When Gielgud was at the Old Vic (1940) he never looked at Ariel but saw him only in his thought, a reading of IV, i, 164 as 'Come, with a thought. I *think* thee, Ariel; come.' To which Ariel replies: 'Thy thoughts I cleave to. What's thy pleasure?' He does all his master bids; sometimes I wonder idly why he has conscientiously to disguise himself as a water-nymph so that he can sing to Ferdinand and 'enter invisible'.

Caliban, son of the dead witch Sycorax (who can be 'blear-ey'd' or 'blue-ey'd' according to choice) is primitive man with forehead villainously low; he has not been acted better than by Robert Atkins (Open Air Theatre, 1930s). Seeing him as a creature striving for articulate speech, and towards something he does not understand, Atkins gave sudden pathos to the passage any Caliban must grasp:

> Be not afeard. The isle is full of noises,
> Sounds, and sweet airs, that give delight, and hurt not.
> Sometimes a thousand twangling instruments
> Will hum about mine ears; and sometimes voices,
> That, if I then had wak'd after long sleep,
> Will make me sleep again; and then, in dreaming,
> The clouds methought would open and show riches
> Ready to drop upon me, that, when I wak'd,
> I cried to dream again. (III, ii, 130–8)

Except for Gonzalo, his Utopian imaginings, and his final 'O rejoice/ Beyond a common joy, and set it down/With gold on lasting pillars', the King and his associates are more or less functional: the shadowy Francisco has the rather fine 'Sir, he may live; I saw him beat the surges under him.' Miranda ('O brave new world that has such people in't') and Ferdinand are a happy pair of innocents, following upon Perdita and Florizel; and the comedians have the customary bravado which can sometimes be trying to the nerves. Directors cannot always make up their minds about the grave and graceful betrothal masque, half spoken, half sung:

> Honour, riches, marriage-blessing,
> Long continuance, and increasing,
> Hourly joys be still upon you!
> Juno sings her blessings on you . . . (IV, i, 106–9)

but it can be 'a most majestic vision'. Brook, in 1956, with his all-white goddesses, turned it to a fertility-rite chanting of key phrases about barns, garners, vines, and plants. In 1963, at Stratford, the goddesses were amorphous shapes like tottering corn-dollies.

Primarily, *The Tempest* is Prospero. We are unsure at first what he intends to do; but everything is clear when, in one of the last talks with Ariel, his project gathers to a head:

ARIEL: Your charm so strongly works 'em
                                    That if you now beheld them your affections
                                    Would become tender.
PROSPERO: Dost thou think so, spirit?
ARIEL: Mine would, sir, were I human.
PROSPERO: And mine shall.
                                    Hast thou, which art but air, a touch, a feeling
                                    Of their afflictions, and shall not myself,
                                    One of their kind, that relish all as sharply,
                                    Passion as they, be kindlier mov'd than thou art?
                                    Though with their high wrongs I am struck to th'quick,
                                    Yet with my nobler reason 'gainst my fury
                                    Do I take part; the rarer action is
                                    In virtue than in vengeance; they being penitent,
                                    The sole drift of my purpose doth extend
                                    Not a frown further. (V, i, 17–30)

Immediately he has the second of his farewell speeches. The first, invariably encouraging to those who believe in Prospero-Shakespeare, is right after the masque:

      These our actors,
   As I foretold you, were all spirits, and
   Are melted into air, into thin air;
   And, like the baseless fabric of this vision,
   The cloud-capp'd towers, the gorgeous palaces,
   The solemn temples, the great globe itself,
   Yea, all which it inherit, shall dissolve,
   And, like this insubstantial pageant faded,
   Leave not a rack behind. We are such stuff
   As dreams are made on; and our little life
   Is rounded with a sleep. (IV, i, 148–58)

The second, invoking the spirits that have served him upon the island, ends simply:

      This rough magic
   I here abjure; and, when I have requir'd
   Some heavenly music – which even now I do –

To work mine end upon their senses that
This airy charm is for, I'll break my staff,
Bury it certain fathoms in the earth,
And deeper than did ever plummet sound
I'll drown my book. (V, i, 50–7)

IV

The end, beginning with the long ground swell of 'Behold, Sir King,/The wrongèd Duke of Milan, Prospero', is golden charity: forgiveness, restoration, unity (we may still wonder about Antonio and Sebastian). The ship is 'tight and yare, and bravely rigg'd, as when/We first put out to sea'. And presently, before the journey on the morrow, through calm seas and with auspicious gales, the company retires to Prospero's cell where he threatens to spend most of the night in discoursing on 'the story of my life,/And the particular accidents gone by/Since I came to this isle'. (He could hardly be expected to miss the opportunity.) When they have gone – sometimes 'Please you, draw near' is to a hesitant Antonio – Prospero speaks the wistful epilogue:

As you from crimes would pardon'd be,
Let your indulgence set me free. (18–19)

Various managers in the past (Tree for one – he preferred to appear as Caliban) have turned the play into a capricious island fling: spangled Shakespeare, with what John Wellington Wells would call 'a first-class assortment of magic'. Few revivals, spangled or plain, are ever wholly satisfying; one creates a mosaic with the voices of Gielgud and Scofield over all, and the island as seen by many designers: Brook's craggy caverns by a 'sea-marge, sterile and rocky hard'; and at the Old Vic in 1961, Leslie Hurry's rocky shore against a sky apparently of veined marble. I would like to have met Barry Jackson's experiment in colour at the Birmingham Repertory long ago. He founded it on the iridescent tones of a seam of copper falling down the wet cliffs of a South Cornish cove. Most sharply now I think of the shabby, thrown-together production I knew first, a curtain or two, a cracked blue backcloth, and the poem declaring itself as infinitely strange and bewildering but with a sovereign voice that could never be dimmed. No question of allegory, the whole condition of man, a 'positive atmosphere of debasement', a study in colonialism, or Shakespeare's grand final gesture, but simply the theatre at its most potently haunted: 'What harmony is this? My good friends, hark!' – 'Marvellous sweet music.'[3]

NOTES

1 He does say to Miranda: 'here/Have I, thy schoolmaster, made thee more profit/ Than other princess' can, that have more time/For vainer hours and tutors not so careful.'
2 One of Sim's stresses lingers. 'Thou *hast* slept well,' he said to Miranda with a bantering emphasis on the second word.
3 III, iii, 18–19.

King Henry VIII
(1612–13)

> I come no more to make you laugh; things now
> That bear a weighty and a serious brow,
> Sad, high, and working, full of state and woe,
> Such noble scenes as draw the eye to flow,
> We now present. (Prologue, 1–5)

I

One evening in the early 1930s, S. R. Littlewood, who was then my chief in drama criticism at the *Morning Post*,[1] returned late from the theatre with his customary urbane bustle. According to ritual he put a sheet of paper into his typewriter and took it out again. He then addressed me solemnly: 'My boy,' he said, 'I don't know who wrote *Henry VIII*, and I don't mind. This is real theatre.' It is. Dogmatism about its authorship is unwise, and divisions are acute, but Shakespeare probably wrote far more of the play than past disintegrators, sieving every phrase, would concede to him.[2] John Fletcher's hand has been confidently traced in the number of 'feminine endings' (or redundant syllables); but not every Fletcherian will applaud the arithmetic. The study can look after these debates; in the theatre we do not argue about detail, for *Henry VIII*, as Littlewood said, is real theatre from its prologue, which has been assigned to various people, the Old Lady, a pedantic chronicler (with chronicle), an anonymous gentleman, and even the King himself.

'In a moment, see how soon this mightiness meets misery.' The play, if ideally staged, thrusts one scene on another so swiftly (as Tyrone Guthrie did at Stratford in 1949 in a long hurtle across his permanent set) that we cannot fail to mark the transience of fame. The night may begin 'all clinquant, all in gold'; it may end with jubilation and christening; until then its theme is one of farewell, decline and fall. Buckingham goes to his 'long divorce of steel', and at once he is forgotten and we are moving towards a royal divorce. Wolsey, King-Cardinal, is broken by the storms of state, and the action speeds into a narrative of the Coronation. Almost before Katharine's dying taper has faded at Kimbolton, Anne across the way is lightly on the throne. Soon she – and Cranmer too – will have fallen, but that is outside the text. Only King Henry will remain unshaken until death (also outside Shakespeare's brief) strips him from the tree as, in gusty Tudor ire, he has spun the leaves that strew his autumnal history.

Besides being a play of farewells – to the world, to life, to greatness – this is a play of greeting: to 'the high and mighty Princess of England, Elizabeth', the new-born glory of the Tudors. We recognise how immediate it must have seemed to its first audiences, listening to a chronicle about their late Queen's father, and with the triumphant palace christening to end the night:

CRANMER: She shall be, to the happiness of England,
An aged princess; many days shall see her,
And yet no day without a deed to crown it.
Would I had known no more! But she must die –
She must, the saints must have her – yet a virgin;
A most unspotted lily shall she pass
To th'ground, and all the world shall mourn her.

(V, v, 56–62)

(Feminine endings here are what prosodists call Fletcherian).

II

Four characters stand above a cast that is more than ten times their length. The first is Edward Bohun, Duke of Buckingham, betrayed 'mirror of all courtesy'. Sentenced for high treason, he leaves the play early in its second act; but his farewell, as he comes from arraignment at Westminster to the bank of the Thames, has impressed itself upon the English stage. The phrasing is direct; its falling rhythms give an ineffable melancholy to such lines as

You few that lov'd me
And dare be bold to weep for Buckingham,
His noble friends and fellows, whom to leave
Is only bitter to him, only dying,

> Go with me like good angels to my end;
> And as the long divorce of steel falls on me
> Make of your prayers one sweet sacrifice
> And lift my soul to heaven. (II, i, 71–8)

There should be a crowd to hear Buckingham, as James Agate said in his notice of the Old Vic revival (1933)[3] when a sensitive actor, Nicholas Hannen, was 'much handicapped by Tyrone Guthrie's staging, which deprived him of the crowd the author prescribed . . . so he addressed the audience directly'. Probably the most touching Buckingham was Johnston Forbes-Robertson, who acted for Henry Irving at the Lyceum in 1892. A recording made more than thirty years later reminds us of his poignantly calm resignation as he stood in plain black velvet in the sunlight:

> Farewell;
> And when you would say something that is sad,
> Speak how I fell. I have done; and God forgive me! (II, i, 134–6)

The second fall is that of Queen Katharine, a part acted during the last half-century by four major actresses of the English theatre, Dames Sybil Thorndike, Flora Robson, Edith Evans, and Peggy Ashcroft. They were in the succession, if not the tradition, of Sarah Siddons who turned to rend Wolsey ('Lord Cardinal, to you I speak') during the trial at Blackfriars:

Q. KATHARINE: Sir,
I am about to weep; but, thinking that
We are a queen, or long have dream'd so, certain
The daughter of a king, my drops of tears
I'll turn to sparks of fire.
WOLSEY: Be patient yet.
Q. KATHARINE: I will, when you are humble; nay, before,
Or God will punish me. I do believe,
Induc'd by potent circumstances, that
You are mine enemy, and make my challenge
You shall not be my judge; for it is you
Have blown this coal betwixt my lord and me –
Which God's dew quench! Therefore I say again,
I utterly abhor, yea, from my soul
Refuse you for my judge, whom yet once more
I hold my most malicious foe and think not
At all a friend to truth. (II, iv, 69–83)

Katharine, personification of noble sorrow, must have presence and
pride. She is a Queen, bred in the royal house of Spain. We hear
her regality with the Cardinals, Wolsey and Campeius, a memorable
scene that for long was regularly omitted:

> My lord, I dare not make myself so guilty,
> To give up willingly that noble title
> Your master wed me to; nothing but death
> Shall e'er divorce my dignities. (III, i, 139–42)

As the Princess Dowager, fading towards death at Kimbolton, she re-
bukes a clumsy messenger:

MESSENGER: An't like your Grace—
KATHARINE: You are a saucy fellow.
        Deserve we no more reverence?
GRIFFITH: You are to blame,
        Knowing she will not lose her wonted greatness,
        To use so rude behaviour. Go to, kneel.
MESSENGER: I humbly do entreat your Highness' pardon;
        My haste made me unmannerly. There is staying
        A gentleman, sent from the King, to see you.
KATHARINE: Admit him entrance, Griffith; but this fellow
        Let me ne'er see again. (IV, ii, 100–8)

Earlier in the scene, when speaking of Wolsey's fall, Katharine
describes the vainglorious prelate: 'He was a man/Of an unbounded
stomach, ever ranking/Himself with princes.' Then, listening to the
quiet tribute of Griffith, her gentleman usher, she adds: 'Whom
I most hated living, thou hast made me,/With thy religious truth
and modesty,/Now in his ashes honour.' Wolsey has made his own
farewell: the man of humble stock in his scarlet robe; the Cardinal,
'lofty and sour', who sought to rule his King, and who ventured 'these
many summers in a sea of glory, but far beyond my depth'. In the
speech that is his own elegy he knows himself as few men do:

> Cromwell, I charge thee, fling away ambition;
> By that sin fell the angels. How can man then,
> The image of his Maker, hope to win by it?
> Love thyself last; cherish those hearts that hate thee;
> Corruption wins not more than honesty.
> Still in thy right hand carry gentle peace
> To silence envious tongues. Be just, and fear not;
> Let all the ends thou aim'st at be thy country's,

Thy God's, and truth's; then, if thou fall'st, O Cromwell,
Thou fall'st a blessèd martyr!   (III, ii, 440–9)

III

Though Henry, as he strides through the play, gives no hint of declining or falling, he does not dominate. He frowns, but Shakespeare rarely lets him blaze. When he does, most actors in remembrance have controlled the fires of a part in which the man should be suggested physically without having his features clamped in a Holbein mask that blurs expression. He came most authoritatively from the picture-frame in Donald Sinden's portrait (Stratford, 1969) of a passionate, easily wrought, self-deceiving monarch. Charles Laughton, of whom much had been hoped, disappointed at the Old Vic in 1933. He had just succeeded in a popular film as the kind of comically gross sensualist Gillray might have caricatured. In the theatre he could not match his husky, sibilant tones to the verse; much of what he spoke had a dull matt finish.

Guthrie, who directed him, came to the play three times, twice at the Old Vic (1934 and 1958) and once at Stratford. Probably we should have had a synthesis of the productions. The surest – in spite of the presence in 1958 of Dame Edith Evans and Sir John Gielgud as the 'scarlet sin' – was the Stratford revival of 1949. Here, though the play has more of lute than spirit-stirring drum, Guthrie did not draw it out slowly. He sustained its pace and animation; he found a balance between the processional and the emotional; and he made of the peers and prelates and the talkative Gentlemen people with a root in the Tudor scene, not just useful mouthpieces exclaiming 'But what follow'd?' and 'You're well met once again!' He provided a toothily excitable First Gentleman with a joyful little leap at 'All the rest are Countesses.' Agreed, he could be too inventive – as directors often are with this play – and he never explained why something cloudingly like a comic cross-talk turn should preface the passing of Buckingham, or why an onlooker's sneeze was allowed to puncture Cranmer's baptismal oration. While keeping the sense of spectacle, he always ignored the extravagances of Jacobean showmanship visible in the stage directions for one pageant after another: the banquet at York Place (and the discharge of 'chambers' which burned down the first Globe Theatre),[4] the order of the trial, the order of the Coronation, the vision of Katharine, and the christening. Wisely, he cut the 'solemnly tripping' Personages of the vision which has been confused so often with inferior ballet matter. We saw everything through the Queen's gaze and in her rapt awakening:

Saw you not, even now, a blessed troop
Invite me to a banquet; whose bright faces
Cast thousand beams upon me, like the sun?
Thy promis'd me eternal happiness,
And brought me garlands, Griffith, which I feel
I am not worthy yet to wear. I shall, assuredly. (IV, ii, 87–92)

Among a crowd of lesser characters Anne Bullen (whom Vivien Leigh once played in Regent's Park) is both meek and adventurous. In her principal scene she is outrun by one of Shakespeare's raciest small creations, the Old Lady who says precisely what she means:

OLD LADY: You would not be a queen!
ANNE: No, not for all the riches under heaven.
OLD LADY: 'Tis strange: a threepence bow'd would hire me,
            Old as I am, to queen it. But, I pray you,
            What think you of a duchess? Have you limbs
            To bear that load of title?
ANNE: No, in truth.
OLD LADY: Then you are weakly made. (II, iii, 34–40)

Another secondary part, much larger than these, has endured both relentless cutting and wanton exaggeration. This is Archbishop Cranmer, the good man who gets his deserts in the play, whatever history may fashion for him. He utters the last salute to the Queen to be and to the glory of her reign:

Good grows with her;
In her days every man shall eat in safety
Under his own vine what he plants, and sing
The merry songs of peace to all his neighbours.
God shall be truly known; and those about her
From her shall read the perfect ways of honour. (V, v, 32–7)

In today's performances the Epilogue is rare. Because *The Two Noble Kinsmen* is not in the general repertory, these lines for the King usually end the last Shakespearian speech the theatre vouchsafes to us:

This day, no man think
His business at his house; for all shall stay.
This little one shall make it holiday. (V, v, 74–6)

It has been nearly a quarter of a century since 'Hung be the heavens with black, yield day to night!'

NOTES

1 The oldest national morning newspaper. It was absorbed by the *Daily Telegraph* in the autumn of 1937.
2 Dr Caroline Spurgeon discovered a typically pervasive image, the allusions to the body, particularly when bowed under a heavy weight.
3 *Sunday Times*, 7 November 1933
4 This was on 29 June 1613.

Some Books

(published in London unless otherwise stated)

Agate, James: *Brief Chronicles*, Cape, 1943.

Boas, Guy: *Shakespeare and the Young Actor* (new edition), Barrie and Rockliff, 1962.

Bridges-Adams, W.:
The Irresistible Theatre, Secker and Warburg, 1957.
A Bridges-Adams Letter Book, edited by Robert Speaight, Society for Theatre Research, 1971.

Brown, Ivor:
Shakespeare, Collins, 1949.
How Shakespeare Spent the Day, Bodley Head, 1963.
Shakespeare and the Actors, Bodley Head, 1970.

Brown, John Russell: *Shakespeare's Plays in Performance*, Arnold, 1966.

Campbell, Oscar J. and Quinn, Edward G., *The Reader's Encyclopaedia of Shakespeare*, Cromwell, N. Y., 1966; pub. by Methuen as *A Shakespeare Encyclopaedia*.

Davies, W., Robertson: *Shakespeare's Boy Actors*, Dent, 1939.

Evans, Gareth Lloyd:
Shakespeare in the Limelight, Blackie, 1968.
Shakespeare (5 volumes), Oliver and Boyd, Edinburgh, 1969–73.

Farjeon, Herbert: *The Shakespearean Scene*, Hutchinson, 1949.

Findlater, Richard: *The Player Queens*, Weidenfeld, 1976.

Gielgud, John: *Stage Directions*, Heinemann, 1963.

Granville-Barker, Harley: *Prefaces to Shakespeare* (5 volumes), Sidgwick & Jackson, 1927–47; illustrated four-volume paper-back edition, Batsford, 1963; preface and notes by M. St Clare Byrne.

Guthrie, Tyrone: *A Life in the Theatre*, Hamish Hamilton, 1960.

Haddon, Archibald: *Green Room Gossip*, Stanley Paul, 1922.

Hale, Lionel: *The Old Vic 1949–1950*, Evans, 1950.

Harwood, Ronald: *Sir Donald Wolfit, CBE*, Secker & Warburg, 1971.

Holmes, Martin:
Shakespeare's Public, John Murray, 1960.
The Guns of Elsinore, Chatto & Windus, 1964.
Shakespeare and His Players, John Murray, 1972.

Hunt, Hugh: *Old Vic Prefaces*, Routledge, 1954.

Irving, Laurence: *Henry Irving*, Faber, 1951.

Kemp, T. C. and Trewin, J. C.: *The Stratford Festival*, Cornish, Birmingham, 1953.

Masefield, John: William Shakespeare, 1964 edition, Heinemann.

Muir, Kenneth, and Schoenbaum, S.: *A new Companion to Shakespeare Studies*, Cambridge, 1971.

Price, Joseph:
The Unfortunate Comedy: A Study of All's Well That Ends Well and Its Critics, Liverpool University Press and University of Toronto Press, 1968.
(Ed.) *The Triple Bond*, Pennsylvania State University Press, 1975.

Robertson, W. Graham: *Letters,* (ed, Kerrison Preston), Hamish Hamilton, 1953.

Rowse, A. L.: *William Shakespeare,* Macmillan, 1963.

Royde-Smith, Naomi: *Outside Information,* Macmillan, 1941.

Salgādo, Gāmini: *Eyewitnesses of Shakespeare,* Sussex University Press, 1975.

Schoenbaum, S.:
  Shakespeare's Lives, Clarendon Press, Oxford, 1970.
  William Shakespeare: A Documentary Life, Clarendon Press and Scolar Press, 1975.

Shakespeare, William: Editions of separate plays in the New Penguin, New Cambridge, and New Arden editions; collected texts: *The Riverside Shakespeare,* Houghton Mifflin, Boston, 1974, and Professor Peter Alexander's edition, Collins, 1951, reprinted many times.

Speaight, Robert:
  William Poel and the Elizabethan Revival, Heinemann, 1954.
  Shakespeare on the Stage, Collins, 1973.
  Shakespeare: The Man and His Achievement, Dent, 1977.

Spencer, T. J. B.: *The Roman Plays,* Longmans, 1963.

Sprague, Arthur Colby:
  Shakespeare and the Audience, Harvard, 1935.
  Shakespeare and the Actors, Harvard, 1944.
  Shakespearian Players and Performances, Black, 1954.
  Shakespeare's Histories: Plays for the Stage, Society for Theatre Research, 1964.
  (with J. C. Trewin) *Shakespeare's Plays Today,* Sidgwick and Jackson, 1970 (reprinted 1971).

Trewin, J. C.:
  Benson and the Bensonians, Barrie and Rockliff, 1960.
  Shakespeare on the English Stage 1900–1964, Barrie and Rockliff, 1964.
  Peter Brook: A Biography, Macdonald, 1971.

Webster, Margaret: *Shakespeare Today,* Dent, 1957.

Wells, Stanley:
  Shakespeare: A Reading Guide, 1969 (2nd edition, 1970).
  Shakespeare: Select Biographical Guides, Oxford, 1973.
  'Royal Shakespeare': Studies of Four Major Productions at the Royal Shakespeare Theatre, Stratford-upon-Avon, in *Furman Studies,* June 1976 (Furman University, Grenville, S. Carolina).

Wilson, John Dover: *Shakespeare's Happy Comedies,* Faber, 1962.

Worsley, T. C.: *The Fugitive Art,* Lehmann, 1952.

285

Index

Adrian, Max 180
Agate, James 71, 173, 216, 223, 278
Ainley, Henry 144, 153, 261
All's Well That Ends Well 183–9
Anderson, Mary 266
Antony and Cleopatra 221–9
Archer, William 177–8
Aris, Doreen 78
Armin, Robert 145, 164
Arnold, Matthew 170
Asche, Oscar 54, 56, 122, 142
Ashcroft, Dame Peggy: as Margaret of Anjou 19, 35; Titania 102; Beatrice 137; Viola 167; Cordelia 206; Cleopatra 223–4; Imogen 255; Queen Katherine 278
As You Like It 16, 43, 98, 140–5
Atienza, Edward 187
Atkins, Robert 18, 38, 103, 184, 248–9, 272
Ayrton, Randle 104, 113, 205, 208, 226

Badel, Alan 36, 130, 152, 210, 271
Bale, John 74
Banks, Leslie 58
Barker, Kathleen 106
Barrymore, John 175
Barton, John 20, 70, 74, 85, 90, 178, 189
Baylis, Lilian 209
Beerbohm, Sir Max 154, 268
Bennett, Vivienne 127, 263
Benson, Sir Frank 18, 21, 23–4, 54, 56, 82, 96, 99, 106, 125, 149–50, 248
Benson, George 130
Benthall, Michael 154, 184
Betterton, Thomas 175
Birmingham Repertory Theatre 17–18, 20, 23, 25, 29, 40, 73, 179, 121–2, 229, 240, 249, 274
Bland, Joyce 252, 255
Bradley, A. C. 205
Bridges-Adams, W. 53–4, 58, 67, 70, 73, 81, 94, 96, 100, 104, 118, 137, 139, 174, 184–5, 187, 223, 227
Bridie, James (O. H. Mavor) 268
Brook, Peter 38–40, 67, 70, 77, 95, 97, 100, 104–5, 195, 208–9, 229, 262, 264, 268–9, 272, 274
Brown, Ivor 213, 230, 270
Brown, John Mason 145
Browne, Coral 101
Bucharest 196

Budapest 176, 222, 229
Burbage, Richard 66–7, 138
Burton, Richard 176
Byford, Roy 117, 122, 136
Byrne, Muriel St Clare 164–5

Carey, Denis 59
Carten, Audrey 101
Casson, Ann 79
Casson, Sir Lewis 94, 182, 212
Chapman, George 73
Chichester 55
Church, Tony 180
Cibber, Colley 26, 31–2, 210
Clarence, O. B. 236
Clunes, Alec 35, 152, 238
Coleman, John 150, 248
Coleridge, S. T. 184
Comedy of Errors, The 13, 45–50
Cooke, George Frederick 32
Cookman, A. V. 39, 237
Coriolanus 43, 62, 235–43
Cottrell, Richard 85
Craig, Gordon 176
Cymbeline 36, 247–58

Daly, Augustin 99
Darlington, W. A. 94, 261
Dean, Basil 100
Dench, Judi 137, 266
Devine, George 58
Devlin, William 205
Digges, Leonard 133, 158–9
Dignam, Mark 72
Dotrice, Roy 130
Doughty, C. M. 204
Dowden, Edward 47
Dryden, John 67
Dunlop, Frank 105

Eddison, Robert 205, 249, 271
Edwards, Philip 244–5
Edward III (Shakespeare Apocrypha) 259
Evans, Dame Edith: as Queen Margaret 35; Katherine 58; the Nurse 94; Helena (*Midsummer Night's Dream*) 101; Rosalind 141, 145; Viola 162; Cressida 177–8; Countess (*All's Well*) 183–4; Emilia 203; Queen Katherine 278, 280
Evans, Gareth Lloyd 205
Evans, Maurice 12, 88
Eyre, Ronald 63

Farjeon, Herbert 36, 39, 243, 264
Farleigh, Lynn 185, 188
Faucit, Helen 133, 266
Ffrangcon-Davies, Gwen 150
Finney, Albert 240
Fleetwood, Susan 255
Fletcher, John 276
Florio, John 73
Fontanne, Lynn 57
Forbes-Robertson, Jean 99
Forbes-Robertson, Sir Johnston 174, 199, 278
Forman, Simon 259
Forrest, Edwin 175
Foss, George 132
French, Leslie 104, 271

Gábor, Miklós 176
Garrick, David 150
Gielgud, Sir John: as Clarence 35; Richard II 85, 89; Benedick 133–4; Julius Caesar 159; Hamlet 173, 175–6; Othello 199; Lear 205, 208; Leontes 262, 266; Prospero 270–2; 274; Wolsey 280
Goolden, Richard 73
Goring, Marius 58
Graham, Morland 130
Granville-Barker, Harley 64, 67, 99, 101, 104–6, 158, 161, 164, 176, 185, 206, 208, 222–3, 235, 252, 257, 261, 276, 278, 280
Green, Dorothy 125, 224
Greene, Robert 260, 264
Guinness, Sir Alec 88, 94, 174, 210
Guthrie, Sir Tyrone 55–6, 67, 79, 99–100, 104, 178, 183–4, 191, 195–6, 230, 232, 237, 276, 278, 280

Hamlet 16, 169–76
Hands, Terry 21
Hannen, Nicholas 216, 278
Hardwick, Paul 181
Harrison, John 73, 179, 249, 260, 271
Harvey, Sir John Martin 54
Hayes, George 40, 44, 81–2, 225
Hazlitt, William 22, 67
Helpmann, Sir Robert 146
Hepton, Bernard 222, 249
Hibbard, G. R. 58
Holinshed, Raphael 19, 31, 149
Holloway, Baliol 35–6, 72, 78, 172, 252, 259
Holm, Ian 36, 152
Holmes, Martin 21, 189
Hotson, Leslie 164
Howard, Alan 114, 138, 148, 152

Hunt, Hugh 67, 157, 164
Hunt, Leigh 232, 234
Hunter, G. K. 204, 219
Hurry, Leslie 274
Hutton, W. H. 248

Irving, Sir Henry 18, 32, 95–7, 236, 278
Isham, Gyles 69, 124

Jackson, Sir Barry 11, 19–20, 23, 65, 73, 77, 146, 221–2, 229, 247
Jacobi, Derek 40
Jefford, Barbara 195, 255
Jew of Malta, The (Marlowe) 39
Johnson, Richard 223
Johnson, Samuel 67
Jonson, Ben 16, 44, 158, 240, 244
Julius Caesar 12, 153–9

Kane, John 105
Kean, Charles 99, 175, 262, 264; Mrs Kean 150
Kean, Edmund 32
Kemble, John Philip 62, 65, 78, 223, 237
Kendal, Dame Madge 220
King Henry IV, Part I 85, 88–9, 113–19
King Henry IV, Part II 98, 115, 119, 121, 127–31
King Henry V 20–1, 90, 121, 147–52
King Henry VI, Part I 16–21, 35, 42, 83
King Henry VI, Part II 20, 22–5
King Henry VI, Part III 20, 26–30, 37, 55, 83, 98
King Henry VIII 263, 276–82
King John 74–80, 83, 86
King Lear 204–11
King Richard II 28, 81–90
King Richard III 26, 30–7, 210
Kipling, Rudyard 98
Knight, Wilson 257
Komisarjevsky, Theodore 48, 112, 122, 206, 223
Krauss, Werner 205

Lacey, Catherine 184
Lamb, Charles and Mary 68, 163, 206, 250
Lanchester, Elsa 271
Lang, Matheson 118
Laughton, Charles 205, 211, 271, 280
Lawrence, T. E. 216
Leach, Rosemary 95
Leigh, Andrew 80
Leigh, Vivien 224, 281
Lindsay, David 65
Lindsay, Helen 95
Littlewood, S. R. 276
Lodge, Thomas 140

Love's Labour's Lost 12, 61, 66–73, 98
Lunt, Alfred 57

Macbeth 16, 115, 212–20
McCallin, Clement 150
MacCarthy, Sir Desmond 104
McEwan, Geraldine 163
Machen, Arthur 25, 227, 236
McKenna, Virginia 146
Macready, William Charles 32, 62, 74–5, 171, 175, 228, 248, 266
Malleson, Miles 72
Marlowe, Christopher 39, 87, 140, 145
Marlowe Society, Cambridge 178
Masefield, John 39, 104, 106, 164, 202, 212–14, 219-20, 236, 257, 269
Maxon, Eric 216
Measure for Measure 190–6, 257
Merchant of Venice, The 107–12, 139
Merry Wives of Windsor, The 98, 120–6, 142, 168, 264
Midsummer Night's Dream, A 42, 69, 98–106
Miles, Sir Bernard 54
Miller, Jonathan 112, 187, 189, 196
Milton, Ernest 82, 124, 175
Mitchell, Yvonne 58
Monck, Nugent 249
Montague, C. E. 82, 171
Morgan, Charles 227
Morning Post, The 276, 282
Morris, Mary 249
Much Ado About Nothing 132–9

National Theatre 112, 142, 159, 175, 199, 270
Neilson, Julia 99
Neilson-Terry, Phyllis 99
Nesbitt, Cathleen 246
Neville, John 83, 146, 152
North, Sir Thomas 159
Nunn, Trevor 223

O'Casey, Sean 26, 30, 67
O'Conor, Joseph 94
Old Vic Theatre: *I Henry VI* 17–18, 20; *II Henry VI* 25; *Richard III* 35; *Titus Andronicus* 38, 44; *Taming of the Shrew* 53, 56; *Two Gentlemen of Verona* 59, 62; *Love's Labour's Lost* 67; *King John* (New Theatre) 79; *Richard II* 87; *Romeo and Juliet* 94; *A Midsummer Night's Dream* 99–100, 103–4; *Much Ado About Nothing* 137; *As You Like It* 141; *Julius Caesar* 157; *Twelfth Night* 164; *Hamlet* 167, 174; *Troilus and Cressida* 178; *All's Well That Ends Well* 184; *Measure for Measure* 196; *Othello* 199, 202–3; *King Lear* 209, 211;

Timon of Athens 232; *Pericles* 248; *The Winter's Tale* 263–4; *The Tempest* 270–1, 274; *Henry VIII* 280
Oliver, Isaac 148
Olivier, Sir Laurence (Lord Olivier): as Richard III 30, 32, 35–6; Titus 42; Hotspur 113, 118; Shallow 130; Henry V 132; Hamlet 173; Othello 199; Lear 205, 210; Coriolanus 240, 243
Open Air Theatre (Regent's Park) 72, 99–100, 103, 246, 271–2, 281
Othello 197–203, 264
Oxford University Dramatic Society 37, 69

Painter, William 185
Parker, H. T. (Boston) 81
Pasco, Richard 145, 152, 249
Pater, Walter 70
Payne, B. Iden 80, 181, 184, 188, 238, 252
Pearson, Hesketh 46, 159
Pericles, Prince of Tyre 11, 244–50
Petrie, D. Hay 72
Phelps, Samuel 73, 248
Phillips, Robin 72
Plowright, Joan 55
Poel, William 177, 182
Porter, Eric 53, 165, 180, 205, 253
Porter, Neil 151
Price, Joseph G. 183, 196

Quartermaine, Leon 223, 254
Quayle, Anthony 40
Quiller-Couch, Sir Arthur 31, 99, 251

Ramage, Cecil 246
Ravenscroft, Edward 38
Redgrave, Sir Michael 118, 138, 150, 205, 216, 223
Redgrave, Vanessa 255
Rehan, Ada 57–8
Richardson, Ian 58, 124, 249, 253, 271
Richardson, Sir Ralph 117, 129, 131
Ridley, M. R. 257
Robertson, W. Graham 256–8
Robeson, Paul 199
Robey, George 117
Robson, Dame Flora 278
Romeo and Juliet 12, 48, 62, 91–7, 243
Royal Shakespeare Theatre, *see* Stratford-upon-Avon
Royde-Smith, Naomi (Mrs Ernest Milton) 184, 189
Rylands, George 74
Rymer, Thomas 203

St George's Theatre, Islington 36, 94, 165

Scofield, Paul 77, 87–8, 95, 205, 208, 233–4, 249, 271, 274
Scott, Clement 45, 95, 170
Seale, Douglas 11, 18–19, 25, 29
Seneca 38
Shakespeare, William, his career 15–16
Shaw G. Bernard 19, 91, 99, 105, 222–3, 251–2, 257
Shaw, Glen Byam 122, 154
Shaw, Maureen 185, 189
Siddons, Sarah 213, 278
Silver King, The (Jones) 85
Sim, Alistair 271
Sincklo, John 55, 58
Sinclair, Arthur 54
Sinden, Donald 137, 205, 280
Sisson, C. J. 50
Slater, Daphne 249
Smith, Logan Pearsall 40
Speaight, Robert 58, 69, 100, 180, 187, 189, 204, 214, 220, 234
Sprague, Arthur Colby 13, 21, 53, 58, 78, 102, 106, 116, 119, 203
Spriggs, Elizabeth 95, 137, 203, 227
Spurgeon, Caroline 282
Stratford, Ontario 72, 183–4, 229
Stratford-upon-Avon (Royal Shakespeare Theatre; formerly Memorial Theatre): *I Henry VI* 18, 20–21; *II Henry VI* 23–4; *Richard III* 35; *Titus Andronicus* 38–40, 44; *The Comedy of Errors* 46, 48; *The Taming of the Shrew* 53–4, 58; *The Two Gentlemen of Verona* 62, 64; *Love's Labour's Lost* 67, 69, 70, 73; *King John* 74, 77–8, 80; *Richard II* 81–2, 85, 87, 90; *Romeo and Juliet* 95, 97; *A Midsummer Night's Dream* 100, 104; *The Merchant of Venice* 112; *Henry IV, Part I* 113–14, 116; *The Merry Wives of Windsor* 122; *Henry IV, Part II* 127, 129; *Much Ado About Nothing* 133, 136, 138; *Henry V* 148, 150–1; *Julius Caesar* 154; *Twelfth Night* 162; *Hamlet* 170, 176; *Troilus and Cressida* 178, 181; *All's Well That Ends Well* 187–8; *Measure for Measure* 195; *Othello* 199, 203; *King Lear* 204, 206, 209; *Macbeth* 214–15; *Antony and Cleopatra* 222, 226; *Coriolanus* 243; *Cymbeline* 256; *The Winter's Tale* 261; *The Tempest* 266, 271; *Henry VIII* 276, 280
Sullivan, Barry 133
Suzman, Janet 223–4
Swinley, Ion 271

Taming of the Shrew, The 51–8
Tate, Nahum 210, 257
Tearle, Osmond 18, 21
Tempest, The 11–12, 268–75
Terry, Dame Ellen 99, 262
Thorndike, Dame Sybil 150, 212, 278
Times, The 21, 39, 44
Timon of Athens 13, 98, 145, 228–34
Titus Andronicus 11, 38–44, 46, 98, 133, 199, 228
Townsend, Genevieve 96
Tree, Sir Herbert Beerbohm 88, 99–100, 118, 158, 174–5, 215, 222, 274
Troilus and Cressida 177–81
Tutin, Dorothy 213
Twelfth Night 17, 49, 132, 160–8, 264
Two Gentlemen of Verona, The 46, 59–65, 98
Two Noble Kinsmen, The (Fletcher/Shakespeare) 105, 270, 281

Valk, Frederick *199, 203*
Vámos, László 222
Volanakis, Minos 157

Walkley, A. B. 132
Waller, Lewis 148
Walter, Wilfred 44, 118, 246
Ward, Dame Genevieve 135
Wars of the Roses, The 19–20
Webster, Margaret 206
Weir, George 106
Wells, Stanley 46, 85, 90
Whetstone, George 191
Winter's Tale, The 259–67
Williams, David 85
Williams, Clifford 48
Williams, E. Harcourt 100
Williams, Michael 209
Williamson, Jane 196
Wilkins, George 245, 248
Wilkinson, Tate 201
Willman, Noel 187
Wilson, J. Dover 77, 139, 259
Wolfit, Sir Donald 36, 167, 180, 201–2, 205, 208, 252–3
Wood, John 37
Woodvine, John 136
Wymark, Patrick 64
Wynyard, Diana 134, 137

Yeats-Brown, Francis 216
Yeats, W. B. 24
Young Vic Theatre 95

Zeffirelli, Franco 136–7